Field of Dreams

Field of Dreams

100 YEARS OF WEMBLEY IN 100 MATCHES

Nige Tassell

**SIMON &
SCHUSTER**

London · New York · Sydney · Toronto · New Delhi

First published in Great Britain by Simon & Schuster UK Ltd, 2023

Copyright © Nige Tassell, 2023

The right of Nige Tassell to be identified as the author
of this work has been asserted in accordance with
the Copyright, Designs and Patents Act, 1988.

1 3 5 7 9 10 8 6 4 2

Simon & Schuster UK Ltd
1st Floor
222 Gray's Inn Road
London WC1X 8HB

www.simonandschuster.co.uk

Simon & Schuster Australia, Sydney
Simon & Schuster India, New Delhi

The author and publishers have made all reasonable efforts
to contact copyright-holders for permission, and apologise
for any omissions or errors in the form of credits given.
Corrections may be made to future printings.

All images © Getty Images, aside from p. 3 (top)
and p. 5 (middle) © Mirrorpix.

A CIP catalogue record for this book
is available from the British Library

Hardback ISBN: 978-1- 3985-1854-4
eBook ISBN: 978-1- 3985-1855-1

Typeset in Bembo by M Rules
Printed and Bound using 100% Renewable
Electricity at CPI Group (UK) Ltd

MIX
Paper | Supporting
responsible forestry
FSC
www.fsc.org   FSC® C171272

To Jane,

courted at an FA Trophy final all those years ago

CONTENTS

INTRODUCTION

Bobby Moore played there forty-seven times and described it as 'the Mecca of stadiums'. Pelé never set foot on its turf but still recognised it to be 'the cathedral of football'. Many millions have made the pilgrimage there – by car, bus or Metropolitan line – over the past 100 years. Watching the beautiful game within its grandstands always was, and still is, a religious experience.

Wembley.

For fans of certain teams, that pilgrimage may only be a once-in-a-lifetime experience. Others who follow more successful clubs, or the national side, have occupied the pews on a more frequent basis. But whatever the denomination, the congregation has been united in prayer, singing its hymns, keeping the faith.

As cathedrals go, the original stadium – the beautiful shape of those twin towers aside – was never a looker. It wasn't St Paul's or Notre-Dame or Lincoln, painstakingly carved from stone by the massed chisels of master craftsmen. It was created more prosaically from 25,000 tons of concrete – and done so in ten short months, a speedy birth that belies its legacy. Originally intended as the showpiece building of the British Empire Exhibition of 1924-25 before being scheduled for demolition within a couple of years, who knew that the stadium would still be hosting cup finals more than three-quarters of a century later? Indeed, one of its two architects – Maxwell Ayrton – admitted that he'd only ever visited one football stadium before designing Wembley, hence the playing area's similarity to Stamford Bridge. A lengthy lifetime wasn't on the agenda.

Nonetheless, over the decades that followed, the stadium became the crucible for the evolution of the national game, its unofficial headquarters, its capital. Other sports got a look-in too – rugby league, greyhound racing, speedway and American football, most notably – along with live concerts and religious rallies and daredevil motorbike shows.

But football is what made Wembley's name, what ensured its survival. Hundreds of trophies have been lifted in its Royal Box and thousands of goals have been scored on its famously big pitch. These goals are seared into the collective recall of the nation, often accompanied by similarly familiar radio or television commentary.

Every year, sporting history has been made here. Tears of joy have been shed. Tears of sadness too. It's been the field of dreams, but it's also the field of nightmares. Dejection and dis-appointment are the inevitable yin to the yang of celebration and ecstasy. Wembley welcomes both winners and losers alike.

Even though the cathedral eventually fell victim to the wrecking ball before it crumbled itself to dust, and even though a new place of worship has been built (at a notably slower pace) on this hallowed ground, the fervour remains. With its arch reaching towards the heavens, Wembley 2.0 has seen plenty of high drama in its relatively young life. It's as magical to today's footballers as the original stadium was to Pelé and Moore. And not just players. In either of its incarnations, the stadium – or at least the *concept* of Wembley – has fuelled the imagination of poets and songwriters alike (although it should be noted that John Betjeman was more than thirty years ahead of Chas & Dave when it came to rhyming 'Wembley' with 'trembly').

Over the course of the next 362 pages, I've selected 100 matches played at Wembley in the 100 years since that first game, the chaotically oversubscribed 'White Horse' FA Cup final of 1923. Although certain matches – for instance, those postmarked 1966 or 1953 or 1996 – were the first names on the team sheet, I've also chosen to turn the spotlight on less well-known encounters, whether obscure exhibition matches or schoolboy internationals or non-league cup finals or the first women's games. These matches are as much a part of the stadium's history as the super-familiar ones – because, at all levels of English football, Wembley means so much to players and fans. Whether seasoned international or wide-eyed semi-pro, the thrill remains the same, the acknowledgement that, for the next ninety minutes plus stoppages, they're playing on the most famous football pitch in the world.

In telling these 100 tales, I've also heard the first-hand testimony of certain protagonists: players, fans, commentators and, in one instance, a cup-final ballboy now in his eighties. In all cases, regardless of the time that has elapsed, their recall remains perfect, spotless, 20/20. These are the days of their lives, and they don't forget a single detail.

So come take your place on the pews and join the congregation. Our opening lesson begins in 1923 . . .

The 1920s

Some people are on the pitch . . .

Saturday 28 April 1923

Bolton Wanderers vs West Ham United

FA Cup final

Young Ernie Thunder wakes early this morning, despite it being a school-free Saturday. He opens his curtains and gazes out across the English Channel. The gunboat-grey sky, matched by the gunboat-grey sea, can't dampen his excitement. A proper red-letter day lies ahead.

In a couple of hours' time, he'll head out of the flat above the Paragon Hotel – the pub his parents run here in Ramsgate – and head towards London, towards the new Empire Stadium. Although he knows this will be the first FA Cup final to be played at Wembley (after years of the showcase match being shunted between the likes of Stamford Bridge, Old Trafford, Crystal Palace, Bramall Lane and Goodison Park), 13-year-old Ernie couldn't possibly imagine how chaotic this afternoon's events will turn out to be. Questions will be asked about it in the House of Commons next week, with the local MP, one Oswald Mosley, being admonished by the Speaker for talk of 'the hooliganism imported there'. Whether hooliganism or good-natured enthusiasm, people will know of this oversubscribed match in a hundred years' time.

Football isn't Ernie's first love. He'll go on to play at a decent amateur level as a young man, but cricket is his calling, a passion far from hindered by his cousin being the England wicket-keeper/batsman Les Ames. But the new cricket season doesn't start for another four days, so today his attentions are elsewhere. A Spurs fan, he has no skin in today's game. It's the new stadium that's his main focus.

His parents are staying behind in Ramsgate to run the pub on what will be a busy Saturday lunchtime in late spring in the seaside town, so Ernie is travelling to Wembley in the company of a chaperone, his 26-year-old aunt, Hilda. The pair are close; she too works behind the bar and lives in the flat above.

Ernie's father knows a man who knows a man. He's called in a few favours and, safely in her handbag, Hilda has tickets for seats in the North Stand at the new stadium. Aunt and nephew head off to the station, skipping as they go.

The stadium has been built for next year's British Empire Exhibition, an ambitious project that aims 'to stimulate trade, strengthen bonds that bind mother Country to her Sister States and Daughters, to being into close contact the one with each other, to enable all who owe allegiance to the British flag to meet on common ground and learn to know each other'. The Empire Stadium represents that rare beast: a building project that's completed ahead of schedule. It's taken just ten months to construct and the Football Association has decided to shift the FA Cup final here, hopeful this will be its permanent home, even though the stadium is due for demolition at the end of the Exhibition. A new railway station is open to passengers for the first time today. It has a snappy name: Exhibition Station (Wembley).

Hilda is an organised sort, and she and Ernie arrive at the new station in good time. But while the train was particularly crowded, neither of them are prepared for the sight that awaits them, for the sheer volume of people at the stadium. The most

Ernie has seen in one place before was two summers back when he watched the Ashes Test at Lord's. He and Hilda do their best to navigate their way down Wembley Way and find the correct entrance for their seats.

Thousands of spectators are pouring off the frequently arriving trains. Like insects, they scuttle along as quickly as the crowds allow. It's a tight, pulsing mass of trilbies and flat caps, a claustrophobic's nightmare. It takes a pair of mounted police – the motorcycle outriders of their time – to carve a channel through the crowd for the motorcade of King George V and his entourage to pass. They fare better than the Bolton team. The Lancastrians' charabanc can get no closer to Wembley than a mile away, such is the swell of the crowd. The players and officials have to walk the final part of their journey, to take their chances in the throng.

This human swarm continues to shuffle forwards, guided by the sight of the new twin towers. Many clamber over whatever obstacle – gate, wall, fence – is between them and the stadium. The turnstiles have now been closed, so climbing prowess is needed for anyone wanting a place on the terraces. A kindly copper, powerless to redirect the swarm, instead offers Hilda and little Ernie safe passage to the entrance of the stand where their seats await.

Once inside, and giving his glasses a wipe, Ernie looks across the vista. He might wake each morning with a widescreen view of the English Channel outside his curtains, but this is an outlook he can truly savour. The stadium is quite magnificent, its scale particularly impressive. Down to Ernie's left is the Royal Box. He'll have a good view of the King today.

Approaching kick-off, the royal seats remain largely empty. The same can't be said for the rest of Wembley. So many people have entered the stadium without either possessing a ticket or paying at a turnstile that the large areas behind each goal are filled with spectators. But still they come, and the pitch is the only place for them to go. By 3 p.m., an estimated 10,000 souls are stood on the turf. A growing cloud of Woodbine smoke hovers above them.

The pitch is completely covered in people. A match looks impossible. But in comes the cavalry – at least, in comes the mounted police. All the horses are dark, save for one light grey horse called Billie, which, on the monochrome Pathé footage to be shown in cinemas in the days to come, appears whiter than he is. Collectively, the mounted police manage to part the human tide and gradually, gently, push the crowd back behind the touchline.

(The Pathé footage is being harvested in an underhand manner. Having not been awarded filming rights, the company decide to smuggle one of their cameramen into the stadium, disguised as a West Ham fan. He looks like any other member of the crowd – flat cap, spectacles and (fake) moustache. He's also carrying a very large wooden hammer, painted in claret and blue stripes and bearing the letters 'Play Up Hammers'. But secreted inside the hammerhead is a film camera, primed to surreptitiously record the action.)

'I saw nothing but a sea of heads,' Billie's rider, George Scorey, will later explain in an interview with the BBC. 'I thought, *We can't do it. It's impossible.* But I happened to see an opening near one of the goals and the horse was very good, easing them back with his nose and tail until we got a goal-line cleared. He seemed to understand what was required of him.' Scorey isn't supposed to be at work today; he was called in earlier when the numbers of spectators spilling off the trains became unmanageable. He'll be seen as a hero over the years, rewarded with a cup final ticket every year as a token of the FA's gratitude. He never takes them up on the offer, though. George Scorey doesn't like football.

Ironically, the final has been transferred from Stamford Bridge, where crowd numbers for the most prestigious game in English football had been shrinking over the last three years. Today, though, the match is chronically oversubscribed. The official attendance is announced as 126,047, not far beyond the official capacity. Presumably this is the number of people who either have a ticket or who paid through the turnstiles before they were locked. The most generous estimates put the number of people inside the stadium to be double that of the official capacity, somewhere around the 250,000 mark. Ernie gazes down at the squash and the squeeze below him, pleased that he and Hilda aren't in that predicament, pleased that his dad knew a man who knew a man.

With the pitch cleared (albeit with the touchlines rammed), the game finally gets under way forty-five minutes behind schedule. It only takes three minutes for Bolton to assert their supremacy, taking the lead with the first goal ever scored at Wembley. It's almost inevitable that David Jack is the scorer. A lean striker whose shyness and modesty off the pitch belies his ruthlessness on it, it's his goals that have brought Bolton to Wembley. The crowd play their part in his goal today. When the West Ham half-back Jack Tresadern gets tangled up among spectators after taking a throw, Jack takes advantage of the extra space to fire past future England goalkeeper Ted Hufton. Jack hits his shot with such power that it knocks out clean cold a spectator stood behind the net.

There's further encroachment from the crowd during the first half, with a lengthy delay caused by Red Cross personnel having to treat injured spectators. There are reports that as many as 1,000 supporters have required treatment for minor injuries this afternoon, with around twenty needing attention at the nearest hospital. After half-time – in which the players, unable to reach the dressing rooms, are forced to take their break on the pitch – the proximity of the crowd comes to bear on the second Bolton goal. West Ham furiously complain that Jack Smith's shot has hit the post, but the referee adjudges it to have gone into the net before being kicked back out by a spectator standing next to the goalpost. The game then dribbles out anticlimactically and Bolton become the winners of the first Wembley FA Cup final. Employing an age-old excuse, West Ham's trainer Charlie Paynter blames his side's defeat on the condition of the turf. 'It was that white horse thumping its big feet into the pitch that made it hopeless.'

In the House of Commons over the next few days, there's talk of the Empire Stadium not hosting a football match again, so disorganised and unprepared were its staff. The MP for Glasgow Gorbals, George Buchanan, suggests an alternative. 'If, in future, it is intended to have a football match like that of Saturday, will the honourable and gallant gentleman consider having it transferred to Glasgow in order that it may be properly conducted?' Mr Buchanan might have a vested interest. He is vice-chair of the Glasgow Trade Council.

The trains are understandably busy after the game, but aunt and nephew arrive back in Ramsgate in time for Hilda to help out behind the bar at last orders. Ernie heads upstairs to his room, drawing the curtains on one of the more memorable days of his young life. He knows he's witnessed history today. He'll visit Wembley many times in future decades – to watch Spurs, to watch England – but never again will he experience the untrammelled chaos, and the sheer volume of people, that he has this afternoon.

And when, more than fifty years later, Ernie tells his grandkids the story of this extraordinary day, there's one detail he insists on repeating: that he and Hilda weren't interlopers, that he and Hilda climbed over no walls or fences or turnstiles.

He and Hilda had tickets. He was supposed to see all that he saw.

Bolton Wanderers 2–0 West Ham United

'May the ball run kindly for you'

Saturday 12 April 1924

England vs Scotland

Home international

It's an unremarkable Thursday afternoon. At least that's what Charlie Buchan thinks.

As usual, he locks up his sports shop on Blandford Street in Sunderland town centre before beginning his walk home. His head – as it is every Thursday – is starting to get lost in thoughts about the coming weekend's game. Tomorrow, the Sunderland centre-forward will be travelling down to London with his team-mates, ahead of their clash with Arsenal at Highbury the following afternoon. He's relishing it. As the season enters its closing stages, Sunderland are top of the First Division, while Arsenal, third from bottom of the table, have yet to escape the spectre of relegation. The match represents another opportunity for Buchan to add to his goal tally; this is his eighth season at Roker Park, a tenure split in half by the war, and he's been Sunderland's top scorer in all but one of those campaigns.

But as he heads home, a well-wisher catches his ear.

'Congratulations, Charlie, and may the ball run kindly for you.'

Lost in thought, Buchan is confused as to why congratulations are being offered. This confusion is clearly painted on his face.

'Don't you know?' asks the well-wisher. 'You're England's centre-forward at Wembley. I've just heard it over the air.'

The news turns out to be true. First-choice centre-forward Harry Chambers has withdrawn through injury and Buchan, at the positively creaky age of thirty-two, is taking the Liverpool striker's place in the starting XI. It will be only Buchan's sixth international cap, his first coming a full eleven years earlier. He understands that, with Saturday's game against Scotland being the final match of this year's home international series, there's a strong possibility it will be his last in England white.

And there's another reason for Buchan to treasure his call-up. Saturday's match will be the first time that the national team has played at the still-new national stadium. History awaits.

Buchan could have been lining up in Scotland blue. He was approached by the Scottish FA back in 1912, the committee's eye drawn to the then 21-year-old's surname. Buchan confirmed that, yes, his parents were both from Aberdeen, but he was born in Plumstead in south-east London. His father, who had served in the Highland Regiment, had relocated to the capital, where he became a blacksmith, and where Buchan Jr appeared on the scene. At this point, to represent a country in an international tournament requires a player to have been born there, irrespective of his parents' nationality. Birthplace is the one qualifying criterion. Buchan could only be an England player.

One of his associates in the England forward line for the Scotland match is a certain David Bone Nightingale Jack, the man who scored the winner for Bolton in the first Wembley cup final fewer than twelve months earlier. He too is of Scottish parentage, but had been born in Lancashire, so also didn't qualify to play for his blood nation. Jack only made his international debut in England's last game, a home defeat at Ewood Park against eventual tournament champions Wales.

Unlike last year, Jack doesn't get on the scoresheet this afternoon. Neither does Buchan. The latter does have a part to play in England's goal, his header being only partially cleared by Scotland right-back John Smith, allowing Aston Villa's Billy Walker to calmly score. But England have already been playing catch-up after trailing at half-time to an own goal from their goalkeeper Eddie Taylor.

Honours are even at the end of this first international to be played at Wembley, a draw which anchors England to the bottom of the table, having not won a single match in the tournament. At least there was no full house to witness the shame. After the previous season's overcrowded cup final, it's perhaps surprising that the crowd is so modest; just 37,250 watch a game that Buchan later describes as giving him 'the greatest pleasure'. Presumably the gate is low because there's a competing full league programme in the First Division. Nine miles away, due east across north London, Sunderland have clearly missed their goal-scoring talisman, falling to a 2–0 defeat that will seriously scupper their title chances.

Buchan is correct in his summation of the significance of the Scotland match to his future. He is never selected to play for his country again.

'In those days,' he later writes in his memoirs, *A Lifetime in Football*, 'professional players had the choice of a match fee or a gold medal. I chose the medal. I am glad I did, for it was the last time I ever played for England. After all, I was thirty-two years old and could not expect more caps.'

But this isn't the end of Buchan's footballing career. At the end of the following season, Herbert Chapman re-signs him for Arsenal, his first club. Three more successful seasons there as captain provide a formidable swansong. And when he finally retires, it takes a world-record signing to fill the boots he leaves. That player's name? David Jack.

England 1–1 Scotland

The Bluebirds' song

Saturday 23 April 1927

Arsenal vs Cardiff City

FA Cup final

After the chaos – and potential danger – of the Bolton/West Ham match in 1923, every subsequent FA Cup final has become an all-ticket affair. Four years later, more than 300,000 fans of both Arsenal and Cardiff City have applied for tickets; less than a third have been successful. Those left empty-handed are instead tuning in to the BBC's radio commentary, the first time that the corporation has broadcast live from Wembley.

This isn't the only cup final tradition instituted this year. In a concert before the match, Henry Francis Lyte's hymn 'Abide with Me' is being heartily sung around the stadium – by those fruity Welsh voices in particular. Nearly a century later, and still sung in shortened form ahead of every final, it will have lost none of its emotive power. One line in particular seems to offer solace to the dejected fan after their team has been beaten: 'Shine through the gloom and point me to the skies.'

There's no gloom for Cardiff's fans this afternoon, either those lucky enough to be in the stands and terraces, or those who've congregated in the city's Cathays Park, listening to the BBC broadcast over loudspeakers. The greatest cheers of the afternoon come with fifteen minutes left of the hitherto goalless game. Cardiff's young outside-right Ernie Curtis embarks on one of his trademark runs before passing to Hughie Ferguson, the team's prolific centre-forward. His shot lacks its usual power and the Arsenal goalkeeper Dan Lewis scoops up the ball in his arms. However, under pressure from advancing Cardiff players, it escapes Lewis's clutches and dribbles over the line. Dressed in his immaculate bow tie and blazer, the referee William Bunnell blows his whistle and gives the goal. A hundred and fifty miles due west, Cathays Park explodes.

While Cardiff's captain Fred Keenor will attribute the apparent mishap to Ferguson having 'put such a spin on it [that] the ball twisted in his hands', Lewis blames his new 'greasy' jersey. As a result, a tradition would be adopted at Arsenal that has been in place ever since: that all box-fresh goalkeeping jerseys must be washed before being worn. More cynical types have come up with a third reason: that Lewis, a native of the Rhondda Valley, deliberately fumbled the ball to let his compatriots win.

On St George's Day, the FA Cup is leaving England for the first and only time, thanks to a goal from a Scotsman. Hughie Ferguson is a goal machine, a man who's scored in excess of 300 times for Cardiff and, before then, Motherwell. Ferguson will head back to Scotland two years later, signing for Dundee, for whom he scores only twice more. His chronic loss of form, coupled with the accompanying criticism from the Dens Park terraces, sinks Ferguson into a deep depression. In January 1930, at the age of thirty-four, he stays behind at the stadium after training and gases himself to death. His body is found the next morning. 'Shine through the gloom and point me to the skies.'

In the spring of 1927, prior to the final, the future of Wembley Stadium had been uncertain. Despite more than 17 million visitors, the British Empire Exhibition had been a financial disappointment and the site was now in the ownership of a boxing promoter and gambler, the charismatic James White. White had already set about selling off Wembley's various buildings, including the stadium, ahead of the site's redevelopment. To do this, he had commissioned a former officer from the Royal Training Corps, Arthur Elvin, whose acquaintance he had made while the latter was working at a tobacco kiosk on the site during the exhibition.

Elvin put his past experience in the scrap metal trade to good use, selling off various buildings and making himself a tidy sum in the process. So successful was he that he made White an offer of £127,000 to buy the stadium. At the time of Cardiff's victory, the deal was progressing well, but two months later, faced with crippling personal debts, White took his own life at his home in Wiltshire.

Having previously agreed to pay White over a ten-year period, Elvin was forced to hurriedly raise the money to buy the stadium outright before its scheduled demolition. This he did, forming the Wembley Stadium and Greyhound Racecourse Company, of which he made himself chairman. He then introduced dog racing, speedway and rugby league to the stadium, as well as giving English football a permanent home. Elvin was Wembley's saviour, while also enjoying an exceedingly comfortable life on its proceeds.

James White's close family weren't so lucky. His death had left them high and dry, penniless and without a home. Indeed, White appeared to have given more consideration to the coroner than to his loved ones. He left a note for him.

'Go easy on me, old man. I am dead from prussic acid. No need to cut any deeper – Jimmy.'

Arsenal 0–1 Cardiff City

Punching above their weight

Saturday 29 September 1928

Ealing Association vs Hastings & St Leonards

Southern Amateur Football League match

Despite being founder members of the Southern Amateur Football League in 1907 and, seven years later, becoming only the second English team to tour Portugal (where they played Benfica twice), Ealing Association Football Club remain a distinctly nomadic set-up throughout the 1920s. They have had a number of home grounds around their corner of west London, including Snell's Farm on Hanger Lane and Gunnersbury Park. Their most notable – and highly surprising – temporary home during this time is where they currently squat, further to the north. They host their opponents at Wembley. Not on some municipal fields in Wembley. At the actual national stadium.

Just how could a team of amateurs receive that honour?

Up until the end of the last season, Richard 'Dick' Sloley – formerly of Brentford and Aston Villa – had been playing inside-right for Ealing Association as they swept to the Southern Amateur League and Cup double, no doubt enhanced by the presence of this former captain of England's amateur XI. At the end of that doubly triumphant season, at the age of thirty-seven, he hung up his boots.

An Olympian who had graced the Great Britain side at the 1920 Games in Antwerp, Sloley is a major advocate for the amateur game, having also previously turned out for the renowned Corinthian-Casuals before the war. And he has a dream. Sloley wants to recruit and develop a team comprising the finest amateur players in the land that can compete with the professional outfits in the Football League. Having named this team Argonauts, Sloley has struck a deal with the owner of Wembley – Arthur Elvin – to hire out the stadium for his new club's initial matches. The choice of location for a still-to-be-formed amateur side is clearly a ridiculously mismatched option, but Sloley believes that renting out the national stadium could be interpreted as a symbol of his unfettered ambition in the eyes of the powers behind the Football League.

He's wrong. The Argonauts' application to join the league has been voted down and dismissed. Not only has the mythical team's dream been extinguished (at least for now; Sloley would go on to launch two more attempts a little further down the line), but he now has a four-month rental deal with Wembley Stadium to honour. With serendipitous timing, his former club Ealing Association are looking for a new home ground while their pitch on Corfton Road in Ealing, which they share with the local cricket club, is undergoing drainage work following flooding issues last winter. They temporarily transplant themselves to Wembley, a shift that the distinctly un-amateur Tottenham Hotspur will repeat almost ninety years later while White Hart Lane is redeveloped.

The move gives the double-winning Ealing Association side a distinct boost as they seek to retain their league title. Calling Wembley your home ground can have that effect. In their first match in the cavernous stadium, they run out winners against Hastings & St Leonards by a single goal. But that bounce soon goes flat as they lose the next game to Ipswich Town 4–0. Things don't really improve after then. By the time their short-term tenancy agreement has elapsed and their return to Corfton Road is confirmed, Ealing Association have lost six of their eight home games. Their only other win is a 4–2 victory over Barclays Bank.

It hasn't been a successful sojourn in Wembley and fortunes won't change once they're back at the cricket ground. By the end of the season, the league champions have been relegated.

The Wembley experiment, although largely born out of necessity for a temporarily homeless club, has derailed a previously high-achieving side. Plus, it wasn't as if it were a savvy business decision either. At none of Ealing Association's eight home games was there a need for a crowd-controlling police horse. In a stadium capable of holding 100,000, the club's average gate has been just fifty.

If Ealing's time at the national stadium failed to turn a coin, Arthur Elvin had plenty of other endeavours up his sleeve. The previous December, following its successful introduction four miles away at White City Stadium, Wembley's owner had opened his doors to greyhound racing. It was the hot leisure activity of the time, a glamorous and increasingly middle-class pursuit. The following year, Hollywood starlet Tallulah Bankhead would open the track at Wimbledon Stadium, while *Tatler* magazine, that arbiter of social standing, announced that few things were more glamorous than going to the dogs.

Elvin rode the wave of the sport's success, with new races such as the St Leger, the Coronation Cup and the Wembley Gold Cup becoming fixtures on the racing calendar. He knew that Wembley couldn't survive on the revenue from a single annual football match (the cup final) and a biannual international fixture against Scotland. He found his cash cow. Wembley hosted races three days of the week, securing the stadium's future. The dogs would run on its track for a further seventy years. Indeed, so important was the sport that even the 1966 World Cup had to step aside, with its match between Uruguay and France forced to relocate to White City when the greyhound promoters refused to surrender, for even just one week, their precious Friday night slot.

Before the 1920s were over, Elvin added more sports to his roster. The Wembley Lions speedway team took to the cinders in 1929; it would be their home track until the late Fifties. The pitch had to be cut away in the corners to accommodate motorbikes, which require a wider track than those lean-as-lean greyhounds, but it was worth it. Crowds were large for these nights of high-octane action: in 1946, 85,000 turned up for a race-meet between the Lions and their rivals Wimbledon Dons, leaving a further 20,000 shut out on Wembley Way.

The Rugby League Challenge Cup final would also make its Wembley bow in 1929. This was less of a sure thing than the introduction of greyhound racing and speedway. The sport historian Simon Inglis notes that it was 'a huge gamble' to shift the climax of rugby league's premier cup competition so far away from its heartland. But without a large-enough stadium in the north to satiate demand, the Leeds-based Rugby Football League felt it had no alternative. Even so, says Inglis, 'requiring the fans of Wigan and Dewsbury to travel south, at a time of immense economic hardship, took some bravado'.

Elvin rolled the dice and it came up six again. Forty-one thousand came down from Lancashire and West Riding for that first final, putting Wembley on an even more secure financial footing. Nearly a century later, Wembley remains the Challenge Cup's spiritual home.

Ealing Association 1–0 Hastings & St Leonards

The 1930s

Eye in the sky

Saturday 26 April 1930

Arsenal vs Huddersfield Town

FA Cup final

As the clock ticks around to four in the afternoon, the skies above Wembley darken prematurely, the sunlight temporarily shaded. Ninety two and a half thousand pairs of eyes look skyward to where the world's largest airship, the German *Graf Zeppelin*, is approaching the Empire Stadium. It looms low and slow, before dipping its nose to replicate a bow before today's guest of honour, King George V. Straightening up, it carries on its way towards the Royal Airship Works at RAF Cardington in Bedfordshire, almost grazing the top tier of the stands as it heads north.

Some fans wave their caps and hats at the flypast; others are more circumspect. There are also a few boos, not just because of the airship disturbing the match but also for what such an aircraft represents, especially to the citizens of London. Fifteen years ago, Zeppelins led bombing raids on the capital, and on towns in Norfolk, with hundreds of British civilians losing their lives. This was only half a generation ago; the memories are still sharp, still sour.

An uncomfortable situation would have worsened had the packed stadium known the identity of today's pilot. It's Captain

Ernst Lehmann, who knows the London skies well. He was one of the leaders of the bombing raids back in 1915.

It's a full house here, despite the plummeting economic prospects in the wake of last autumn's Wall Street Crash. Whether finding a couple of shillings for a spot in the standing enclosures way behind either goal, or being able to fork out twenty-one shillings for a seated, halfway-line view from the upper tier of the South Stand, financial hardship is put on hold for now. This is the cup final, after all. Who knows when your team might be there again? By the end of the year, though, the depression will truly kick in. The UK's exports will have halved, with unemployment increasing by 150 per cent over a single calendar year. Dark skies indeed.

As the airship passes low over the stadium, Lehmann and his crew may be able to see the scoreboard. At this point, early in the second half, Arsenal are leading by a single goal, scored by their quixotic playmaker Alex James in the sixteenth minute. The Scot is distinctive and easily recognisable, even to those in the highest rows of the stands; he wears voluminous shorts over the top of long johns, the latter worn to aid his rheumatoid arthritis. Donny Davies, the *Manchester Guardian*'s chief football correspondent, calls him 'the baggy-trousered Napoleon'.

The *Graf Zeppelin* has already docked in Bedfordshire by the time Arsenal double their lead just a couple of minutes before the final whistle. The scorer is the prolific Yorkshireman Jack Lambert, a robust centre-forward who has notched up four goals in the previous rounds. Even so, Lambert might consider himself fortunate to be in this afternoon's starting XI. Arsenal manager Herbert Chapman only made room for him by dropping Dave Halliday, despite the Scot scoring four times in an extraordinary six-all draw against Leicester City last Monday.

After winning an FA Cup and two league championships while in charge at Huddersfield, this afternoon Chapman has proved that his forward-thinking ways are perfectly transferable between football clubs. He is undeniably a visionary. And it's not just his creation of the revolutionary 'WM' team formation that marks him as such.

This is a man who conceived of the notion of shirts bearing numbers; who advocated the playing of matches under floodlights; who believed that transfers should be restricted to a particular point on the calendar; who called for European club competition; who happily signed overseas players; and who considered the introduction of artificial pitches as a way of deftly sidestepping the mud-clagged fields of England in winter.

Not all measures will be adopted in Chapman's lifetime, but for decades to come, the game will wear his indelible mark and will be shaped by his progressive thinking.

Today has been a final of firsts. It's the first time that the two teams have taken to the cup final pitch side by side, shoulder to shoulder, an advance suggested by Huddersfield to show the fraternity between the clubs, linked as they are by their respective manager's offices having been graced by Chapman.

That's not all. While this afternoon isn't the first time that the BBC has carried a live radio commentary of the game, it is the first time that the corporation has paid for the honour. The age of broadcasting rights is upon us.

Today also marks Arsenal's maiden FA Cup win. Having lost three years ago to Cardiff, their trail of triumphs in this competition – fourteen over the next ninety years – starts here. Also starting here is Arsenal's domination of English football throughout the 1930s, a period when the Highbury trophy cabinet will bow under the weight of five league titles, two FA Cups and five Charity Shields.

Not that Chapman, the great architect, will live to see the extent of what he's constructed. In 1934, he'll die suddenly at fifty-five. And he won't be the only protagonist of that afternoon in April 1930 to die prematurely. Three years after Chapman's death, Captain Ernst Lehmann will perish in the Hindenburg airship disaster in New Jersey at the age of just fifty.

Arsenal 2–0 Huddersfield Town

The cup final without a cup

Wednesday 21 March 1934

Greenwich Trafalgar vs Walthamstow Fellowship

London Occupational Football League final

The Prince of Wales – the future abdicator King Edward VIII – isn't used to Wembley being so empty. A regular face at the FA Cup final, he's more familiar with the terraces being noisy and full. Today, though, aside from a hardy cadre of rattle-spinning fans in the North Stand, the seats and terraces are vacant and silent.

But the prince is familiar with his duties today. Before him on the pitch, two football teams – all short back and sides, and Brylcreemed on top – are lined up and waiting to shake his hand and perhaps swap a pleasantry or two. He's shaken the hands of many of the era's top players in the past. But waiting before him today are no internationals, no household names. Instead, greetings are shared with the anonymous players of Greenwich Trafalgar and Walthamstow Fellowship, who are

28

about to duel it out in the final of the little-known London Occupational League.

Such a level of football wouldn't normally come by royal appointment, but the prince is here to show solidarity. For these twenty-two men of Greenwich and Walthamstow have one thing in common: they are all currently unemployed. The London Occupational League is populated by teams that are exclusively composed of jobless men. Indeed, today's line-ups are only revealed at the eleventh hour; had a player accepted a job offer this morning, he would have been ineligible to take part this afternoon.

Neither team would have trouble replacing any late drop-outs; unemployment among London's male population currently stands at 14 per cent. That's notably better than many other regions across Britain, especially in north-east England. In Jarrow, a town previously buoyant thanks to its shipbuilding might, three in every four men are without work. Five years on, the country continues to feel the deadening economic effects of the Wall Street Crash and the resultant Great Depression.

In being here, the prince is showing sympathy for the players' plight. He might be wearing a Bond Street scarf and carrying a reassuringly expensive trilby, but his facial expression appears gracious and empathetic.

Sat in a half-empty Royal Box, he chews on his pipe through-out the match. He's seen better teams here, and seen better games. But although the match isn't the tidiest, and is decided in Walthamstow's favour by a single scrappy goal, what's more important this afternoon is the pride, dignity and self-respect that's on show. Furthermore, for these men of south-east and north-east London, this is an exercise in escapism. For ninety minutes, they can pretend they're Raich Carter or Cliff Bastin or Arthur Rowe. They can be superstars. Real life can be shut out for a couple of hours. Ignored, forgotten.

The prince warmly shakes each player's hand again as they collect their medals afterwards. But one cup final staple is missing: a trophy. 'It is a cup final without a cup,' explains the Pathé newsreader, 'because a cup's a permanent thing.' Unlike, hopefully, the current employment status of these twenty-two men.

Greenwich Trafalgar 0–1 Walthamstow Fellowship

Disappearing act

Saturday 29 April 1939

Portsmouth vs Wolverhampton Wanderers

FA Cup final

It might now boast a half-timbered, mock Tudor frontage – one that's incongruously paired with an art deco sign out front – but The Bird In Hand, in the Hampshire village of Lovedean, goes back a couple of centuries. In the 1800s, it was home to both the local baker and greengrocer. These days, it's a country pub known for its cuisine, where discerning diners can salivate over the Thai-spiced salmon and prawn fishcakes or the pan-fried rillettes of pork belly, while their vegetarian companions can tuck into the harissa-roasted celeriac steak.

Between the nineteenth and twenty-first centuries, The Bird In Hand was notable for more than supplying the locals with their daily bread, or satisfying the appetites of visiting gastronomes. It made a sizeable – if secretive – contribution to English football history.

It's the late April of 1939 and the respective first XIs of Portsmouth and Wolverhampton Wanderers are making their way to Wembley to contest the FA Cup final. Wolves have won the cup twice before, but both triumphs came in pre-Wembley times, winning at Fallowfield Stadium in Manchester and Crystal Palace. Even though this is Portsmouth's third Wembley visit in ten years, Wolves are the favourites, having notched up no fewer than nineteen goals in their five matches in the competition thus far, including a 5–0 hiding dished out to Grimsby Town in the semi-final.

But it's Portsmouth who take the firmest of grips on the game, making Wolves goalkeeper Alex Scott, in the words of the ridiculously plummy Pathé announcer, 'as busy as a flea at a party'. After a goalless first half-hour, Portsmouth edge ahead, thanks to a cross-shot from their inside-left Bert Barlow. It's a particularly sweet strike for Barlow, who joined Pompey only two months ago from today's opponents; he played just three times in the gold of Wolves. Centre-forward John Anderson hooks in another a minute before half-time and, a few seconds after the break, outside-left Cliff Parker makes it 3–0. Wolves belatedly become energised and pull a goal back, but this is soon neutralised by Parker's second. The FA Cup is heading to the south coast, although the Portsmouth manager Jack Tinn puts the triumph down not to his coaching and selections, but to the 'lucky spats' he's worn in every round.

The outbreak of the Second World War in little more than four months' time will mean the suspension of the competition. Perhaps for a year, possibly for two. It turns out to be seven years until the next FA Cup final, seven years that the trophy stays in Portsmouth's possession. It will become the only fact about the 1939 cup final that every pub quiz contestant knows. No other club has ever been in possession of the trophy for anywhere close to that long.

At first, the famous cup lives exactly where it would expect to live: in the trophy cabinet at the holders' home ground. But once the war starts in earnest and Portsmouth's naval base, barely a couple of miles to the west of Fratton Park, begins to attract the attentions of the Luftwaffe, the silverware is shrewdly removed and secreted at various points across the city, including being held at a police station, and under lock and key at a bank. But, whenever the air-raid siren rings out across the Portsmouth skyline, a shifting cast of protectors ensure the trophy accompanies them down into the shelters below ground.

The cup then spends a couple of years at The Bird In Hand, in the comparative sanctity of the countryside to the north of the city, outside the expected drop zone of German bombs. There it takes pride of place behind the bar, perched on top of the pub's radio – during opening hours, at least. After the doors are locked, off upstairs goes the cup. 'Father took his role very seriously,' the landlord's daughter, Joan Wilkinson, will confide to the BBC many years later. 'At night, it could not be downstairs, so it would go under the bed.'

After six years of a peripatetic existence, at the end of the war the famous trophy will re-emerge from hiding. It's quite possibly in better nick than when George VI had presented it to the winning team back in 1939. In the days following the Wembley triumph, goalscorer Barlow had elected to take the cup on a night out to South Parade Pier in Southsea, whereupon the decidedly refreshed Yorkshireman dropped it down some steps.

It would prove to be an expensive fumble. The silversmith's repair bill came to £70. Barlow only earned £7 a week.

Portsmouth 4–1 Wolverhampton Wanderers

The 1940s

Friendly fire

Saturday 13 April 1940

England vs Wales

Wartime international

For the 40,000 permitted into Wembley for the stadium's first wartime international, the match-day programme offers unusual reading. In the centre pages – and flanked by some feeble puns advertising a certain beef-flavoured beverage ('BOVRIL "feeds" the Inside Right', 'BOVRIL quickly intercepts a chill') – are the teams' line-ups. Not only is the referee announced as Pilot Officer A. J. Jewell (RAF), but seven of the starting XI for England are listed with their current serving rank in the armed forces, whether corporal (goalkeeper Sam Bartram), private (full-back Joe Bacuzzi and centre-forward Dennis Westcott) or sergeant instructor (Stan Cullis and a couple of others). Rather neatly, Arsenal winger Denis Compton is a gunner.

The outbreak of the Second World War hasn't stopped football in England. While the 1939–40 Football League season was soon abandoned after war was declared, a series of ten regional mini-leagues was established, albeit with teams weakened by the loss of players to the war effort. Wartime internationals involving the England team have been taking place – including away matches in Cardiff and Wrexham, and a home game in Newcastle – but the record books don't deem them full internationals. Today's is the first match at Wembley since Portsmouth won the FA Cup two weeks shy of a complete calendar year ago.

It's also the first appearance – unofficial international match or not – of the Wales national team at Wembley. It's the third time that the teams have met since the previous November, and thus the third time they've played each other since war broke out seven months ago. 'Even the war hasn't affected the billiard table smoothness of the famous Wembley grass,' the Pathé announcer will later declare – although it's uncertain why the condition of the turf would be affected. The Battle of Britain, bringing the conflict to these shores, was still three months away.

Playing in 'red shirts and white knickers', Wales are pretty irresistible today, with Cullis and England captain Eddie Hapgood working tirelessly to repel the five-strong Wales attack. The only goal comes shortly before half-time when the debutant Bartram fumbles a twenty-yard shot from Bryn Jones, Arsenal's record signing a couple of years ago when he joined from Wolves for the princely sum of £14,000. England should equalise from the penalty spot with five minutes left, but the Spurs inside-right Willie Hall puts his kick wide.

Wales's defence is the equal of its strike force and receives gushing praise from George Casey, the boisterous Londoner who holds the position of sports editor at the *Sunday Pictorial*. 'The tackling and covering of the Welsh defence was superb,' his report will read in the morning, commendably stripped of any bias, intentional or otherwise. 'Not once did it show signs of crumbling against the bull-like rushes of Westcott and the spasmodic artistry of Matthews.'

Although the programme doesn't list his military rank, Matthews – that chap Stanley – is another conscript, an RAF man currently stationed in Blackpool, to where he has moved his family from their native Stoke. Matthews is presumably quite pleased that a certain Welshman isn't playing today – the tough-tackling QPR wing-half Ivor Powell. Had he been, and had Matthews and England notched up a better result, there might have been hell to pay on the parade ground come Monday. Sgt Powell is Matthews' commanding officer.

England 0–1 Wales

The magnificent seven

Saturday 1 May 1943

Arsenal vs Charlton Athletic

Football League (South) War Cup final

'In the event of an Air Raid Alert, in the course of which information is given by the Spotters that Enemy Aircraft are in the immediate vicinity of the Stadium, an announcement will be made over the loudspeakers. Spectators will then be requested to leave the enclosures and make their way quietly to the Circulating Corridors under the Stands, as directed by the Stewards and Officials. Those wishing to leave the Stadium may do so by any of the usual Exits.'

After several years of after-dark visits from the Luftwaffe, London barely bats a collective eyelid to public warnings such as this one from the front page of the programme for the 1943 Football League (South) War Cup final. Certainly the 75,000 who've streamed here from across the capital appear not to be put off by the airborne threat.

The back page of the programme offers additional confirmation that this is a match being played during wartime. It contains a cartoon-cum-advert encouraging today's spectators not to spend their money on frivolities, not to succumb to the temptations offered by a fictional creature called 'the Squander Bug'. 'Wherever you carry your money, there you will find him,' it cautions. 'Give him half a chance and he's on your shoulder, whispering his insidious propaganda into your ear.' The use of the phrase 'insidious propaganda' is an undiluted attempt to suggest that selfish spending is an unpatriotic act. Indeed, the advert is promoting the weekly purchase of Savings Certificates, asking people to put their money behind the war effort. If people don't, the advert claims, 'before you know where you are, you have bought some footling thing with money that should be doing battle for Britain'.

No Arsenal fan who's paid six shillings for a seat in the South Grandstand this afternoon – or ten shillings and sixpence for a posher perch – would believe they've acted unpatriotically this afternoon. This is no frivolity. This is their team in a cup final. Indeed, it turns out to be money very well invested, with the Gunners notching up seven goals this afternoon.

Whether or not the Arsenal players have any inkling that this afternoon will be such a smooth, dominant and easy victory, they certainly seem confident in the dressing room beforehand. In his shirt, tie and RAF greatcoat, Ted Drake looks every part the dapper, at-ease airman, while Denis Compton, wearing the uniform of the Territorial Army, beams heartily before changing into his cherry-red kit, pulling his number 11 jersey over his head. The Arsenal manager, the bowler-hatted George Allison, is his usual unflappable, semi-detached self.

The confidence is justified. Charlton, playing in their first

Wembley final, look more tentative in their dressing room and are quickly put to the sword. The north Londoners are 4–1 up at half-time. Three more goals arrive in the second half.

The Arsenal centre half-back Bernard Joy will later write a history of the club, in which he declares that Reg Lewis and Drake 'wrought devastation' on the Charlton defence. It's a fair summation, with the pair sharing six goals between them. Drake jointly parades the trophy afterwards with the Arsenal captain, George Male. They couldn't look more different. Whatever hair the balding Male is still in possession of is straggly and a little out of control. He has a touch of the science boffin about him. Next to him, Drake doesn't have a single Brylcreemed hair out of place, looking every inch the matinee idol.

The biggest post-match smile, however, belongs to Reg Lewis. His four goals this afternoon ensure it's one of the landmark matches of his career. He will be a particular victim of the war's effect on English football. Whereas the sun had already set on the careers of some of his team-mates – including Drake and Cliff Bastin – by the time the war was over, Lewis was still only twenty-six. He carried on scoring. His Arsenal record in official matches, right up to his retirement in 1953, reveals an impressive 118 goals in 176 appearances. That puts him, even today, within the top dozen Arsenal strikers of all time. But factor in Lewis's wartime games and that career-wide tally becomes three times more impressive – as many as 392 goals in 451 matches. Furthermore, a chunk of these war years was spent on the front line in Germany with the British Army of the Rhine. He's a man whose exploits should be more widely celebrated.

The zenith of Lewis's career will undoubtedly be reached one Saturday afternoon in the April of 1950 when he scores both goals in the FA Cup final as Arsenal beat Liverpool 2–0. He's nearing the end of his playing days by then, and the world is a different place. For starters, match–day programmes no longer need to carry warnings of possible aerial bombardment.

Arsenal 7–1 Charlton Athletic

War is over

Saturday 26 May 1945

England vs France

Victory international

Perhaps it was right that honours were even, that this afternoon would produce a draw.

On the fourth Saturday in May, fewer than three weeks after the Allied countries had exploded in rapture with news of Germany's surrender, and widespread celebrations had broken out on what became known as VE Day, the national football teams of England and France march out at Wembley.

Despite regular wartime internationals involving the home countries, this is England's first match against non-UK opposition since a 2–0 defeat against Romania in Bucharest in May 1939. It's also the first of three matches dubbed 'Victory internationals', the other two being home games against Switzerland (at Highbury) and Belgium, back here at Wembley next January.

The sense of mutual respect and relief is palpable in the eyes of both captains as they shake hands. The tall and imposing

England skipper, Tommy Lawton, leans forward slightly, lowering himself to the height of his French counterpart, Oscar Heisserer. *We're all equal here*, Lawton's body language seems to declare. *We've all been through it.* There's a twinkle in each man's eyes, a smile on their faces. The handshake is gentle and genuine; no bone-crushing signal of intent here.

This is a football match of solidarity, comradeship and brotherhood, a celebration that the dark days of the last six years effectively ended with Hitler's self-inflicted gunshot less than a month ago. Football can now properly resume, even if today's game – along with those two other forthcoming Victory internationals – doesn't qualify as a full international.

Lawton's strike partner, Horatio 'Raich' Carter of Sunderland, scores first, with just ten minutes of peace-time football gone. Any expectation that England – with the likes of Lawton, Carter, Stanley Matthews, Joe Mercer and Bert Williams in their line-up – are going to walk away with a comfortable victory soon evaporates when, first, Brentford's Leslie Smith has a penalty saved and, second, when Ernest Vaast equalises for the visitors. England regain the lead with ten minutes left through Lawton and it looks to be enough. But a penalty is conceded in the ninetieth minute and Heisserer is only too happy to make sure the spoils are shared.

'Congratulations, guys,' says the French newsreel announcer. 'You surprised the English, the masters of the football world.' Indeed, Heisserer's goal prompts a collective sigh within the England camp, a sense of disappointment justified by one look at that impressive, four-strong attack that should have put France to the sword: Lawton, Matthews, Carter and 'Sailor' Brown.

An inside-forward for Charlton, Brown was given his nickname for apparently sharing his physique with that of Popeye; a 'rolling gait and muscularly stocky build', according to one obituary nearly sixty years later. Brown will be in the starting line-up for the next Victory international at Wembley, scoring in a 2–0 win over Belgium. It's his sixth and final appearance for England in either wartime or Victory internationals. He will never earn a full cap.

His story is not dissimilar to that of the other goalscorer against the Belgians. Jesse Pye, a former South Yorkshire coalminer who served in North Africa and Italy during the war, does at least win a single full England cap, against Ireland in 1949. But despite, like Brown, going on to become a record signing for his club – Wolves in Pye's case, Aston Villa in Brown's – he never becomes an established international. One match, one cap.

Contrast this with another player making his England bow in that Belgium match, a future team-mate of Pye's at Molineux. With that trademark Billy Whizz quiff, Billy Wright will become both the first England player to reach 100 caps and one of the national team's most popular captains in history. He will play at three World Cups, manage Arsenal, become head of sport at ATV and Central Television, marry one of the singing Beverley Sisters and twice be the recipient of the big red book on *This Is Your Life*.

Jesse Pye opened a sweet shop.

England 2–2 France

Heroes and villains

Saturday 27 April 1946

Charlton Athletic vs Derby County

FA Cup final

Bert Turner is an experienced player with some notable achievements etched onto his CV. Prior to the outbreak of the Second World War, he won back-to-back promotions with Charlton before they went on to finish runners-up in the First Division in 1937, just three points away from winning the title. This son of Caerphilly has won several full caps for his country too, as well as appearing in numerous wartime internationals. And let's not forget his guest appearances for Newport-based Lovell's Athletic, the works team of the confectionery manufacturers of the same name.

But it is ninety short seconds in 1946 – by which time Turner has reached the grand old age of thirty-seven – that truly make his name, that stamp his indelible mark on FA Cup folklore. It's 0–0 between Turner's Charlton and red-hot favourites Derby in a final that's the climax of a competition longer than any other in its seventy-four-year history. With the ending of the war, there hasn't been a regular 1946–47 league season. Instead, each round of the FA Cup, up to and including the sixth round, has been a two-legged affair. It's a one-off departure with two purposes: to give fans as many matches as possible in a league-free season, while also bolstering the coffers of cash-stricken clubs.

Charlton have played thirteen matches to reach Wembley, Derby one more on account of their semi-final against Birmingham having gone to a replay. And now, with eighty-five minutes gone of a pulsating but scoreless final, extra-time looms. At least, that's until Bert Turner intervenes. Dally Duncan – one of Derby's impressive front three alongside Raich Carter and Peter Doherty – pounces on a punched clearance by Charlton keeper Sam Bartram and fires towards the goal. In attempting to clear the ball from danger, full-back Turner miskicks and sends it into his own net.

With just minutes left, it looks like the cup is heading to the East Midlands. But Turner has other ideas. Within sixty seconds, Charlton have been awarded a free-kick on the edge of the Derby box. Ready to wipe the slate clean, Turner nominates himself to take it. His attempt strikes Doherty's heel and completely wrong-foots goalkeeper Vic Woodley. It's 1–1 and that period of extra-time is back on the agenda. Not only has Turner become the oldest player to score in an FA Cup final, but he has also become the first player to score at both ends, a tradition later upheld in the 1980s by both Manchester City's Tommy Hutchison and Tottenham's Gary Mabbutt.

Into extra-time, Derby's status as pre-match favourites proves justified as they run in three goals in fourteen quick-fire minutes. First, the Northern Ireland international Doherty puts the Rams back in front, before two goals from their centre-forward Jackie Stamps (who had also scored twice in that semi-final replay) seals Derby's first – and still only – FA Cup triumph. As well as the fifteen matches they'd played to secure the silverware, they've had other hurdles to surmount. At the start of the campaign, captain Jack Nicholas visited a gypsy camp in order to have a supposed curse on the club lifted. Then, a players' strike was averted just before the cup final after the players discovered that the wives of the directors had superior seats at Wembley compared to those allocated to the players' partners.

In short, it's a hard-won triumph. The post-war gold shortages mean that the winners' medals are fashioned from bronze, but no one minds. A victory is a victory is a victory.

Still, Derby's serpentine cup run could have been half an hour shorter. With the game in the dying embers of normal time after Bert Turner's dual cameo as both villain and hero, Stamps – possessor of one of English football's fiercest shots, the Peter Lorimer of his day – took aim and unleashed what he thought would be the winning goal. But the shot was comfortably gathered by the hands of a surprised Sam Bartram. Stamps had hit the ball with such force that it had burst, much to his frustration.

'The bloody thing just went PHUT ...'

Charlton Athletic 1–4 Derby County

The raggle-taggle brigade

Wednesday 11 August 1948

Great Britain vs Yugoslavia

Olympic Games quarter-final

Matt Busby visited Wembley recently. Four months ago, he was here with his Manchester United side, leading them to their first FA Cup win for almost forty years as they overcame Blackpool

4–2. Today is a wholly different proposition. He's here as the boss of the Great Britain Olympic football team, a raggle-taggle brigade of strictly amateur players who, a month earlier, had never clapped eyes on each other before. Indeed, Busby had seen only one of this twenty-six-man squad play prior to taking the job: Bishop Auckland's Bob Hardisty, alongside whom the Scot had played for Middlesbrough during the war.

To have steered this makeshift team to the last four of the competition was success beyond which Busby could only have dreamed. After all, as he will later write in his memoirs (the imaginatively titled *My Story*), he knew the Olympic playing field wasn't an even one – and wouldn't be for quite some time.

'Russia, Hungary, Bulgaria, Yugoslavia ... These are leaders in international amateur football, yet they are represented by players who, by our standards, would be classed as professionals. Some of the big stars in these countries, though they may all have other jobs for the benefit of the casual enquirer, play football all year round – and they are obviously paid money, often big money, to help attend to the necessities of life.'

Busby declares the situation to be 'a gross distortion of the Olympic ideal'. Britain faces a dilemma, he says: whether to refuse to take part or to do so 'knowing they have no earthly chance of victory'. The authorities always plump for the latter, 'presumably on the assumption that it is better to have the Union Jack trampled into the turf than not to show the flag at all ... even though, every four years, it exposes Britain's footballer-clerks, footballer-grocers and footballer-pitmen to something akin to ridicule'.

Busby's new charges are men with rugged, everyday names and rugged, everyday professions. Inside-right Andy Aitken is a steelworker from Motherwell, while outside-left Bill Amor is a policeman. Eric Fright is a shopkeeper, Kevin McAlinden a bookmaker and Tommy Hopper a greengrocer. During the war, striker Dennis Kelleher escaped from a prisoner-of-war camp and spent three weeks traversing Germany under cover until he reached his native Northern Ireland. These are men of character, spirit, fight.

In order to be a firm part of Matt Busby's plans, including attending a training camp in rural Berkshire, each player is foregoing their regular wage from their regular job. And unlike their backhander-accepting counterparts from Eastern Europe, in line with those Olympic ideals there's not a penny of FA money heading their way. In return, though, these amateurs not only have the personal attention of one of the most promising young managers in the country, but they are being coached by a handful of off-for-the-summer Manchester United players.

And now – at least for eleven lucky ones – there's the dream of playing at Wembley.

To get to today's semi-final, the Great Britain team have had to beat the Netherlands and France. Both were tight games, held respectively at Highbury and Craven Cottage. With the Olympic athletics events having vacated the Empire Stadium last weekend (the stand-out performances being four sprint gold medals for the Netherlands' Fanny Blankers-Koen and long-distance gold and silver for Emil Zátopek from Czechoslovakia), the tournament's final four games will be held here. It's a far cry from some of the grounds used in the early rounds; these include Champion Hill in Dulwich and Green Pond Road, home of Walthamstow Avenue FC.

This evening, though – in front of a nation watching live on television – Busby's side will run out of road, undone by the Iron Curtain's definition of 'amateur'. Yugoslavia are just too strong. Great Britain put up a plucky performance, with a goal from the Welsh winger Frank Donovan, an electrician from Pembroke Dock, immediately cancelling out Yugoslavia's opener, but the East Europeans ultimately emerge 3–1 winners.

Busby will generously give a few other players the chance to play on the sainted Wembley turf in the bronze-medal match just forty-two hours later, but Denmark take the medals with a 5–3 victory.

While he hasn't replicated the success he tasted here at Wembley back in late April with his professional charges, Busby is nonetheless basking in the glow of a near-impossible job well done. And that glow doesn't remotely dim by the time he gets round to writing those memoirs nine years later.

'Steering Manchester United to the championship of the Football League was child's play besides the problems of sorting out a winning team from twenty-six spare-time footballers from four different countries.

'I got a great kick out of working with such a grand team of amateur footballers.'

Great Britain 1–3 Yugoslavia

Day trippers

Saturday 23 April 1949

Bromley vs Romford

FA Amateur Cup final

In Romford, Saturday dawns and the air crackles with the optimism of what just might be this afternoon. Today, the town's football team travels to north-west London for its first – and what will be its only – appearance in the FA Amateur Cup final. More significant to the football historian is the fact that the competition will be reaching its denouement at Wembley for the first time. Until now, it's been played at grounds all over the country – Roker Park, The Den, Ayresome Park, the Boleyn Ground, Selhurst Park – but such is the popularity of the competition in these post-war years that the FA has elected to relocate the final to a permanent home. That decision will be thoroughly vindicated this afternoon when 94,000 expectant souls swing through the turnstiles.

A large proportion will arrive from Essex. Romford is experiencing a mass exodus; one of the town's factories has hired no fewer than *forty* coaches to take its workers to the match. Among the motorcade heading west is the team bus, carrying the squad and officials in a manner to which they're not accustomed. Not only do they stop off for lunch at the Manor Cottage Tavern in East Finchley but, from there on in, two police motorcycle outriders escort them along the final seven miles around the North Circular to the stadium.

Their opponents, though, are rather formidable, a side perfectly capable of bursting Romford's balloon. Bromley are enjoying a terrific season, one that will see them win both the Athenian League title and the Kent Amateur Cup. Despite featuring two players from the Great Britain Olympic squad from last summer (Tommy Hopper and their captain Eric Fright), their star player is actually the centre-forward George Brown, whose goal tally this season alone has reached *triple* figures. Included in that total are a phenomenal *thirteen* hat-tricks.

Despite their amateur status, neither side appears to be over-awed by playing at Wembley. As it is, their respective semi-finals took place at other cathedrals of football. Bromley drew with Leytonstone at Highbury before winning the replay at Stamford

Bridge, while Romford dispatched Crook Colliery Welfare at West Ham's Boleyn Ground.

But Romford will do no dispatching today. Bromley take the lead in the first half, when Hopper finishes off a slick move, and the Essex men have little in the way of a reply. Indeed, such is Bromley's dominance that, in these substitute-free days, when two of their players can do little more than hobble round the pitch thanks to injuries sustained, their nine fit men can still see the game out. It's the third time Bromley have lifted the Amateur Cup, although it will be their last. Romford never darken Wembley's doors again, nor do their fans. Those factory workers are back in position come Monday morning, that excursion to north-west London a once-in-a-lifetime affair.

Bromley 1–0 Romford

The 1950s

Gentlemen and scholars

Saturday 21 April 1951

Bishop Auckland vs Pegasus

FA Amateur Cup final

Wembley Stadium will witness much over its first 100 years of existence, but rarely will it see a doctor of philosophy in goal.

But that's the situation this afternoon with Ben Brown, of Oriel College, Oxford, wearing the goalkeeper's jersey for amateur side Pegasus. He's not alone when it comes to academic pedigree. Pegasus full-back John Maughan is a modern history student shortly to head off to theological college and life thereafter as a vicar, while forward John Dutchman is another notable scholar who served in South Africa during the war, where, in his spare time, he wrote a dissertation on ostriches.

In fact, all eleven Pegasus players are well-read, intellectual men. Their club's curious name reveals why. A combination of the Oxford centaur and the Cambridge falcon, Pegasus is a team featuring the best footballers from both universities, a concept dreamed up by the academic Dr Harold Thompson, later chairman of the FA. The ink is still fresh on the blueprint; Thompson conceived of the idea only three years ago. Despite such a short time in existence – and despite the fact that they don't play in a league, nor do they have a home ground – the club, constructed along similar 'gentlemanly' principles of fair play and sportsmanship as the famous Corinthian-Casuals, have already reached the final of the Amateur Cup.

This isn't the first time that university students have taken to the Wembley pitch. In 1929, London University took on Cambridge University, the latter running out 3–0 winners. Eight years later, a combined Great Britain universities side hosted a team of students from Germany; it was the first time a German side appeared at Wembley. And, having played each other for decades at various grounds across London, from 1953 until 1988 the Oxford/Cambridge varsity match will become a staple of the Wembley calendar.

This afternoon's contest – against County Durham's greatest amateur side Bishop Auckland – isn't quite the culture clash it might first appear. The Bishops' kit combines the dark blue of Oxford and the light blue of Cambridge, and this is no mere coincidence. Sixty years earlier, they too were formed by students of both universities who were studying together at Auckland Castle.

Bishop Auckland have won the competition seven times before, but never at Wembley. Their only appearance at the national stadium was last year, when they were surprisingly thrashed 4–0 by fellow County Durham side Willington. They'll improve on that result this afternoon, but the silverware won't be heading back north with them.

Playing in front of a full house of 100,000 (some of whom have opted to sport mortar boards), after a goalless first half Pegasus run out 2–1 winners at the final whistle. It's a thoroughly deserved victory. Coached by former Tottenham player Vic Buckingham, they favour a highly attractive style similar to the 'push and run' approach that's currently propelling Spurs towards the league title. Indeed, one newspaper report will declare that 'it was almost possible to imagine that these white-shirted men were the Spurs themselves'.

Just three years into their existence, Pegasus have flown to the top of the amateur football tree. They will regain the cup in 1953 in front of another full house, but that will be the only addition to their palmares. In 1963, fifteen years after they first convened, the players of Oxford and Cambridge go their separate ways. 'Pegasus came and went like a shooting star,' *The Times*' correspondent remarks, 'but in their short life, they shed a light on the game as a whole. They were something different.'

Any despondency Bishop Auckland feel heading back north this afternoon will dissipate over the next few years, when they'll amass a further handful of victories in the competition. They make six appearances in seven finals up to 1957.

Indeed, such is their domination of the competition during this time, it's small wonder that, with an eye on a certain other club's supremacy in the nascent European Cup, the north-east football writer Harry Pearson will declare them 'the Real Madrid of amateur football'. All except the patronage of a fascist dictator, that is.

Bishop Auckland 1–2 Pegasus

A tilt at redemption

Wednesday 9 May 1951

England vs Argentina

Festival of Britain international friendly

'On the result of this game, our international prestige, buried beneath the soil of Brazil last year, will either be resurrected or dragged through the mire once more.'

The correspondent from the *News of the World* understands the importance of this afternoon's match. It's little more than ten months since the England team returned from the World Cup in Brazil, little more than ten months since they experienced the greatest humiliation in their history. Right there, in Belo Horizonte. Right there, attempting to teach the world how to play football, having arrogantly refused to participate in the three World Cup finals held up until then. Right there, losing to the part-timers of the USA, sunk by a goal scored by Joe Gaetjens, a man usually found up to his elbows in soapy water, washing dishes in a Brooklyn restaurant.

Walter Winterbottom, your boys took one hell of a beating.

For subsequent England managers, such abject failure in an international tournament by failing to progress from the initial group stage, coupled by the shame of that USA defeat, would be more than sufficient for them to be served with their cards. Not so Winterbottom. Still in his thirties, he's only five years into his sixteen-year tenure. And he's England's first ever national coach. The suits at the FA have yet to develop the skills of hiring and firing.

Although he's led England to victory at Maine Road in Manchester, Leeds Road in Huddersfield, Highbury, Goodison Park, Villa Park, White Hart Lane and Roker Park, Winterbottom has yet to register his first win at Wembley – although, admittedly, this is only the third time that the national team has played at the national stadium since 1946.

Ten months on from Belo Horizonte, this is – as the man from the *News of the World* declares – a test of character, a tilt at redemption. It's England's second match against overseas opposition since returning from Brazil ashen and embarrassed. The first match, an inconclusive 2–2 draw with Yugoslavia back in November, didn't rebuild reputation, didn't restore faith, didn't forgive and forget. The wound is still open and weeping and sore. Only a win today will help to anaesthetise the pain.

Today's game – the opening match of a series of friendlies involving the home nations and visiting sides to celebrate the Festival of Britain – is not only the first time the hosts have played in red but also it's the first ever encounter between the future fierce adversaries. Argentina are something of an unknown entity. Although they were runners-up at the inaugural World Cup in 1930, they didn't take part in either 1938 or 1950. They're known as a mobile side who like to pass the ball quickly and sharply. As such, their style is in marked contrast to that of Winterbottom's England, who are more direct, more physical, both up front and at the back.

There's a debutant in England's defence this afternoon – and he's the oldest player on the pitch. It's the Fulham centre-half Jim Taylor, who's making his international bow at thirty-three, having travelled to the World Cup last year without playing. Quite how Taylor, an avid pipe-smoker, will cope with the fast-moving Argentinians isn't clear. This is a man who's been described by one newspaper as 'no graceful stylist in his floppy shorts and thick boots'.

The contrast in styles is proved in the eighteenth minute when a swift Argentinian move finds England goalkeeper Bert Williams out of position and outside-right Mario Boyé heads into an empty net. That the visitors didn't expect to find it this easy to breach England's defence is hinted at by Geoffrey Green of *The Times*. 'Boyé, flushed with the excitement, ran back to the centre as if he had conquered the world.'

England's best efforts to equalise come from that reliable pair of Stan Mortensen and Jackie Milburn, but neither can get past the Argentinian goalkeeper Miguel Rugilo. Something of a showman, the thickly moustachioed Rugilo pulls off unconventional save after unconventional save. 'Three times he stunned the crowd, receiving ovations by holding his hands up like a boxer,' the *Daily Herald* will report tomorrow morning. 'He saved at least six sure goals.'

The last thirty minutes of the match are televised live, commentated on by Jimmy Jewell, a man enjoying his third incarnation in football, having previously been both a referee (one who officiated the 1938 FA Cup final, no less) and the coach of Norwich City. Armchair England fans tuning in for this final third of the match will have liked what they saw. With ten minutes left, Mortensen equalises with a point-blank header before Milburn, who scored twice here just four days ago in the FA Cup final, slides in to score the winner.

England have avoided another grave post-mortem, but the manner of their victory can't be described as assured. Tomorrow morning, the *Manchester Guardian*'s headline offers a five-word verdict: 'Late goals after many failures'. The ex-footballer journalist Charles Buchan is more complimentary. 'The game provided a contrast in defensive styles and I can say with certainty that our method with the "stopper" centre-half was much more the convincing of the two.'

While the famously astute Buchan clearly took some pleasure in England reasserting themselves against overseas opposition, another crisis isn't too far over the horizon. In two years' time, Hungary will arrive in north-west London.

England 2–1 Argentina

Cover version

Saturday 3 May 1952

Arsenal vs Newcastle United

FA Cup final

It's a charming tableau, one rendered in pencil and paint by 11-year-old hands. It shows four footballers. On the left, there's the blue jersey of a goalkeeper, his arrow-straight arms attempting to divert the passage of a heavy, brown leather ball. Next along is a player, with neatly parted hair, wearing a red shirt with white sleeves – presumably an Arsenal player. Whether he's a striker or defender isn't quite clear. Next to him is a player in black-and-white stripes. Newcastle United? Notts County? Grimsby Town? Juventus? The final player is just watching on, standing stock-still. The number on his back – 9 – suggests the stripes are attacking and that the Arsenal player, rather than attempting to score, is actually proving ineffectual in preventing what looks to be a goal.

Bearing in mind the age of the artist, these players are impressively drawn, their limbs in proportion, their heads not outsized. But whatever its merits, it's an artwork that would have never been seen again, after a spell on a classroom wall, were it not for the identity of the young artist. Instead, it adorns the sleeve of an LP released more than twenty years later, an LP made by this very person, by then a man in his early thirties. His name? John Winston Lennon.

While many record buyers knew not what the artwork for this album, *Walls & Bridges*, depicted, followers of football of a certain vintage knew exactly which moment it captured – a moment caught by the shutter of a camera and reproduced in paint by the prepubescent Lennon. The date written at the top of the painting – June 1952 – confirmed it. This was the young artist's impression of the George Robledo goal that won Newcastle the FA Cup the previous month.

The Robledo brothers – inside-left George and left-half Ted – were mainstays of the Magpies. Born in Chile, their English mother brought them to Wath upon Dearne in South Yorkshire at the ages of five and four respectively. Starting out as players at nearby Barnsley, they both signed for Newcastle in 1949, with George refusing to join the club unless Ted was part of the deal. They both also played for the country of their birth, despite neither of them speaking Spanish. Instead, the Chile dressing room resonated with hearty Yorkshire vowels. After retirement, George would move back to South America, becoming a PE teacher in Viña del Mar. Ted would work in the oil industry and was lost at sea in 1970 in the Persian Gulf, falling from a tanker allegedly after a fight with the ship's captain, who was charged with murder but acquitted. Ted's body has never been found.

That cup-winning goal of George's – running on to a Bobby Mitchell cross to nod the ball past George Swindin, the keeper with the arrow-straight arms – represents the crowning glory of a career that also saw service in the 1950 World Cup. The narrow victory over Arsenal should have been more comprehensive, bearing in mind that not only has injury forced their opponents to be reduced to ten men for much of the match, but that they finish the game with only seven fit players. Nonetheless, Newcastle have broken new ground in the competition. They are the first twentieth-century team to win the FA Cup in successive years.

The Newcastle captain Joe Harvey makes the climb up the steps for the second time in thirteen months, following last season's victory over Blackpool. Waiting for him in the Royal Box, ready to hand over the silverware, is a man whose presence at the match might well provide the reason why this particular encounter grabbed the imagination of that young painter from Liverpool. Handing over the trophy was the provider of Lennon's middle name – a certain Winston Churchill.

Arsenal 0–1 Newcastle United

The bridesmaid's big day

Saturday 2 May 1953

Blackpool vs Bolton Wanderers

FA Cup final

In the winter of 2018, in a cavernous warehouse in the Derbyshire countryside, the match ball from the 1953 FA Cup final came under the auctioneer's hammer. Metaphorically, at least. It sold for the sum of £5,250. The purist observers were pleased; it was purchased by a lifelong Blackpool supporter.

Up to that point, this ball had had rather a nomadic existence for a piece of football memorabilia of such significance to the English game. At the tail-end of the 1980s, it was a raffle prize at an FA charity evening and was won by one of the event's waitresses, who promptly passed it on to her football-crazy brother. He possibly wasn't as football-crazy as she thought. One Christmas Day, the power failed at his house, requiring him to call out his electrician. For making himself available at this distinctly unsocial hour, the electrician was given the ball as extra recompense and he marched back to his Christmas dinner with this additional present under his arm. Eventually, it fell into the possession of the son-in-law of one of the electrician's closest friends, who kept it for eleven years before deciding to put it up for sale. The auctioneers were only too happy to add it to the inventory of their next event.

This ball holds such significance because it represents the only time, in a hundred years of FA Cup finals at Wembley, that one has been given to a player to take home, the only time that a player has earned the honour by scoring a hat-trick in the final. That man is Stan Mortensen, centre-forward for Blackpool and England.

Mortensen scores his first after thirty-five minutes, cancelling out Nat Lofthouse's second-minute opener with a heavily deflected shot that he's fortunate to be credited with (indeed, BBC commentator Kenneth Wolstenholme is insistent it's an own goal). Ten minutes into the second half, though, Bolton are 3–1 up. If they're not home and hosed, then they at least look likely to be imposing a third cup final defeat in six years on Blackpool.

But this doesn't reckon on Mortensen. After sixty-eight

minutes, he gets his second, scrambling home an over-hit Matthews cross at the far post. And with two minutes left, he fires a blistering free-kick past shell-shocked Bolton keeper Stan Hanson to make history.

In homes across the country, the audience for the FA Cup final is greater than it's ever been before, thanks to many families either buying or renting television sets ahead of the Queen's coronation in exactly a month's time. The 1938 final, between Preston North End and Huddersfield Town, was the first to be televised. Then, fewer than 10,000 households boasted a television set, a number dwarfed by the 93,497 inside the stadium that day. Fifteen years later, one in every five British homes has a set, around which friends and relatives have gathered this afternoon.

And these viewers have been served up a doozy of a cup final, which reaches even greater heights when, in the second minute of injury-time, Matthews squares to outside-left Bill Perry, who shoots home to claim a win more dramatic than any cup final before it. Such an exciting match will help to crystallise the cup final as an annual national television event, a must-see. As such, it's the first of several events to become a bolted-on fixture of the televisual calendar. The first Queen's Speech will be broadcast at Christmas 1957, with the maiden live transmission of the Grand National following in 1960.

The '53 final is far from Stanley Matthews' greatest ever performance, yet it remains his most famous match. While it was his trickery that set up Perry for Blackpool's winner, the accuracy of his crosses this afternoon hasn't been at his usual standard. But the match is universally referred to as 'the Matthews Final' anyway. At the age of thirty-eight, and twice a runner-up in the final, he has finally won the trophy, a fitting climax to a career that many presume he will now draw the curtain on. (No one would have expected him to be playing top-flight football for another dozen years to beyond his fiftieth birthday.)

To be fair to Matthews, he's ill at ease with the state of affairs that sees Mortensen cast into the shadows by the wholesale use of the phrase 'the Matthews Final'. 'Every time I hear [those] words,' he reveals, 'I cringe with embarrassment because quite simply it's not true.'

It didn't matter if it weren't true. It was preordained. The *News of the World* had, six days ahead of the match, determined that a Blackpool victory 'will go down in soccer history as the Stanley Matthews final'. The *Sunday Chronicle*'s coverage isn't atypical. The headline 'Magnificent Matthews' is followed by the mildly bemusing declaration: 'Matthews 4, Bolton 3 is more correctly the result'.

What must Stan Mortensen be thinking as he scans those Sunday papers? Only the leather ball next to him is a conclusive acknowledgement of his achievement. He could have scored six, but the spotlight would still have fallen elsewhere. He has a winner's medal, he's scored a hat-trick, but he's fated to be the bridesmaid, doomed to play second fiddle.

In later life, Mortensen is eulogised in song by indie satirists Half Man Half Biscuit, who anoint him as 'the Jesus Christ of Bloomfield Road'. He dies in 1991, on the very day that Blackpool, in beating Scunthorpe in the Fourth Division play-off semi-final, reach Wembley for the first time since the '53 final.

One wag suggests that 'they'll probably call it the Matthews funeral'.

Blackpool 4–3 Bolton Wanderers

People from outer space

Wednesday 25 November 1953

England vs Hungary

International friendly

Running a hand through his slicked-back hair, Pat Ward-Thomas takes a long sigh and gazes down at his notes. They are plentiful, and studded with exclamation marks right from the very first line. He has little time to make sense of them; he needs to dictate his copy down the line to the office in Manchester post-haste. After all, what has just happened over the last two hours could well be front-page news.

Ward-Thomas is much better known as the golf correspondent of the *Manchester Guardian*, a man at ease with whipping up illuminating pen-portraits of the players of the day or poetically describing the arc of an approach shot at the seventeenth hole at St Andrews. But this isn't a sun-kissed, high-summer afternoon on the links. This is Wembley in misty, malcontent autumn, and Ward-Thomas is in his off-season role as football reporter.

While there has been plenty on show here in front of him this afternoon that earns his purple prose, Ward-Thomas the poet needs to also be Ward-Thomas the obituary writer. Has English football just been served its death notice by the magnificent Magyars? Even a part-time football correspondent fears the worst. He picks up the phone and prepares himself to speak to Manchester.

Tomorrow morning, his verdict will be read across the

nation's breakfast tables: 'England will never match this efficiency unless the progress of international teams becomes, as in Hungary, of more importance than the interminable league programme.' As if the scoreline hadn't alone told the story, his words confirm that Hungary had delivered 'a severe lesson in the arts of Association Football'. No stranger to the 'delights' of Eastern Europe after a lengthy spell as a prisoner-of-war at Stalag Luft III in Poland during the war, Ward-Thomas nonetheless can do nothing but heap praise on the visitors.

With all the bluntness he would normally employ to describe a tee shot sliced into the trees, Ward-Thomas reserves particular opprobrium for the home side's attacking players, who muster just five shots to Hungary's thirty-five. 'England's refusal to shoot quickly was pathetic in its pottering hesitancy, arising from that accursed disease of making sure.' Hungary's players were liberated and free range. England's weren't. The shackles were on.

The ever-astute Charles Buchan doesn't shy away from what needs to be said either. 'It is no use blinking at the facts,' he announces. 'The plain truth is that we are many years behind Hungary and the other continental teams in all the essential points: speed, ball control, distribution and teamwork.'

As Jonathan Wilson will later write in *The Guardian*, exactly sixty years to the day, it's not just that it's England's first defeat at Wembley. It's that they've been handed an absolute pasting while surrendering that unbeaten record. Seismic tremors will now rumble through the fault-lines of English football.

'This had not been a defeat in Madrid in May,' notes Wilson, 'or in Belo Horizonte in July. It had been a defeat at Wembley on a damp pitch on a misty November afternoon, in conditions most believed football was meant to be played.' The complacent national team have been forced to surrender their misguided belief to be the godfathers of world football. England's approach has been confirmed as blinkered, their ideas stagnant. Lessons are to be learnt.

Not that England are the best at learning lessons, at heeding advice. The humiliation dealt out by the United States three years earlier at the World Cup in Brazil appears not to have been interpreted as a wake-up call by the cigar-and-scotch brigade at the Football Association. To them, it was a blip, an anomaly. Nothing more. Despite being the current Olympic champions, the Hungarians are still being viewed with amused curiosity when they walk out for kick-off. Their star man – the barrel-torsoed army major Ferenc Puskás – doesn't look too much of a threat. And look at those lightweight boots of theirs, strangely cut under the ankle. How can they play the game, *our* game, with such inadequate footwear?

It takes just seventy-five seconds for that amused curiosity to disappear in the mist, the Hungarian centre-forward Nándor Hidegkuti hitting a first-time, crowd-silencing shot past Gil Merrick. Hidegkuti is key to England being split open time and time again today. Unconventionally, he drops deep – so deep that he's often found in his own goalmouth – in a proto false-nine role, one that the home side can't cope with, despite having encountered such a development when touring Argentina two years earlier. The England players have been, as ever, instructed to mark their opponents in conventional fashion – the number 3 marks the opposition 7, the 5 takes care of the number 9 – but Hungary's fluid numbering system simply bamboozles the hosts. Accordingly, the retreating Hidegkuti pulls England centre-half Harry Johnston up the pitch and out of position, leaving his athletic, mobile fellow forwards to simply swamp the space behind.

After Jackie Sewell fashions an equaliser after fifteen minutes, Hungary reapply the gas and are 4–1 up before half an hour has elapsed. The third goal features Puskás's soon-to-be-legendary drag-back that leaves England captain Billy Wright chasing shadows, looking 'like a fire engine rushing to the wrong fire', as *The Times*' Geoffrey Green astutely observes.

Another couple of Hungarian goals after the break put the issue to bed early in the second half. They've notched up six before there's been even an hour's play. The potential to reach double figures wasn't an outlandish thought. 'No one present would have been surprised had they scored ten,' Ward-Thomas will announce down the line to Manchester.

Those present, the 100,000 England fans in the seats and on the terraces, are dumbfounded rather than angry. Many will admit to being beguiled by the Hungarians' play. Indeed, on the final whistle, generous applause rings out to salute the visitors' superiority. There has been no mass exodus during the second half, very few England supporters have taken an early train home, opting not to escape the embarrassment, the pain.

That England kept a clean sheet for the final half-hour is of no consolation – not to the fans, not to the players, not to Walter Winterbottom. Humiliated. Ashamed. Anachronistic.

They're a team trapped by tactical awareness, training methods and fitness levels that have outlasted their shelf life. They're standing still in a world that's accelerating away. They are prisoners of the past. And they need to catch up.

It takes time though. Six months after this first Wembley defeat (actually their first home defeat in ninety years of international football), England travel to Budapest to test themselves against Hungary once more. They are beaten 7–1. The thoroughly dominant, thoroughly modern Magyars dish out another thrashing. Once again, their free-form attacking play leaves the England back line bewildered, as centre-half Syd Owen will admit. The experience, he sighs, was 'like playing people from outer space'.

By then, though, Pat Ward-Thomas isn't around to

draft another obituary. He's back on the fairway, back in the sunshine.

England 3–6 Hungary

The light fantastic

Wednesday 26 October 1955

London XI vs Frankfurt XI

Inter City Fairs Cup group match

The clocks go back in four days' time, plunging teatime Britain into premature darkness. We're still in British Summer Time for now, but a 7.45 p.m. kick-off in late October means the sun has long since set. But that's no matter for Wembley any more. Tonight, its bright floodlights will be used for the first time for a football match.

Not only is their use an innovation, but tonight's competition is new too. Alongside the just-announced European Cup, UEFA has pulled the wraps off a parallel tournament: the Inter-Cities Fairs Cup. Invitations have been made to those European cities that hold trade fairs to participate (hence its name) and accordingly Barcelona, Basel, Birmingham, Cologne, Copenhagen, Frankfurt, Lausanne, Leipzig, London, Milan, Vienna and Zagreb have taken up the offer, although Vienna will drop out before a ball is kicked.

Managed by Chelsea chairman Joe Mears and captained

by his club skipper Roy Bentley, the London XI have been recruited from other sides across the capital, including Spurs, Millwall, Charlton, Leyton Orient and Fulham. Having travelled to Switzerland back in June to stick five past the Basel XI, the Londoners tonight step onto home turf – albeit home turf that's strangely illuminated.

The Germans acclimatise quicker to the 160 lamps firing out bright white beams and are two up by half-time. Mears's side get their eyes in by the interval and, in the first minute of the second half, the luxuriantly named Fulham striker Bedford Jezzard pulls one back for London. Then his Cottagers teammate Bobby Robson equalises before the prolific Jezzard – who scored thirty-nine league goals the season before last – grabs the winner to ensure that London continue to sit pretty at the top of their group.

Seven weeks later, Wembley turns on the lights again when England host Spain in a midweek friendly – even though their use isn't planned. Despite it being a 2 p.m. kick-off, the return to Greenwich Mean Time, along with the misty weather, is having its effect. At half past three, with fifteen minutes still left, the switch is flicked and on come those 160 lamps to illuminate the gloomy vista. Kenneth Wolstenholme, for one, is bathed in delight.

'Oh, the lights! The floodlights! The floodlights have been switched on!' the BBC TV commentator gleefully announces. 'Now we really can see the fog as it swirls in the floodlighting.'

By this stage, England are four goals to the good, but fail to add to their tally under the lights. They do seem to help the Spanish eyes, unused to playing in such misty conditions; within four minutes they've scored a consolation.

Surprisingly, England won't play an entire match under the Wembley floodlights for another eight years, when they're deployed for an evening game against Northern Ireland in late

November 1963. (They were, though, used back in June when Henry Cooper took on Cassius Clay in the first of their famous bouts.) England beat the Northern Irish 8-3. Playing on mid-week evenings at Wembley will now become the norm.

It's not the only innovation in 1963. That year, the open terraces at Wembley become a relic of the past when a glass and aluminium cantilever roof, offering protection from the rain right around the stadium, is installed. A state-of-the-art electronic scoreboard is also erected. On its fortieth birthday, Wembley Stadium moves into the modern era.

London XI 3–2 Frankfurt XI

'It was the noise. I heard the crack'

Saturday 5 May 1956

Birmingham City vs Manchester City

FA Cup final

At 9 a.m., as the London train steams into Chichester station, 16-year-old Fred Knotts moves forward to climb aboard, his stomach a tangle of nerves. A couple of hours later – with those nerves even tighter and more intense – he alights at Victoria Station and heads down the steps into the Underground. His destination is Wembley Stadium. His destiny is to be one of the eight ballboys on duty at this afternoon's FA Cup final.

All eight have been selected from along the Sussex stretch

of the south coast; Knotts is here as a reward for his work as a junior coach. The ballboys don't know one another and, after today, will never see each other again. But for the next few hours, they will be united in the service of English football's most glittering occasion, faithfully gathering every wayward shot and every hoofed clearance, returning the ball to play as swiftly as possible. These teenagers are vital cogs in the smooth running of the day. No pressure, boys. No pressure.

Having changed into matching cream tracksuits and wandered around the empty pitch, the ballboys are given a tour of behind-the-scenes Wembley, beyond the velvet curtain, deep in the stadium's bowels. They visit the dressing rooms, they meet the players, and they shake hands with the officials, including the one-armed referee Alf Bond. But they're given little or no steer on their duties this afternoon. There's no briefing, no rehearsal, no drill. Each is simply allotted his own position around the pitch – two behind each goal and two patrolling each touchline – and nothing more. Quick and efficient, that's all they have to be. Not that this simple instruction stops Manchester City captain Roy Paul pulling young Knotts aside for a half-joking whisper in his ear. 'If we're leading 1–0 and there are five minutes left to play, make sure you don't hurry getting the ball.'

Then comes the moment that, back in his home village in Sussex a full sixty-five years later, Knotts remembers the most. 'We stood in the tunnel and that was the thing that got us going – to stand there, with the sunlight pouring in, next to all those professional footballers. When they went out, the sun hit them and then came the roar from the crowd. The hairs on the back of your neck stood up. It was one of those moments. Then we ran out, following them, round to our allotted positions. I was right behind Bert Trautmann's goalposts.'

Although Birmingham are favourites, Manchester City – with

Don Revie selected as their number 9 just a few hours before kick-off – take the lead in the third minute. A fast-flowing counter-attack finds Revie, whose back-heel is met low and hard by Joe Hayes for the opener. Birmingham draw level after fourteen minutes through their inside-right Noel Kinsey, finishing a move in which commentator Kenneth Wolstenholme applauds the use of a throw-in 'for attacking purposes, instead of just getting the ball into play, rather like the American tennis players use their serves'.

From his vantage point to the right of Trautmann's goal, the teenage Knotts – a county-level player in his own right – is learning plenty about professional football. 'Everything was so much faster than what we'd been used to,' he later remembers. 'We thought we were quite quick, but we just weren't.' It's a lesson Knotts will re-learn four years later when he experiences another fleeting FA Cup adventure: playing at left-back for Chichester City against Bristol City at Ashton Gate in the first round of the cup in 1960. 'We were winning everything in county football, beating teams 8–0, 9–0. I really thought we stood a chance against Bristol City. Then I realised I still had a lot to learn. While I was thinking about doing something, their players had already done it. The speed of it was just completely different.' They lost 11–0.

Back in 1956, Manchester City regain the lead seventeen minutes into the second half, prompting another Wolstenholme observation: 'The ladies who are sitting in front of me, who one time looked happy, then very worried, are now hugging each other and kissing each other.' Two minutes later, a long clearance from Trautmann finds Scotland international Bobby Johnstone, who fires home the Mancunians' third. It's the second successive FA Cup final in which he's scored. He's the first player to do that at Wembley.

This isn't Trautmann's last significant contribution to the

match. With seventy-five minutes on the clock, the German does what he's been doing all game – diving bravely at the feet of Birmingham's marauding forwards. This time it's Peter Murphy, whose right knee smashes into Trautmann's neck.

Other than the line of photographers to the side of the goal, Knotts the ballboy is the closest non-player to the incident. 'I was right behind Trautmann. It was the noise, the break. I heard the crack.'

With the FA not permitting substitutes in the English game for the best part of another ten years, the former prisoner-of-war soldiers on towards the final whistle. No one has a clue that the collision between goalkeeper and opposing inside-left is what will come to define today's match as one of the most notable cup finals of the twentieth century. Trautmann awkwardly holds his neck for the remaining fifteen minutes of the game, as well as when he climbs the famous stairs towards the medal presentation. In the Royal Box, Prince Philip passes comment on how crooked the neck looks. It's not until four days later that Trautmann discovers he's dislocated five vertebrae, one of which has cracked in two.

The cup is raised and medals are pocketed, and the eight ball-boys shuffle off backstage. 'There were no celebrations for us,' remembers Knotts. 'At the end, it was simply a case of getting changed, having a quick cup of tea and going home. That was it. The tracksuits were very nice, but we had to return them after the game to be used the following year. All we were given were a pair of socks, a pair of shorts and a little rough shirt. That was all we got.' Then it was a trudge back to the Tube station, back to Victoria, and back aboard the puffer down to the south coast.

'We didn't realise the significance of the match at the time. It was just a good day out for us boys. We were sixteen. We were teenage lads doing something special that weekend and that was it.' On the Monday morning after the final, Knotts is back to work as an apprentice painter and decorator, back among the paint pots and brushes.

'Still, I was there. I was there when it happened. I was part of that game. I've watched it back a few times over the years, of course. "That's me!"'

'But it's just a glimpse and then it's gone.'

Birmingham City 1–3 Manchester City

Jimmy, Jimmy

Wednesday 16 October 1957

England under-23s vs Romania under-23s

International friendly

In a terraced house in Liverpool, a 15-year-old boy is practising hard on his guitar, trying to nail the solo on the Arthur Smith instrumental 'Guitar Boogie'. On Friday night, at the New Clubmoor Hall in the suburb of Norris Green, the teenager will be lining up for the first time in the ranks of local skiffle outfit The Quarrymen. His name is James Paul McCartney and the band, after adopting several different options, will later settle on their own name. They will be known as The Beatles.

That same evening 200 miles away in north London, another teenager, another James, is preparing for his own date with destiny. At the age of seventeen, Jimmy Greaves is slipping on the white shirt of England, ready to represent his country at under-23 level. It's not his first match for the side; that came three weeks ago at Stamford Bridge when he scored twice, and missed a late penalty, in a 6–2 win over Bulgaria.

But tonight is just as special. Tonight will see Greaves play at Wembley Stadium for the first time, the first of many. The striker, who burst into the Chelsea first team just a couple of months ago, is more than two years younger than the rest of the under-23 side. Indeed, his Chelsea team-mate Peter Brabrook had been the only other teenager in the starting XI against Bulgaria.

The rest are positively veterans in comparison. Greaves' fellow striker Brian Clough is nearly five years older; there's an even wider age gap between him and Johnny Haynes. Nonetheless, it was Greaves and Haynes who won most praise following the Bulgaria victory. One newspaper reporter likened their apparently innate partnership to that of a certain couple of football immortals: 'There has been nothing quite like this from an England pair since the great days of Raich Carter and Wilf Mannion.'

It was high praise indeed. Neither Clough nor Haynes are in the side for tonight's Romania match, but Greaves doesn't need the presence or protection of more senior players. Fresh-faced and spiky-haired, he oozes the confidence of youth as he walks onto the sacred turf for the first time. He looks every inch the international footballer – as defined and instructed by the FA in the official confirmation letter sent to Greaves' parents' house in Hainault. Alongside issuing instructions as to the correct attire to be wearing on arrival at Wembley (as well as informing him that only third-class train travel to the stadium would be reimbursed), the letter also made clear how Greaves' boots must be 'in pristine condition and studded in such a way as to make them most suitable for play at this level, with the laces washed, bearing no unseemly marks of mud'.

His boots are most certainly suitable for play at this level. This he shows within a minute of kick-off, within a minute of his first appearance at Wembley, when he gives England the lead, driving home a low shot after Alan A'Court's cross is knocked down by Brabrook. Nerves? What nerves? Twenty-two minutes later, he doubles his tally, and doubles England's lead, when his diving header flies past Iuliu Utu in the Romanian goal. Greaves' momentum has him somersaulting into the net.

Romania score twice to bring the scores level before half-time, but Bill Curry's scrambled goal on the hour mark tips the game in England's direction. It's Greaves – who's also denied what appears to be a clear penalty – who steals the headlines and plaudits again. *The Official FA Yearbook* will later note that 'young Greaves will retain pleasant memories of his first game at Wembley'.

Tonight's match is only the second full game played under the Wembley floodlights – and will be the only under-23s encounter to be played at the national stadium. Greaves will appear a further ten times for the side, notching thirteen goals overall. The precocious teen will then graduate to the senior team – scoring on his debut, of course, as he did everywhere he went.

But Greaves always was a precocious lad. Five months after that Romania game, he got married to his childhood sweetheart Irene Barden. He was barely eighteen years old. And he'd be a father before his twentieth birthday.

England under-23s 3–2 Romania under-23s

Great escapes and early endings

Saturday 2 May 1959

Luton Town vs Nottingham Forest

FA Cup final

Reginald Dwight is in hog heaven. It's five minutes to three on cup final day. He's in the living room at home in Pinner, surrounded by a bounty of chocolate eggs, impressively untouched from Easter Sunday six weeks ago and saved just for this afternoon. For not only is it cup final day, but 12-year-old Reg has a vested interest in today's match. His cousin Roy plays on the right wing for Nottingham Forest.

Wembley is only a handful of miles down the road, but Roy's not been able to get his pre-teen cousin a ticket. That's no matter, though. Reg will become intimate with the stadium in years to come. He'll be there at the cup final in twenty-five years' time as the owner of one of the finalists. Nine years before then, he'll headline a concert there, with the Beach Boys as his support act. This will come three years after he changes his name to Elton John.

But it's Roy who'll be the headline act this afternoon – for good and bad reasons.

The Forest side has travelled south in high optimism. Not only have they beaten holders Bolton Wanderers on the way to the final, but they've also finished higher in the First Division table than today's opponents, Luton Town. Forest's manager Billy Walker is so assured of his team's destiny that earlier in the week he brought them to Wembley to practise climbing the steps to the Royal Box.

It's not the only unorthodox pre-match custom. In his impeccable book *My Father and Other Working-Class Football Heroes*, the broadcaster and writer Gary Imlach will later reveal the peculiar ritual of his father Stewart, Forest's left-winger today. Imlach Sr likes to crack an egg into a glass of sherry before downing it – 'for stamina', apparently. This is a familiar tradition for the Scot. Less familiar is the sight today of Frank Chambers, Forest committee member and local lingerie manufacturer, in the team's dressing room. He circles the players, handing each one a pair of frilly knickers – in Forest colours – for their wives and girlfriends to wear at tonight's (hoped for) celebration dinner at the Savoy. It's an extraordinary intervention, but it successfully breaks all and any tension in the room. (A pair of these knickers – unworn – will be sold at auction in 2008 for £250, one of the more esoteric items of football ephemera to come under the hammer.)

With the edge taken off any unease, Forest start the match impressively. It takes them fewer than ten minutes to take the lead, thanks to their two wingers, Imlach and Dwight. The former neatly turns the Luton right-back Brendan McNally before pulling the ball back for his team-mate to slot home. In Pinner, Reg Dwight experiences a rush that's not just chocolate-induced. His cousin is the possible cup hero. The younger, yet-to-be-born Imlach will later describe it beautifully: 'The ball hits the net and the goal slips untouched into the past. Unmediated, self-contained, perfect. It nestles into the memory, bedding in for posterity.'

Forest's dominance is rewarded by a second goal just four minutes later when their unmarked centre-forward Tommy Wilson rises to meet a long, floated cross. A cricket score could be in the offing, especially when Dwight waltzes through the Luton defence and almost scores a third. But this will be his last contribution to the game. Just beyond the half-hour mark, he's injured in a tackle with McNally. It looks relatively innocuous, but when Dwight eventually rises to his feet, he collapses. On comes the St John Ambulance volunteers, on comes the stretcher. It will later be revealed that he's broken his right fibula.

The FA's 'no substitutes' rule applies even for a game as important as the cup final, so Forest must now ride out the remaining fifty-five or so minutes with ten men. Unsurprisingly, the numerical advantage allows Luton to come back into the game and midfielder Dave Pacey capitalises on Forest's defence tiring on the softening pitch and slots home. But no equaliser arrives in that last half-hour, despite Forest effectively being down to nine men when right-back Bill Whare begins to suffer from acute cramp. He can only hug the touchline of Wembley's big pitch, out of harm's way, unable to run.

The triumphant Forest side climb the steps to the Royal Box, just as they practised a few days ago, and the Queen hands captain Jack Burkitt the trophy. But it could all have been very different. Back in January, in the third round, Forest were nearly dumped out of the cup before their run had even got going. Drawn away to Tooting & Mitcham of the Isthmian League, they encountered a pitch every bit as firm as the Wembley pitch was soft. The turf was ridged and rock hard, with a coating of snow for added jeopardy. Indeed, at lunchtime on the day of the game, Billy Walker – showing more of that trademark confidence – told his players the match would be off.

But it wasn't. Instead, roared on by 14,000 locals, Tooting & Mitcham took a surprise 2–0 lead, their second goal a thirty-yarder that flew into the Forest net. The amateurs seemed to be able to handle the unnatural, unpredictable bounce of the ball – which was behaving as if made of Indian rubber – better than their First Division foes. Until, that is, a back pass bobbled embarrassingly past the home keeper to give Forest a lifeline. A second gift came in the form of a dubious penalty awarded for an unobvious handball. Billy Walker's men escaped to fight another day, emerging comfortable 3–0 winners in the replay a fortnight later.

Had they succumbed to the south London amateurs and their bone-hard pitch, the Forest players would be sat on their sofas come Saturday 2 May, mere spectators with a light ale within easy reach. Among them would be Roy Dwight, his leg fit and functioning, never to suffer the injury that accelerated the end of his playing days.

Instead, still in his kit, he watches the remainder of the match on the television set in Barham Ward at Wembley Hospital, refusing to be wheeled to the X-ray department until the final whistle. It's the most bittersweet of days for him. His cousin Reg, watching back home in Pinner, shares these mixed emotions. He might even be feeling a little crook himself after all those Easter eggs.

Luton Town 1–2 Nottingham Forest

The 1960s

The singing goalkeeper

Saturday 15 April 1961

England vs Scotland

Home international

When Bobby Smith scores the ninth, Frank Haffey's dive isn't the most convincing. He moves to his right but the ball is already past him and he sinks onto his backside. It's been a bad day at the office for the Scotland goalkeeper. And it's his last day at the office too.

A couple of hours ago out on Wembley Way, the Scottish fans had been bursting with optimism, waving their tam-o'-shanters with gleeful abandon and snapping up the hawkers' giant rosettes – dark blue and tartan affairs with an embroidered thistle at their centre – by the dozen. Their mood is further enhanced by spying – and demanding autographs from – Lawrie Leslie, the Airdrie goalkeeper who in recent times has become Scotland's first-choice number 1. He's injured today, though. His face carries two lines of stitches, one above and one beneath his right eye. Come teatime, Frank Haffey will wish Leslie wasn't crocked.

Today marks Haffey's second full international. In the first, twelve months ago and also against England, he saved a Bobby Charlton penalty. This afternoon, he's saved very little. He was definitely at fault for a couple of goals – a soft parry that

85

delivered the ball right onto Jimmy Greaves' bootlaces for the third; a fumble of Bryan Douglas's daisy-cutter that dribbled over the line for the fourth – but England have been absolutely rampant this afternoon. Few other teams in world football would have kept up with their ruthless, swashbuckling ways. Nevertheless, in choosing never to select Haffey to represent his country again, the Scottish footballing authorities will make it clear who they believe to be most at fault for this calamitous result. It's a diagnosis that ignores the fact that the Scots have four debutants in their starting XI. It's men versus boys.

Greaves helps himself to three goals this afternoon and has a fourth disallowed for handball. He's only a couple of months beyond his twenty-first birthday, but this is already his third hat-trick for the national team. Smith and captain Johnny Haynes weigh in with a couple each. Three goals down at half-time, Scotland rally after the break and narrow the score to 3–2. The faces of their fans move from anguished to encouraged, but then England move up a gear. The final five goals are scored in a ten-minute spell late on. Back to anguished. Deeply, deeply anguished.

You might have expected Haffey to have been mortally embarrassed by the previous two hours, possibly even to be in the early stages of an existential crisis. Certainly, one newspaper report describes his exit from the pitch as 'head bowed, alone, for the darkness of the tunnel'. This is at odds with what then occurs in the Scotland dressing room. While his team-mates sit in stony silence, Haffey gets into the bath and breaks into song. 'He was singing his head off,' Denis Law reported, 'like it was us who'd won 9–3.' There was method in his behaviour, as Haffey would tell *The Scotsman* several decades later. 'I was just singing to get over my troubles.'

He embraces the media attention that comes his inevitable way after such a thrashing, allowing himself to be photographed below Big Ben as it strikes the hour of nine. He also plays to the camera on the journey back to Scotland, posing for snappers underneath the Platform 9 signs at both King's Cross and Glasgow Central.

Haffey may not have even been at Wembley that day had his sister had her way. She was concerned about the effect that the capital's bright lights might have on her 22-year-old sibling, so she locked him in a bedroom in the Haffey family's tenement flat in Glasgow. It wasn't the most foolproof of plans; the flat was on the ground floor, allowing young Frank to make an easy escape through the bedroom window.

He'll make another escape relatively soon. After three more seasons at Celtic, and a brief spell with Swindon Town, he and his wife emigrate to Australia's Gold Coast, where he plays domestic football for another five years. On retirement, though, his career heads in an unlikely direction, albeit one possibly hinted at in that Wembley dressing room. He becomes a cabaret singer, even recording a couple of singles – 'The Dear Little Shamrock' and 'Slattery's Mounted Fut'. Haffey also finds work as a bit-part actor, his most high-profile role coming in the cult Second World War drama *Spyforce* alongside a young Russell Crowe. Plus, there's even a turn as a stand-up comic. 'Old people's homes were the best,' he told the *Sunday Times*. 'The residents couldn't walk out.'

Having moved halfway around the world to help escape any ongoing ignominy about that fateful afternoon back in 1961, forty-odd years later Haffey bumps into his former team-mate Denis Law, who's on holiday on the Gold Coast. The old goalkeeper explains how he's thinking of returning home to Scotland.

'Don't,' advises Law. 'It's still too soon . . .'

England 9–3 Scotland

The free-thinkers

Saturday 6 May 1961

Leicester City vs Tottenham Hotspur

FA Cup final

'You think you've been getting away with it all this time, standing by. Well, son . . . your bystanding days are over! You're in it now, up to your neck!'

As they sit in the dark on velveteen seats, the words of Gregory Peck fill the ears of the Tottenham Hotspur squad. They're a warning. Tomorrow afternoon, these men can't be bystanders. There's the small matter of facing Leicester City in the FA Cup final. Victory will mean the just-crowned league champions will become the first club to win the Double in the twentieth century.

For now, though, on this Friday night, these players are being transported to wartime Greece where, cast as members of a crack Allied commando unit, Peck, David Niven and Anthony Quinn are attempting to wipe out a German fortress on a fictional island in the Aegean Sea. This is *The Guns of Navarone*, the film of the moment, released last week.

It's an unlikely works outing on the eve of such an important occasion. But it's been officially sanctioned. It's the idea of the manager, Bill Nicholson, and serves as a smokescreen, a distraction technique. Rather than having his players kicking their heels as they mooch around the Hendon Hall Hotel, ticking off the hours until bedtime, he's arranged a special late-night showing of the film here at the Odeon in Leicester Square.

Nicholson could have taken his players to the local Odeon in Hendon, barely half a mile from the hotel. But convenience wasn't paramount. The Yorkshireman wants to keep his players out late to wear them out, to make sure getting to sleep won't be an issue. Indeed, when the team bus arrives back at the hotel around midnight, he even lets them have a light ale or two before they head for their beds. But it's also a distraction technique for himself, to stop his mind being turned inside-out by tomorrow's historic possibilities. Nicholson has accompanied them into the West End, willing to be absorbed by this high-action tale of wartime derring-do.

The following afternoon's cup final is no high-action tale of derring-do. For a side whose league performances this season have been so free-flowing, so energetic (they were out of the blocks from the start, winning their first eleven games in the First Division and not suffering their first defeat until mid-November), it's a lacklustre showing. Everyone knows it, and most admit it. Danny Blanchflower, their straight-talking captain, will later call it 'the worst match the 1961 team played'.

Nevertheless, a below-par performance is still sufficient to dispose of the average Leicester City side, a team incapacitated when right-back Len Chalmers suffers a broken leg early in the game but remarkably soldiers on until almost the end. Bobby Smith and Terry Dyson take advantage of the disadvantage, adding two more goals to the 134 the team have scored on their way to the Double. A victory is a victory, a trophy is a trophy. But Spurs haven't won it in style. They haven't made history with any particular flourish. They haven't won it the Bill Nicholson way.

Nicholson is a graduate of Arthur Rowe's Spurs side of the early 1950s, the 'push and run' team that played with as much positivity as his Double winners. He took charge of the first team in October 1958, at which point they sat in the bottom six in the league. His attacking intentions were laid bare in his very first match, a 10–4 win over Everton. Within two years, Spurs – his Spurs – were untouchable at the top of the league.

Outwardly conservative, Nicholson actually has an unorthodoxy streaking through him. While most other managers of First Division clubs would choose to live in middle-distant suburbia, in homes endowed with the latest mod cons, Nicholson and his wife live in a modest Victorian terraced house just around the corner from White Hart Lane. The couple will still be living there when he resigns in 1974 after almost sixteen years in the job. He'd shown this free-thinking side as a player, too. He earned his first England cap in 1951 against Portugal when, even though he was a defender, he scored with his very first touch in international football. There were just nineteen seconds on the clock. But it was to be his only England cap, a situation that was voluntary. Nicholson decided that Spurs, his wage masters, were his priority.

When he took the manager's job, Nicholson inherited Blanchflower as captain but demoted him for neglecting his defensive duties, before reinstating him as the fulcrum of the side he was rebuilding. His skipper was an intellectual, an admirer of the football-loving musicologist/wannabe psycho-analyst Hans Keller, with whom he shared the belief that people couldn't – or, at least, *shouldn't* – be coached into doing certain things ('You can drill people into doing things like they do in the army, but you don't get the best out of them').

Blanchflower could think for himself and Nicholson trusted those instincts. Ten years after the Double success, the manager sang Blanchflower's praises to the writer Hunter Davies. 'I ran everything, but as today, any player in the team talk can suggest ideas or changes. I want them to talk about the game, to think about it, but few of them do today. But Danny, he always did. He was a good captain in that sense and I backed to the hilt any decisions he took on the field.'

Exactly three months ago today, Blanchflower was ambushed by *This Is Your Life* presenter Eamonn Andrews and his big red book, having been lured to a BBC studio on false pretences. The player wanted nothing to do with the idea and disappeared into the night, the show's first refusenik. 'Danny Blanchflower keeps his life to himself', said *The Guardian*'s headline the next morning.

The following year, on the TV interview programme *Face to Face*, Blanchflower will try to explain his disappearing act. 'I don't exactly know why. I did this instinctively. I felt I was trapped in the situation – shanghai'ed into a situation – and I instinctively revolted against it and I ran away from the cameras. It developed into a sort of Keystone comedy after that.'

Blanchflower might not have understood why he had rejected Eamonn Andrews' advances, but his manager had an idea. It was the captain's free-thinking nature. 'There we are,' Nicholson tutted, although almost certainly appreciating the refusal to have his privacy invaded.

'Typical Blanchflower.'

Leicester City 0–2 Tottenham Hotspur

Hoodoo child

Wednesday 22 May 1963

Benfica vs Milan

European Cup final

As Eusébio da Silva Ferreira takes his place in the front row of Benfica's line-up, a needy wall of photographers before him, he's thinking back to eighteen months ago, to the day he last set foot on Wembley's turf. The Mozambique-born-and-bred teenager had been in the colours of Portugal back then, his team failing to qualify for the 1962 World Cup after a 2–0 defeat to England. As it was, the Portuguese side had only the most outside chance of qualification that evening, needing to beat the hosts by a significant score to cancel out England's superior goal difference and make it to Chile.

That night, Eusébio had appreciated that Portugal's prospects weren't favourable, severely dented two weeks earlier by conceding four (*four!*) against Luxembourg (*Luxembourg!*). Tonight, back in north-west London, Eusébio knows the odds are better.

All that separates Benfica from a third successive European Cup triumph is Nereo Rocco's Milan, a side that boasts a seemingly formidable midfield force, including Cesare Maldini, Giovanni Trapattoni and Gianni Rivera. That's *all*.

It's the first time that Wembley has hosted the European Cup final. After visiting Paris, Madrid, Brussels, Stuttgart, Glasgow, Bern and Amsterdam, the competition's climax has finally reached the cathedral of English football. If it's surprising that it's taken as long as it has to arrive here, the attendance possibly hints at why: fewer than 46,000 are in the stands, not much more than a third of those at Hampden Park for the final three years ago. A 3 p.m. kick-off for a midweek match might also explain plenty.

A banner in English praising 'The glorious Benfica' is raised high, suggesting there's a strong expat presence in the stands. The Milan fans are in particularly strong voice. 'It-al-ia! It-al-ia!' is the pre-match chant of choice, hinting that they're not exclusively Milan devotees, that they are just keen for Italian hands to raise the European Cup for the first time. The noise they generate is impressive considering their reduced number. At times this afternoon, Rocco's barked instructions won't reach the ears of his players.

Never mind an Italian win, a third title for the Portuguese side looks increasingly likely when, with the clock approaching twenty past three, Eusébio opens the scoring, outpacing the Milan defence and hitting a low drive into the far corner. Having scored twice in last year's final against Real Madrid, his personal streak is continuing. And that Benfica hat-trick is on, too.

In those eight years, the European Cup has been won only by attack-minded, free-flowing sides. Milan are out to break that tradition. Unlike the cream of the Iberian Peninsula, they are more pragmatic, more calculating, more *cynical*. This is seen by the selection of the robust Gino Pivatelli ahead of the creative Paolo Barison. It's a matter of what Rivera calls 'practical intelligence'.

This approach particularly comes to bear during the second half, both before and after José Altafini's equaliser. Having squandered numerous clear-cut chances before the break, the centre-forward brings the scores level just prior to an hour passing, swivelling and shooting from the edge of the area. By now, the threat of Eusébio, not dealt with in the first twenty minutes, has effectively been snuffed out, with Trapattoni increasingly man-marking him, leaving souvenirs of lumps, bumps and bruises on the Benfica striker's body. That the star man is being neutralised means their captain, Mário Coluna, has stepped up when it comes to creative play. He's running the show, a consequence of which is that he becomes the next prime target of Milanese attention.

Within sixty seconds of Altafini's equaliser, Coluna gets nobbled – and the nobbler is that man Pivatelli. He breaks his foot. Benfica's potent playmaking edge has been blunted. And the nature of the European Cup changes in an instant. 'The Pivatelli foul did not just symbolise a new era,' the journalist Miguel Delaney will later write in the pages of *The Blizzard*. 'It set the template for it.'

Ten minutes after the foul on Coluna, Altafini strikes again, surging through the opponents' half, leaving the chasing defenders for dead. Although his first shot is parried by Benfica keeper Costa Pereira, the Italian stabs home the rebound. In the final twenty minutes, and shorn of their attacking flair, Benfica find no way of getting back into the game. Three shrill blasts from the whistle of English referee Arthur Holland signals that the dream of a hat-trick of European titles is over.

To the dejected Eusébio, it's a second Wembley heartbreak. And his record at the national stadium won't ever improve. In 1968, at the next Wembley-hosted European Cup final, Benfica will be overrun in extra-time by Manchester United. Two years prior to that, the England team's momentum will take them past Portugal in the World Cup semi-finals in '66. These were the extent of his Wembley experiences. Four games. Four defeats.

'I'm not sad about my experiences at Wembley,' he later reflects to *FourFourTwo*. 'I played there, I scored goals. For me, it will always be one of the best stadiums in the world.'

Benfica 1–2 Milan

The war of the roses

Saturday 1 May 1965

Leeds United vs Liverpool

FA Cup final

As pre-match preparations go, it seems a tad unusual – especially for an FA Cup final. Under the East Stand at Wembley, the Liverpool dressing room is a place of mirth. Jimmy Tarbuck is telling jokes, Frankie Vaughan is singing songs. The players are loving it. The players are relaxed.

It's not that unusual. Tarbuck – wearing, as he himself quips, 'a rosette as big as a bloody house' – is a regular in the Liverpool dressing room. Bill Shankly offers frequent invites. He likes Tarbuck to crack the tension, to ease the pressure. The cup final might be kicking off in a matter of minutes, but Shankly finds no reason to do things differently. If anything, he needs Tarbuck's gags – and the songs of Tarbuck's mate Vaughan – even more. This is the club's third appearance in the final. They've yet to win one.

Across the corridor in the Leeds dressing room, there's no

comedian, no singer. It's quiet, very quiet – a funeral compared to the cabaret across the way. It's certainly very hard to imagine the dour Don Revie countenancing such an invasion into the Leeds inner sanctum. Instead, he prefers the quiet focus, the deep concentration.

The buzzer goes in both dressing rooms and the teams gather in the corridor. The Pathé news bulletin will later describe the match as 'the soccer War of the Roses' and here indeed they are: Leeds in Yorkist white and Liverpool in Lancastrian red.

Sixth in line among the Leeds players is Albert Johanneson, the South African winger who's just about to become the first Black player to appear in an FA Cup final. He's been in England four and a half years now, having swapped the dry heat of his homeland for the brutal winters of West Riding. Although a shy, introverted man, Johanneson has become a fans' favourite on the left wing. This afternoon, though, as he walks out towards the Wembley pitch, he's more nervous than ever. He's spent most of the last hour in a toilet cubicle, throwing up. And then, as the teams emerge into the Wembley bear-pit, it hits him.

'All I could hear was a cacophony of Zulu-like noises coming from the terraces,' Johanneson later tells his biographer Paul Harrison, author of *The Black Flash*. 'I could barely hear myself think for those screams. I wanted to run back down the tunnel.' What should have been an historic moment rocks him to his bones.

(Although only revealed decades later, Johanneson is actually sharing this historic moment with his team-mate, Paul Reaney. The full-back is mixed race, when everyone assumes him to be white, rather in the way that Ryan Giggs will be regarded in a future age.)

Shocked by the racist abuse, and targeted by Liverpool for some rough treatment early on, Johanneson has a poor game, one of his worst in a Leeds shirt. And Revie – without the luxury of replacing him mid-match in these substitute-free times (although they'll finally be introduced into the English game next season) – will tell him so, in no uncertain terms, at the final whistle.

The game itself is poor too – the first ninety goalless minutes, at least. The correspondent from *The Times* will be generous in his appraisal, describing it as 'a tense battle of human qualities' full of 'careful shadow boxing that led up to a pulsating finish'. The *Daily Mirror*'s Ken Jones will be less munificent, singling out Johanneson and the Liverpool winger Peter Thompson for failing to puncture the boredom, 'men who could and should have lifted the game with their talent'.

But the thirty minutes of extra-time do provide that pulsating finish. Liverpool's Roger Hunt breaks the deadlock, stooping to head home a cross from left-back Gerry Byrne. That Byrne has made it this far into the match is noteworthy. He broke his collarbone early in the game, thanks to a stiff challenge from the Leeds captain Bobby Collins. Again, the lack of substitutes meant Shankly's team also had to carry a weak link.

Seven minutes after Hunt's opener, Billy Bremner equalises with a classy half-volley past Tommy Lawrence. With the final heading towards its first-ever replay, another Scot – Ian St John – leaps like a salmon towards Ian Callaghan's cross, contorting his body sufficiently to send a diving header past Gary Sprake in the Leeds goal. It's the dramatic moment that the afternoon has been crying out for. Liverpool have won the FA Cup for the first time in their history, the first of many such triumphs in the competition over the next few decades.

While Liverpool will go from strength to strength, that's not the case for Albert Johanneson. Dogged by injuries and the arrival in the first team of another left-winger in Eddie Gray, over the next five seasons he'll take his place in a Leeds starting line-up on only ten more occasions. A two-season spell with York City will fail to rejuvenate Johanneson's career and he'll drift out of the game, taking numerous low-grade jobs and continuing his troubled relationship with alcohol. It's no existence for such a pioneer. Eventually he will die prematurely in 1995 at the age of fifty-five. A week will elapse until his body is found in his rundown tower-block flat.

Who knows, perhaps Revie's post-match words that May day in 1965 – words both brutal and insensitive – constantly replayed themselves in Johanneson's head for decades, feeding the insecurity, feeding the demons.

'Albert, you let yourself and your family down today. You went hiding.'

Leeds United 1–2 Liverpool

The dress rehearsal

Wednesday 19 May 1965

TSV München 1860 vs West Ham United

European Cup Winners' Cup final

Bobby Moore knows exactly how many steps he has to climb to reach the Royal Box from the cinder track surrounding the Wembley pitch. Three hundred and eighty-two days ago, he made this very ascent to lift the FA Cup. Tonight, it's the European Cup Winners' Cup that he's raising to the delirious

West Ham fans after the team's victory over TSV München 1860. And in another 437 days' time, he'll make the journey again, this time to get his hands on the biggest prize of all following the defeat of another team of West Germans. These Wembley steps are rapidly becoming as familiar to him as the staircase of his mid-terrace home in Gants Hill.

As he reaches the thirty-ninth and final step and makes the left turn towards the waiting dignitaries, Moore has the chance to reflect on a tumultuous season off the pitch. His first child, Roberta, was born in January. Two months earlier, though, had come a secret diagnosis and a secret operation: Moore had testicular cancer. It would only be after his death in 1993 that this earlier illness was publicly revealed. Team-mates who knew that Moore had undergone an orchidectomy would, after he later received an OBE, rather insensitively joke that it stood for One Boiled Egg.

The previous ninety minutes had shown West Ham at their potent best, all technique, flair and fitness, with their wide men John Sissons and Alan Sealey causing no end of danger. Not that the West Germans are themselves slouches; Jim Standen, the Hammers' goalkeeper, saves his team's bacon on several occasions, swiftly off his line to absorb the waves of 1860 counter-attacks.

Despite both teams' attacking intentions, the first seventy minutes don't produce a goal and, during a lull in play, the BBC's Kenneth Wolstenholme becomes distracted by a female photographer behind one of the goals. In his defence, she does stand out, resembling – in both looks and dress sense – a real-life Lady Penelope from *Thunderbirds*. 'Now you can have a good look at the lady photographer,' Wolstenholme creepily suggests to the viewers. 'Why don't we have things like that at Wembley more often? Lovely blonde photographers like that make football a much better game.'

The West Ham fans are too wrapped up in the game to notice her. They break into a chorus of 'I'm Forever Blowing Bubbles' in an attempt to puncture the mounting tension, but it's a fierce strike from Sealey that calms the nerves and opens the scoring. A second Sealey goal, this one a tap-in, comes along within two minutes. And this will be enough. The local lads – only the Hexham-born right-back Joe Kirkup didn't grow up in or on the outskirts of the capital, with most being born within a handful of miles of the Boleyn Ground – have conquered Europe.

The scorer of just three goals all season, tonight is Sealey's moment in the sun. 'He didn't shout his name from the rooftops,' his son Anthony will explain many years later, 'but he basically lived out a dream that night.' But it will be his last moment in the sun. Sealey breaks his leg that summer in pre-season training, and will appear in his beloved claret and blue only five more times before leaving the club. A handful of appearances for Plymouth Argyle will be followed by a spell in non-league football before he hangs up his boots in 1971, still shy of his thirtieth birthday.

A premature retirement would then be followed by a premature death. Alan Sealey suffered a fatal heart attack in 1996. He was just fifty-three.

His team-mate, his captain, had passed away three years before, at the even younger age of fifty-one. A nation remembers Bobby Moore a certain way; he never looked better, never looked more natural, than when he was lifting a trophy at Wembley. It seemed like a task he was born to do.

As Moore lifts the Cup Winners' Cup, Wolstenholme has finally forgotten about the Lady Penelope doppelganger and instead offers some wiser – and prophetic – words. 'Who knows, in just over a year's time, he might be standing on the same spot with the World Cup in his hands.'

The man with the mic seemed to know tonight was a dress rehearsal.

TSV München 1860 0–2 West Ham United

Rhapsody in blue

Saturday 14 May 1966

Everton vs Sheffield Wednesday

FA Cup final

It's been an extraordinary twenty-four hours for the teenage Everton fan Kenny Jones. Yesterday, he and his pals boarded a Euston-bound train at Lime Street Station, travelling south for the FA Cup final against Sheffield Wednesday, only to discover that several members of Everton's 1933 cup-winning side were sharing their carriage. Among them was the club's most prolific goal machine, one Dixie Dean. Young Kenny hadn't brought his autograph book on the trip, so Dixie and the old boys signed his blue-and-white-striped plastic hat instead.

This morning, cup final morning, the Jones gang have decided to walk from their hotel in Soho to Downing Street, optimistically hoping for a glimpse of off-duty prime minister – and MP for the Liverpool constituency of Huyton – Harold Wilson. 'There were a load of us singing "We want Harold!",' Jones will later recall to the *Liverpool Echo*. 'And he came out, shook our hands and wished us all the best. As for security in those days, I just remember there being two policemen outside Number 10.'

The group's serpentine pilgrimage towards the twin towers then takes in Hyde Park, where – extraordinarily – a certain Muhammad Ali is training for his rematch with Henry Cooper at Highbury next weekend. Ali is shadow boxing on the grass, the hood of his training top pulled tight around his head. The dozen or so young men, some carrying 'Everton for the Cup' banners, stand transfixed. Kenny Jones, wearing both that autographed hat and a scarf that reaches to his knees, is smiling at their discovery. 'Within about an hour, I'd shaken hands with the prime minister and the world heavyweight champion.'

When the Metropolitan Line finally deposits him at Wembley, Jones misses out on another celebrity spot. Taking their seats, presumably to cheer on Everton as they seek to match Liverpool's victory in the final twelve months ago, are John Lennon and Paul McCartney. The use of 'presumably' is required as neither Beatle – at this time, at least – unequivocally nails his colours to the mast when it comes to their football allegiance. After all, why alienate one half of the record-buying public of your home city when you can dodge answering direct questions on the matter and retain their goodwill and custom? So while the pair might be seen at an Everton cup final (and McCartney will return to Wembley in two years' time for the Toffees' encounter with West Brom), the only footballer to appear on the cover of *Sgt Pepper's Lonely Hearts Club Band* will be the former Liverpool striker Albert Stubbins. Hats tipped to both sides, bets surely hedged.

(Decades later, McCartney will come clean to *The Observer*. 'My father was born in Everton, my family are officially Evertonians, so if it comes down to a derby match or an FA Cup final between the two, I would have to support Everton.

They are both great teams, but if it comes to the crunch, I'm an Evertonian.')

Whether teenage fan or pop star, what the crowd is served up this afternoon is a match every bit as thrilling and dramatic as the World Cup final will be in a couple of months' time. Everton are probably favourites, having become the first team to reach Wembley without conceding a single goal in the preceding rounds, but they find themselves behind after just four minutes when a deflected Jim McCalliog shot gives Wednesday the lead. The winger David Ford doubles the Owls' advantage just before the hour mark and the cup is halfway to South Yorkshire.

But this doesn't factor in the near-immediate intervention from Everton's Mike Trebilcock. The young Cornishman has been at Goodison Park for only five months, during which time he's largely been in the treatment room. So there's no better way to make an impression on your new(ish) club than by scoring the goal that brings them back into contention in the cup final. More than that, it's his first goal in Everton blue. And just five minutes later comes Trebilcock's second goal in Everton blue. Scores level and honours up for grabs. With quarter of an hour to go, left-winger Derek Temple outstrips the Wednesday defence and buries the orange ball in the far corner. The comeback, the rapid turnaround, is complete.

Trebilcock makes tomorrow's headlines, his contribution to Everton's history and heritage now indelible – even though he will play only eleven more times and score just three more goals for the Toffees. But another hero will be toasted this evening too. Eddie Cavanagh was once on Everton's books, without ever making the first team. But he got on the pitch this afternoon, staging his own one-man pitch invasion – arguably the most famous interloper onto the Wembley pitch until Scotland's fans arrived in 1977.

Once Trebilcock's half-volley equaliser flashed into the net, Cavanagh was off, over the barriers and across the pitch. Several policemen were in his wake. One got hold of his suit jacket but, in a terrific piece of physical comedy worthy of Buster Keaton or Harold Lloyd, Cavanagh merely slipped his arms out of its sleeves and left the officer grasping at air. It took a rugby tackle by Special Constable Edward New to bring Cavanagh, now in his braces, to justice. 'He got me down,' he would later recall in the oral history *Three Sides of the Mersey*. 'I just put my hands back and I think six of them had me pinned down like I was one of the train robbers.'

Cavanagh's antics are richly relived when tens of thousands of Evertonians ride the rails back to Merseyside this evening. Kenny Jones is presumably also regaling his fellow passengers with one of the more colourful days of his life. How many actually believe this star-studded tale involving Dixie Dean, Harold Wilson and, most unlikely of all, Muhammad Ali is moot, but Jones is floating like a butterfly nonetheless.

Everton 3–2 Sheffield Wednesday

A tale of two tackles

Wednesday 20 July 1966

England vs France

World Cup group match

The first World Cup to be held on English soil has started slowly for the hosts. And World Cup fever – despite all manner of commercial opportunities featuring the tournament mascot, the cartoon lion World Cup Willie – has yet to truly dig its claws into the nation. England's first group match, a goalless draw against Uruguay this time last week here at Wembley, was 5,000 under capacity. Saturday's win against Mexico was played before a full house and started to build some momentum, but tonight's result is the one that matters, the one that will take the side into the knock-out stages. It's then that the fever will send temperatures rising.

With fifteen minutes remaining, they're not home and hosed, but they are hopeful. Although they lead by only a single Roger Hunt goal, they've looked comfortable throughout and the current France side is little match for them, especially as they've effectively lost the services of Robert Herbin, injured early in the game and hobbling around the pitch ever since.

Another man who looks like he'll be seeing out the game in a similar crocked fashion is the elegant French midfielder Jacques Simon. He's the unwitting victim of a challenge from England's enforcer Nobby Stiles, who's just gone right through the back of him, leaving him flattened on the turf. Had that tackle occurred fifty years later, the red card would be out of the referee's pocket before you could say 'Grievous bodily harm'. Instead, the Peruvian official simply waves play on.

'He attempted to sell Nobby a dummy,' Bobby Charlton will later recall. 'Unfortunately, he didn't sell him anything. He just bought himself the tackle from hell, one that from the moment of its inception was destined to land somewhere between the Frenchman's thyroid gland and his crotch.' To make matters worse for the French, England score their second while Simon is still writhing around on the floor, when Hunt rises to meet an Ian Callaghan cross.

(An aside: despite providing the assist, Liverpool winger Callaghan will have to wait more than eleven years for his next appearance in an England shirt.)

FIFA is swift to issue a statement about Stiles's challenge, although it stops short of dishing out further punishment. It warns him that 'serious action' will be taken if there's a repeat of such behaviour in subsequent matches and the Mancunian is under no illusions that he's drinking in the last-chance saloon. FIFA has more teeth than him.

The FA steps in, requesting Alf Ramsey drop the combative midfielder for the next match, the quarter-final clash against Argentina. The England boss refuses, saying that the FA would be in swift receipt of his resignation should it interfere with his selections. 'RAMSEY DEFIES THE STILES WITCH HUNT' screams the *Daily Mirror* headline. In this battle of attrition, the FA blinks first, Ramsey stays in charge, and Stiles lives to tackle another day.

That's more than can be said about Jimmy Greaves.

To confirm that unnecessarily violent and over-zealous challenges aren't the exclusive preserve of England's ankle-biting defensive midfielder, France's right-half Joseph Bonnel elects to run his studs down the shin of Jimmy Greaves. It's like a can opener slicing open a tin of soup – or, as Greaves himself will later recall, 'my leg opened up like a red rose'. The England trainer, Harold Shepherdson, treats the wound. It's deep. He winds bandages around it for now; the stitches it's crying out for will have to wait until the final whistle. Walking wounded or not, England need the numbers on the pitch. The blood soaks through Greaves' bandages and into his sock.

Fourteen stitches are put into the wound after the final whistle. Greaves has no chance of making the quarter-final against Argentina, but adequate rest should put him into contention should England make the last four. This plan, though, doesn't legislate for the impact that Geoff Hurst makes against the South Americans. The young West Ham striker, with just six caps for his country, scores the only goal against Argentina in a cantankerous match. Greaves in comparison hasn't scored for five successive England games, the longest dry spell of his international career.

The shin injury heals sufficiently to give Ramsey a choice between Hurst and Greaves for the striker's spot against Portugal in the semi-final. Glancing at their recent scoring records, Ramsey decides not to disturb the momentum that's gathering within the team. He names an unchanged XI for the semi.

It's a decision that doesn't surprise Greaves. 'I knew I'd be out from then on once Geoff had scored the goal against Argentina,' he later conceded. 'It was all over for me. I knew that. Unless somebody else got injured, I was never going to get my place back.'

Having recently survived a nasty bout of hepatitis, one that caused him to miss three months of the regular season, it's a cruel blow. On the bench at the final, gazing on in his shirt and tie as his replacement fires himself into sporting immortality, Greaves admits he's 'the loneliest man in Wembley Stadium'.

No matter how deep the scar on his shin is, it will heal eventually. The scar on his soul may never disappear.

England 2–0 France

The other guy

Saturday 30 July 1966

England vs West Germany

World Cup final

Hugh Johns places his microphone down, takes off his headphones and lets out a long sigh. Although cast in late-afternoon shadow, it's still very warm up here on the Wembley gantry, high above the noise and the colour and the buzz. Johns has played his part today, a longer-than-expected shift transferring that noise and colour and buzz to homes across the country. He's exhausted. Only the prospect of a few gins and a lie-down is what gives him the energy to clamber down from his eyrie.

There's a strong sense of relief in both directions along the gantry that England's World Cup win, secured just twenty minutes earlier, wasn't decided by Geoff Hurst's controversial second goal. While most of the press pack believe his snapshot to have ricocheted off the crossbar and behind the goal-line, Hurst's net-busting third, in the dying embers of a crackling match, put the result beyond doubt, extinguishing any rancour come the final whistle.

As ITV's lead commentator, Johns is satisfied with his afternoon's work. Yes, there were a few minor slips – prior to the start of the game, he declared that England had 'won the cup' before correcting himself with a chuckle: 'won the *toss*' – but he's happy with the words that he, a former print journalist, selected to describe England's fourth.

'The referee looking at his watch. Seconds ticking away.' Johns' rich voice – seasoned by a twenty-a-day habit and lubricated by a daily self-prescription of two pints of Brains Dark – gives the appropriate grandeur to the occasion. 'Geoff Hurst goes forward. He might make it three . . .

'He has! He has! And that's it! That's it!'

(Let's give Johns the benefit of the doubt that the 'three' to which he refers describes Hurst's personal tally this afternoon and not that of England.)

'And that's it! That's it!' The finality and excitement of Johns' description should ensure that it passes into immortality, the last word on English football's most monumental day. He knows history has been made in the last hour. Perhaps his chronicle of it – from this pumped-up latter-day Venerable Bede – will become the definitive account, the iconic commentary to be cherished for decades to come.

It won't. Johns' employment with ITV will ensure that. Of the 32 million watching at home, almost 90 per cent of households have been tuned into the BBC's coverage, described by the plummier-voiced Kenneth Wolstenholme. It's a monopoly, a landslide. Although only two years older than Johns, Wolstenholme has been a TV commentator since the early 1950s; Johns, by contrast, was recruited to the commentary ranks only this year. And when he watches the BBC highlights later, Johns realises the words of his more experienced counterpart further along the gantry will be the ones to crystallise in the public memory.

It's probably only fair. Not only is Wolstenholme's exclamation as Hurst's bullet of a shot bulges the back of the net every bit as conclusive as Johns' 'That's it!', he also welcomes those premature pitch invaders into his commentary, those excitable interlopers seemingly unspotted by the ITV man. Plus, those fourteen spontaneous, immortal words of Wolstenholme boast a superior, immaculate rhythm. They could be a comedian's three-part gag. They're almost a haiku.

> *Some people are on the pitch*
> *They think it's all over*
> *It is now.*

If they were even momentarily remembered by the minority ITV audience, Hugh Johns' words are soon forgotten. He doesn't grumble, though. While his colleague Brian Moore is increasingly engaged with presenting duties, Johns will continue to be the channel's lead commentator at a further three World Cups. By 1974, usurped at the BBC by David Coleman, Wolstenholme will be employed by ITV regional channel Tyne Tees, where his brief includes manning the wintry, wind-whipped gantry at Victoria Park, home of lowly Hartlepool United. That same year, Johns is still riding the crest of his game, installed at the World Cup final at Munich's Olympiastadion to apply his descriptive skills to the elegance of Cruyff and Beckenbauer, Neeskens and Müller.

It's just that on that July afternoon in 1966, thanks to the sheer imbalance of the viewing figures and regardless of the words chosen, Hugh Johns' destiny was sealed. Had Shakespeare been employed by ITV, even he would have been the other guy.

England 4–2 West Germany

The third degree

Saturday 4 March 1967

Queens Park Rangers vs West Bromwich Albion
League Cup final

It was perhaps a surprising move. No, it was more than that. It was *definitely* a surprising move, the kind of downward transfer that a player doesn't agree to unless they're a young gun eager to get some game time under their belt or an ageing stalwart keen to carry on for one more season before being put out to pasture.

Rodney Marsh was neither of these. Although still only twenty-one, he was already proven in the First Division, having ended the 1964–65 season as Fulham's top scorer. Across his first spell in SW6, the young man scored twenty-two times in sixty-three games, a return that made it all the more eyebrow-raising when, in March 1966, Marsh crossed west London to sign for Queens Park Rangers, then of the Third Division.

The reason was regime change at Craven Cottage. Marsh had blossomed under the stewardship of Bedford Jezzard, the former England forward forced into management by a career-ending injury while still in his twenties. But when Jezzard grew disillusioned with the direction of the game, in particular the rise in player power since the maximum wage had been abolished, he retired to run a pub. His replacement was the former Ajax manager and future Barcelona boss Vic Buckingham, with whom Marsh didn't get along. Marsh didn't respect his authority; Buckingham retaliated by not playing him in the first team. The end was nigh down by the Thames.

Having dropped two divisions, a player of Marsh's calibre unsurprisingly flourished at Loftus Road. In his first full season, he scored thirty league goals as QPR romped to the Third Division title. He also fired the Hoops towards the first League Cup final played at Wembley.

As well as now being hosted at the national stadium, the final's format was slimmed down from the two-legged affair it had been for the first six years of the competition's existence. QPR have been fortunate with how the draw has unfolded: today's opponents, West Bromwich Albion, are only the second top-flight side they've faced, the other being Leicester City, dispatched in the fourth round.

QPR – playing in all white and shorn of their trademark hoops (West Brom had also lost their familiar stripes, instead playing in red) – found themselves two down at half-time, both goals coming from their former left-winger Clive Clark. It feels as though it's already over. Certainly Kenneth Wolstenholme thinks so as he delivers his summary of the first forty-five minutes to the BBC cameras. 'Albion are moving so well around Wembley Stadium. It looks as if they've got fifteen or sixteen players on their side compared to Rangers' eleven. And that in itself tells its own story.'

It's a different story that gets told in the second half, though. With a player called Mark Lazarus in QPR's line-up, surely fate has decreed that one of the greatest comebacks seen at Wembley is about to unfold. The winger Roger Morgan – whose twin brother Ian, another winger, is on the bench – starts the fight-back, nodding home a floated Les Allen free-kick.

Twelve minutes later, Marsh decides to make a proper impression on the game. He picks up the ball deep in his own half, then makes a run sideways across the pitch. He jinks back in on himself, before heading forwards, beating one Albion defender, pushing the ball a little wider to set up the shot and then hitting it low from twenty yards, in off the far post. And with nine minutes left, a sharply struck winner comes courtesy of that man Lazarus. Dead and buried at half-time, QPR have been resurrected.

It's a comeback started and completed within eighteen minutes. Rodney Marsh's has been rather longer. And he may never have been on the pitch. Back in 1963, in one of his earliest games for Fulham, he scored the winning goal against Leicester, but in doing so he had collided with the opposition full-back John Sjoberg. It was a nasty collision. Marsh broke both his jaw and his skull, as well as being left permanently deaf in his left ear. Doctors had advised that he should never play again.

This afternoon's goal was for them.

Queens Park Rangers 3–2 West Bromwich Albion

A boy's own story

Wednesday 29 May 1968

Benfica vs Manchester United

European Cup final

It's approaching quarter to eight on a Wednesday evening in late May and people are getting excited in the White household – just as people are in all the other houses on this street in Altrincham, just as they are on many streets across south Manchester and beyond.

It's a school night but young James White – later to be known as Jim White, broadsheet football writer and author of several books on Manchester United – has special dispensation to stay up late. The club are making their first appearance in a European Cup final and he, his mum and his dad (James's older sisters are away at university) have gathered in the sitting room in front of the black-and-white TV set. A plate of cheese sandwiches is placed before the youngster, essential sustenance to see his way through the unfolding drama of the next two hours.

Although his parents aren't the most dyed-in-the-wool United fans, young James has already nailed his colours to the mast; Old Trafford is just six miles north-east of his hometown. 'In the playground, you were either George Best or Mike Summerbee,' he explains more than half a century later. 'It was quite a halcyon time because City had won the league that season. Manchester seemed the centre of the footballing world. It was like Beatlemania. But I'd gone for Best.

'He was the fashionable one who everybody went for. Or Denis Law, but he didn't play in the final because of injury. Best and Law were the lads. That one-armed goal salute, with your shirt sleeve pulled up over your fist, was very common in the playground.'

The first half tonight is goalless, the main talking point being the rough, tough treatment meted out to James's favourite player. Whenever he looked like hitting his stride, Best has been unfailingly, and mercilessly, chopped to the ground by a Portuguese defender. The closest the game has come to a goal was when Eusébio hit the bar. James knows he's Benfica's most dangerous player, the one that United's enforcers needed to shackle. 'We'd seen him in '66, of course, and I knew he was the one to worry about. Back then, my dad had said to me: "He's the man. He's the boy."' Kenneth Wolstenholme's commentary confirms to James the accuracy of his dad's observation. 'This man can manufacture a chance out of nothing,' Wolstenholme tells the young lad as the ball comes back off Alex Stepney's crossbar.

After the break, United turn the gas up on Benfica and within eight minutes they break the deadlock when David Sadler's floated cross from the left is met by Bobby Charlton's glancing header, which leaves José Enrique glued to his line. Surprisingly, it's Charlton's first goal in the entire European Cup campaign. The bulk of their goals have come from Sadler, Best and Law.

United hold that slender lead until eleven minutes are left on the clock when a cross-shot from Benfica's right-midfielder Jaime Graça sinks Wembley into near silence. There is now the spectre of extra-time to consider. More than that, there's the spectre of a United defeat too, as Eusébio is put through on goal. Bottom dollars would confidently be put on Portugal's greatest player finishing off Matt Busby's men there and then, but that doesn't legislate for the bravery and brilliance of Stepney, who manfully blocks Eusébio's rocket of a shot. The striker understands the importance of that moment. After Stepney bowls the ball out to his left-back Tony Dunne, Eusébio remains in the six-yard box, warmly applauding the keeper for his point-blank save. He thought it was a certain goal, as did young James back in Altrincham. 'I was thinking, *This is it.*'

Then comes extra-time and a quick negotiation between son and parents. The conference was swift, with mum and dad caught up in the occasion. 'Discipline went out the window,' laughs Jim now.

'My mum was very confident going into extra-time. I don't know why. Maybe that was a hangover from '66. Because England had won the World Cup in extra-time, perhaps there was a general consensus that we'd be all right. We'd be stronger, we'd be fitter than these foreigners.'

Mrs White's confidence is borne out by a seven-minute spell in the first period of extra-time, when United score three times, dashing Benfica's hopes of lifting that heavy old trophy for the third time. First, Best finally evades the attentions of the heavy mob to slice his way through the defence and weave around Enrique to restore United's lead. Then Law's replacement, the teenager Brian Kidd, adds a third on his nineteenth birthday, nodding home after his initial header is parried by the keeper. The fourth arrives shortly after, when Kidd's cross is converted by a deft near-post Charlton flick.

That first period of extra-time has been the most exciting fifteen minutes of James's life so far. 'It was fantastic. I was dancing around the sitting room after Best had danced around the keeper. But I was slightly behind the curve though, not always realising the importance of something, such as when Kidd's header went in. I wasn't sure what had just happened and had to look at my dad for confirmation.'

And to think he might have been sent to bed after ninety minutes, the howls and cheers of his parents tantalisingly coming up through the floorboards of his bedroom. 'I have absolutely no memory of the team going up to the Royal Box and lifting the cup, though. I may have been dispatched to bed before that happened. It would have been about half-ten by then, which was late for a primary school kid in those days.'

Jim does remember there being tears in his father's eyes. 'I know this sounds awful, but I was only young and I didn't have the Munich connection that he had. He saw it as destiny.' The Munich air disaster had happened ten years earlier, as United were returning from a European Cup tie. To win that very competition a decade later couldn't have been more poignant – to the grown-ups, at least. Jim shakes his head. 'It didn't seem to be a thing for us kids at that time.'

The following morning, James met up with his best friend Malcolm Brooks for their usual walk to school. There was only one topic of conversation of course, although in the days of black-and-white television coverage and monochrome morning newspapers, it was quite some time – possibly not until the full-colour football magazines came out a week or so later – before the pair realised United had played their most significant match in an uncustomary all-blue kit.

'I remember the headmaster announcing it at assembly – "Manchester United are the European champions" – and everybody cheering, even those who'd been Mike Summerbee in the playground. Then we couldn't wait until break when we could get out and play football.'

Despite his two goals barely twelve hours earlier, no one wanted to be Bobby Charlton, then at the positively ancient age of thirty. 'He was in the prime of his game, but he felt more of an establishment figure. Instead, everybody was George Best, trying to replicate his goal from the night before, rounding the keeper and slotting home.

'Being Best was the prime aim of us all.'

Benfica 1–4 Manchester United

The ides of March

Saturday 15 March 1969

Arsenal vs Swindon Town

League Cup final

In the half-century since Third Division Swindon Town took on mighty Arsenal, an urban myth has grown. Most mentions of this particular match, of this particular giant-killing, make reference to the deplorable state of the Wembley turf – sodden, muddy, cut up – and to how the ground staff have worked tirelessly to make it a playable surface, covering huge patches of the pitch in golden sand. These are correct observations. But the reason given for its state is what has become miscued over the years since.

The blame is almost always attributed to the Horse of the Year Show taking place here a few days earlier. It's an unsafe accusation. The Horse of the Year Show didn't take place either here or then. It was held seven months later, under the roof of Wembley Arena next door. Perhaps there's some confusion with the Royal International Horse Show that *did* take place here in the stadium itself that year. But, again, no. That wasn't held until late July. (Indeed, a similar erroneous excuse will be given the following year about the 1970 cup final between Chelsea and Leeds: that, again, the Horse of the Year Show is to blame for the appalling state of the turf.)

It appears that time is an unreliable witness. Perhaps the source is a throwaway quip that has been reshaped into fact? And each time the myth has been repeated, it has crystallised that little bit harder, moved that little step further from the réalité. And, without fail, when a journalist revisits the match come a certain anniversary, out comes the story. And it's not just repeated by journalists who weren't even alive at the time. Those who actually played in the match have allowed memory to mislead them. They've repeated the myth, giving it extra legitimacy.

Put simply, there is no record of any equestrian event being hosted at Wembley in the preceding days, or even weeks, of this League Cup final. The turf – already ailing having not been replaced since prior to the 1966 World Cup – has been broken up by a week of rain and by an international friendly played here just three days ago. Football boots have cut up the pitch, not horses' hooves. Had it been the latter, then ITV commentator Brian Moore would have made reference to it in his pre-final spiel; instead, he describes it as 'a pitch that has been hammered by the England–France game on Wednesday night and so much rain since'. Similarly, the Pathé report on that international match merely calls Wembley 'windswept', with no reference to any showjumping event a few days earlier.

On this March afternoon, the red carpet is doing its work, saving the heels on Princess Margaret's shoes from sinking into the mud as she's introduced to the teams. After Frank McLintock handles the formalities for his familiar Arsenal side, the Swindon captain Stan Harland does likewise for his. Even if Margaret was the keenest follower of football, she'd still need to be introduced to these players. The men of Swindon Town, the men of English football's third tier, are largely unknown, largely anonymous.

The pleasantries over, the Swindon players strip off their tracksuit tops and let them drop onto the red carpet, from which their manager Danny Williams scoops them all up, like a father retrieving discarded clothes from a teenager's bedroom floor.

Both sides are in their away strips today – Arsenal in gold shirts and blue shorts, Swindon in all white. It's a curious decision not to allow one of the teams to wear their usual red kit, especially as the match is being broadcast in black and white. As soon as Swindon's players get their shorts muddy, for television viewers they become indistinguishable from their opponents. But Swindon won't worry about the mud. It's to their advantage. They're used to it. In fact, one or two of them quip that, as deplorable as the pitch is, it's still better than some they regularly encounter down in the Third Division.

Swindon are out of the traps quickly, their speed and athleticism belying their league status. The winger Don Rogers particularly stands out, a man universally believed to be punching below his weight, a player who belongs at a higher grade of football. The fitness of Rogers and his team-mates should pay dividends on this claggy pitch, especially if the Robins can take the Gunners into extra-time. This fitness is a product of manager Williams' strict regime, specifically the regular Thursday morning training session that forces his players to run thirteen laps of their County Ground pitch.

It's no surprise that Swindon take the lead before half-time, a calamitous goal that neither Arsenal goalkeeper Bob Wilson nor central defender Ian Ure will want to revisit on the TV highlights. In the second half, Arsenal throw everything at Swindon as they seek an equaliser. Swindon's keeper Peter Downsborough pulls off at least a dozen top-class saves. Indeed, as *The Times'* Geoffrey Green will later report, 'for quarter of an hour, it was Downsborough versus Arsenal, and Downsborough won'.

It is cruel, then, that it's a Downsborough mistake, his first of the match, that gifts Arsenal their equaliser with just three minutes left, rushing out but failing to block Bobby Gould, who is then able to head into an empty net. However, Swindon's superior fitness comes to bear in extra-time, thanks to two goals from Rogers, one a scrappy piece of opportunism, the other a gloriously taken solo effort.

Here, on the Ides of March, Brutus has slain Caesar.

Thirty thousand Swindon fans are jubilant in a way they've never been jubilant before. It is – and will remain – one of Wembley's biggest acts of giant-killing. Among the Arsenal fans is an 11-year-old Nick Hornby. It's his first time at Wembley. He is not enjoying the experience. 'When the final whistle went, my father betrayed me,' he would write in *Fever Pitch* more than twenty years later. 'He rose to his feet to applaud the extraordinary underdogs, and I ran for the exit.'

The two heroes – Rogers and Downsborough – had differing fates. Both would stay at Swindon for a few more seasons, perhaps surprisingly in Rogers' case, bearing in mind he was regarded as one of the hottest properties outside the First Division. He eventually moved to the top flight in 1972, signing for Crystal Palace. Downsborough went in the opposite direction – to Bradford City of the Fourth Division – before a post-retirement life as a school caretaker.

While the schoolkids of Halifax were probably unaware of Downsborough's heroics that particular March day back in 1969, Rogers would relive those events on a regular basis. He opened a sports shop in Swindon – the unsubtly named Don Rogers Sports – which meant that the final was a frequent topic of conversation over the shop counter. 'The League Cup was actually in the shop window for a while,' he would later tell *The Guardian*. 'You wouldn't have that now, would you? I'd need a bodyguard.

'And I had it at home for a couple of nights. I slept with it.'

Arsenal 1–3 Swindon Town

The 1970s

Ten stone of barbed wire

Saturday 11 April 1970

Chelsea vs Leeds United

FA Cup final

Mathematicians with a speciality in probability would be fascinated with these numbers. Over the forty-one FA Cup finals held at Wembley before this afternoon, as many as thirty-six have been decided after ninety minutes. The remaining five have gone to extra-time, but all produced a winner before the second final whistle. It's a quite amazing anomaly that not one final – and these are games, in the main, played between the best, most closely matched teams of the day – has remained level after 120 minutes.

Until today, that is.

Perhaps ITV commentator Brian Moore possesses some psychic qualities. He informs his viewers that neither Chelsea nor Leeds have won the FA Cup before, 'so whatever happens today, provided the match is decided, a new name will go on the cup'. *Provided the match is decided.* It's a caveat that'll be borne out at about quarter past five this afternoon.

The final is being played a month earlier than usual, with the FA believing that a successful defence of the World Cup in the stifling heat of Mexico this summer requires the England squad to have an extended period of acclimatisation. It's a fair point. Six of this afternoon's players – Jack Charlton, Allan Clarke, Terry Cooper and Norman Hunter of Leeds, Peters Bonetti and Osgood of Chelsea – were named in Sir Alf Ramsey's squad last month and will be beneficiaries of the rescheduling.

This being mid-April, though, means that the Wembley turf hasn't seen as much sunshine as it would otherwise by cup final day. It's a dog-rough pitch that, in places, seems to be cutting up just from the marching of the pre-match military band. Elsewhere, there are patches of new turf, recently laid and possibly yet to have a decent chance to properly take root.

The condition of the pitch precludes a match of fast-flowing football – although, that said, Leeds' twinkle-toed left-winger Eddie Gray keeps his balance well to earn the man-of-the-match award. It's an intriguing game nonetheless: combative, sturdy and with plenty of incident. Jack Charlton gives Leeds the lead after twenty minutes, his header from a Gray corner creeping over the line as two Chelsea defenders – Ron Harris and Eddie McCreadie – can't get any purchase from the turf to stop it rolling in. If the opener was poorly defended, so too is Chelsea's equaliser, a speculative twenty-yard shot from Peter Houseman that slithers under Leeds keeper Gary Sprake and into the far corner. Honours even at half-time.

The second half continues in the same evenly matched way until, with six minutes left, a Clarke header hits the post and Mick Jones slams home the rebound. Leeds, usually tricky to haul back once they're ahead, need to prevent Chelsea equalising for a second time. On the bench, Don Revie chews his gum and takes a long look at his watch, trying to calculate the time remaining. He doesn't look too nervous, though. He's a veteran of Wembley, as a player for both club and country, and as a manager. His Chelsea counterpart Dave Sexton has never been here before, either as player or boss.

Sexton urges his players on. For seven of his squad, the disappointment of losing to Spurs in the cup final three years ago is still fresh. Charlton concedes a free-kick wide on the left, John Hollins curls the ball in and Ian Hutchinson outjumps the defence to bring the scores level. Several Leeds players slump to the deck. In four days' time, they've got the second leg of their European Cup semi-final against Celtic. Extra-time is all they need. Four minutes later, the final whistle sounds. Honours even at the ninety.

Before the match, the ITV computer predicted a 3–2 win for Leeds and, in the extra half-hour, they do their darnedest to prove the hardware correct. Only a goal-line clearance from David Webb stops a Johnny Giles volley from finding the net. Shortly after, a Clarke snapshot hits the bar. But that's it. History – a reluctant history in the eyes of double trophy-chasing Leeds – has been made. Honours even after extra-time.

With the forthcoming home internationals also having been brought forward in the calendar, the FA has already decided the replay will be at Old Trafford rather than at Wembley. It will take place a full eighteen days after the original match and will be one of the filthiest, dirtiest matches in English football history. Chelsea will eventually settle the two-match encounter when, in another helping of extra-time, Webb – given a torrid time by Gray in the first game – meets Hutchinson's long throw with his cheekbone to put the Blues 2–1 up. His goal finally settles the issue after 240 minutes of high-intensity football. Leeds' one-time hopes of an extraordinary league/FA Cup/European Cup treble have evaporated. Not a single trophy will be going back with them to West Riding.

The brutality of the replay means it's remembered more than the original game. Late challenges and petty retaliations abound. One of the more severe challenges features a kung-fu style clearance by McCreadie where his boots are as high as the head of Billy Bremner, who collapses in a heap. No foul, no free-kick, no card of either colour. Another altercation involves England team-mates Osgood and Charlton, and ends with a retaliating Charlton flooring the Chelsea man with a well-directed knee (and possibly a head-butt). 'The referee is surely going to take some action here,' says Brian Moore. He doesn't.

Eric Jennings is in charge of his final match before retirement and, as in the first game, elects to play it leniently, choosing not to properly punish some truly X-rated challenges. In 1997, the referee David Elleray will be invited to watch the replay back in its entirety and to assess it according to the interpretation of the laws of the game in the 1990s. Elleray, no stranger to sending players off, especially if Roy Keane is on the pitch, will conclude that six red cards and twenty yellows would have been dished out under modern refereeing standards. By 2020, another referee, Michael Oliver, will up the ante, suggesting there were eleven red-card offences alone.

Again, those probability experts might well have predicted such a feisty match. If the tone and tenor of an organisation is set at the top and trickles down to the underlings, then the events of the replay are possibly unsurprising, bearing in mind the two sides' respective captains. Ron Harris is known to wingers across the First Division as 'Chopper', while no less an astute observer than John Arlott has brilliantly described Billy Bremner as 'ten stone of barbed wire'. No five words better encapsulate him. He's always in one tangle or another.

Chelsea 2–2 Leeds United

Jesus of the North Bank

Saturday 8 May 1971

Arsenal vs Liverpool

FA Cup final

Wembley is a place of goalscoring celebrations, spontaneous expressions of joy and elation, unchoreographed dance moves made up on the hoof. There's Stuart Pearce's demon-dissolving rant after smashing home his penalty in the shoot-out against Spain at Euro 96. There's the ten-man pile-on near the corner flag that greeted Ben Watson's late winner in the 2013 FA Cup final. There's Kenny Dalglish treating the advertising boards like a high-hurdle sprinter would as he leaps over them to celebrate his goal in the 1978 European Cup final. And then there's long-haired Charlie George in 1971 – taking to the turf, lying down on the job, arms outstretched in a Christ-like pose.

It's unclear whether he hits the ground through exhaustion – it is the 111th minute, after all, of a game played in blazing heat and bleached-out sunshine – or whether it's a deliberate, not-playing-to-the-cameras gesture by a don't-give-a-fuck footballer, a player who does his own thing, who lives his own life. Either way, 20-year-old George has scored the goal that means two possible things: Arsenal may just have won the FA Cup, and Arsenal may just have won the Double. If he does nothing else in his career in the decade to follow, he's just been anointed as Arsenal royalty, beatified as a latter-day saint.

The celebration is remembered more than the goal itself. The winning strike is relegated to second billing, despite the snapshot's pinpoint accuracy from twenty yards out. 'He sees his moment and then "Whack!",' observes ITV's summariser Jimmy Hill, running the rule over the slow-motion replay. 'Look how far it is from the post. Inches? Fantastic goal.'

Not everyone is lost in the moment. 'Get up, you lazy fucker!' Arsenal's centre-forward John Radford is bellowing at him, grabbing at George's arm to get the goalscorer back on his feet. 'There are still nine minutes left.'

Nine minutes or not, it feels too golden a moment not to be the decisive few seconds of this final, a glorious way for Arsenal to secure their first Double, having claimed the league title five days earlier. Unwittingly, Liverpool play ball; their failure to equalise in the remaining minutes ensures Charlie George's moment is trapped in amber.

No one will ever ask George to re-enact the goal; for the Gunners faithful, the celebration is all. Decades later, fans will spot him walking down the street and throw themselves down onto the pavement to faithfully replicate those few seconds from the Double-securing cup final win. Still in the foothills of his career, it becomes his defining moment as a player. He won't mind, though. He's happy to belong. Having been gracing the Highbury terraces since he was five years old, he's always been one of their own, a North Bank regular who became a North Bank idol. He's cut from the same cloth as the suedeheads and longhairs who today have swapped the tightness of Highbury for the long-distance view from Wembley's West Stand. As Nick Hornby observes, George represents 'one of the few genius misfits to have jumped straight over the perimeter fence into a club shirt and shorts'.

If George's little lie-down is as idiosyncratic as the man himself, his celebration on the final whistle is no more auspicious.

He attempts a forward roll on the run, which he doesn't quite execute correctly, falling backwards and landing on his backside. George won't worry. No one saw it.

Arsenal 2–1 Liverpool

The coronation of Cruyff

Wednesday 2 June 1971

Ajax vs Panathinaikos

European Cup final

Johan Cruyff already has a paper cup of champagne when one of the Ajax directors hands him a glass of the fizzy stuff. Backstage here at Wembley, the Ajax dressing room is a mixture of suited-and-booted club bigwigs and fresh-out-of-the-bath players. Cruyff is yet to get in the bath, standing there in the green of his just-procured Panathinaikos shirt, a drink in either hand, holding court. His smile is as wide as the Zuiderzee.

Cruyff is dissecting the previous ninety minutes to anyone who'll listen. He's also considering what might now be: what new era, what new dynasty may just have arrived in European football. New kings have just been crowned.

His smile might not be beaming like Cruyff's, but Rinus Michels can be one satisfied man this evening. Tonight represents the culmination of what, as head coach, he's been trying to achieve at Ajax over the past six years. As the architect of

'Total Football', Michels has led them to four Eredivisie titles and three Dutch cup victories. Now comes the big prize. After the collective dejection of being runners-up to Milan two years ago, his charges are the champions of Europe. It's a position they'll hold for three years, winning a hat-trick of successive finals. Tonight's is the first.

But the next two European Cup triumphs won't be secured with Michels in the dug-out. The Romanian Ştefan Kovács will be in charge in 1972 and 1973. In exactly four weeks from now, Michels will leave Amsterdam, heading to Barcelona's Camp Nou, and taking his revolutionary thinking, his thoroughly modern ways, with him. (Michels will, though, pop back to Amsterdam in the summer of '73 to sign Cruyff for Barcelona for the handsome sum of 6 million guilders, roughly 2 million US dollars.)

Perhaps his imminent departure is what's separating Michels from an all-out celebration. His mood is one of satisfaction and contentment rather than uncontrolled ecstasy. He's happy to stand on a bench here in the dressing room to receive and absorb the cheers of his players, directors and backroom staff, but it's bittersweet. At the age of forty-three, his time at Ajax – for whom he was a free-scoring forward during the 1950s – is almost done. For now, at least.

Nineteen years his junior, Johan Cruyff will, from now on, be the person most associated with Ajax's brand of Total Football. His performance tonight will earn him a landslide victory in the ballot for European Footballer of the Year. All night he's been teasing and tormenting the Panathinaikos full-backs, turning them this way and that. A dropped shoulder sends a defender the wrong way. A shimmy lands another on his backside.

From the fifth minute, the identity of tonight's winners is pretty much decided. As some evening sun warms the players,

Piet Keizer finds himself in possession of the ball wide on the left. This is usually Cruyff's position, but the fluidity and inter-changeability of the Ajax side permits Keizer, a centre-forward with 11 on his back, to be where he's not expected. He floats a teasing cross into the box, exactly the kind of ball he'd love to be served with. Instead it's Dick van Dijk, the team's right-sided striker, who's ghosted in to direct a delicious glancing header into the Panathinaikos net.

Radiating easy dominance, Ajax strangely don't then go on to score a hatful. They're not timid in front of goal, but they seem to lack a killer instinct to put the Greeks to the sword. And a one-goal lead is always a slender one. But their saving grace is that Panathinaikos – conquerors of Everton and Red Star Belgrade on their way to Wembley – are intimidated by the Dutchmen's mobility and invention. They never look like scoring, despite the competition's highest scorer, Antonis Antoniadis, leading their forward line.

The game is edging towards a predictable denouement when Cruyff feels he needs to enliven it. That golden sun having been replaced by the floodlights' beams, the number 14 slowly walks the ball to the edge of the Greek box, his step entirely without spring. But it's the ability to play the kind of pass he supplies to the onrushing Arie Haan, a delightful nudge that bisects two Panathinaikos players, that forgives his slightly pedestrian ways. Haan shoots for goal first time, the ball coming off the studs of Anthimos Kapsis and looping over the goalkeeper Takis Ikonomopoulos. That first European Cup victory is secure.

Perhaps it's this particular moment of brilliance that Cruyff is revisiting so enthusiastically in the dressing room afterwards. When he has no audience left, he finishes his two drinks, strips off his green Panathinaikos shirt and heads towards the Wembley baths. Tonight, the prince has become a king.

'Playing at Wembley was something totally special,' he'll later declare. 'Wembley has always been different.' Wembley loved Cruyff in return. When he died in 2016, the arch was lit up in orange. The king is dead, long live the king.

Ajax 2–0 Panathinaikos

The invisible adieu

Saturday 29 April 1972

England vs West Germany

European Championship quarter-final first leg

He doesn't have the gait of a disappointed man, that Geoff Hurst. His number's been called and he trots off the pitch, under the Wembley lights, with little attitude or disdain. As he approaches the bench, a tracksuit top is tossed in his direction. He catches it, turns the inside-out garment the right way and sits back to watch the remaining half-hour of the match.

Hurst doesn't know at this point that, at the age of thirty, he's just kicked the last ball he'll ever kick in an England shirt. His international career is over, annoyingly stalling one cap short of a half-century.

Hurst will be hoping that he'll at least get to be part of the remainder of England's campaign in this European Championship. For now, though, there's the small matter of squeezing past West Germany in this two-leg quarter-final.

When Hurst goes off, England are a goal down and deservedly so. Alf Ramsey has been uncharacteristically gung-ho in his selection, opting to not include an out-and-out defensive midfielder to disrupt the West Germans' flow. *The Observer's* legendary sage, Hugh McIlvanney, isn't impressed, questioning the wisdom of 'Ramsey's unexpected policy of manning the midfield with three players noted for what they can do with the ball, rather than what they can do to get it'.

Without protection in front of them, there's every danger that England's ageing central defence partnership – Bobby Moore and Norman Hunter – are going to be exposed by the creative and sharp partnership of striker-in-chief Gerd Müller and the flaxen-headed longhair Gunther Netzer, playing at number 10. Netzer in particular has been taking advantage of the gappy England midfield, launching a number of galloping counter-attacks.

England become the architects of their own downfall. When, after twenty-seven minutes, an under-pressure Moore curiously elects to dribble the ball into the heart of his own penalty area rather than lump it into row Z, he loses possession to Müller. This allows outside-left Sigfried Held to tee up Uli Hoeness, whose edge-of-the-box, first-time shot takes a slight deflection off Hunter's studs to deceive Gordon Banks at his near post. It's all that West Germany deserve.

This is their first visit to Wembley since *that day* back in 1966. The wounds are probably now largely invisible, especially as there are only three West German players – Held, Horst-Dieter Höttges and Franz Beckenbauer – who played six years ago. The rest are largely undented by what Geoff Hurst did to their national team that afternoon.

Nonetheless, the West Germans must be relieved to see the back of Hurst after sixty minutes, replaced by Manchester City's Rodney Marsh, earning his second cap. From his position on the darkened bench, Hurst can now only watch. As it is, the most interesting passage of the match comes in the final stages. With twelve minutes left, a snapshot from Colin Bell is parried by German goalkeeper Sepp Maier, right into the path of Bell's Manchester City team-mate Francis Lee, who walks the ball into the net.

Should England escape tonight with a draw ahead of the trip to Berlin in a fortnight's time, it wouldn't be catastrophic, especially seeing how outplayed they've been. But instead England keep pushing players forward, seeking the win. The gaps at the back keep expanding and, with six minutes remaining, England are caught out by the raw pace of Held, his progress eventually being halted by Moore, who brings him down illegally just inside the area. Pushing his hair to one side, Netzer sets up the spot-kick and just squeezes it home via Banks's gloves and the inside of the post. Back in front.

In search of a second equaliser, England continue to flood forward, but with a minute remaining, Müller – the scourge of England two years ago in León at the 1970 World Cup – grabs a third goal, a neat turn and shot after England had gifted possession away. It's a cheap goal to concede, especially in the home tie of a two-legged quarter-final. It makes the Germans' lead that bit more comfortable.

In the press box, McIlvanney loads both barrels. To him the result is 'a disaster' and 'the worst defeat a Ramsey team have ever suffered at Wembley'. Most in the stadium would have to agree. That it's Hurst's final game in England colours is unknown at this juncture and thus he's denied an appropriate send-off. Instead, he quietly slips into the sunset.

While Hurst's international career terminates here, England will very soon be shunted into the sidings. Defeat tonight, when married with the goalless second leg in Berlin in a fortnight's time, kicks off an eight-year period in which the national side will fail to qualify for a single international tournament, a barren spell that will deeply embarrass the English game.

England 1–3 West Germany

Fanfares and farewells

Wednesday 3 January 1973

The Three vs The Six

Exhibition match

'Britain has much to contribute to, as well as much to gain from, the new Europe which is being created. We can look forward with excitement to the venture on which we are embarking.'

Prime Minister Edward Heath has welcomed 1973 with the widest-open arms. It's the third day of January, the third day that the UK has been a member of the Common Market – or, as it's officially known, the European Economic Community. And today is the first day of Fanfare for Europe, an eleven-day cultural festival celebrating the country's welcome into the bosom of western Europe.

More than 300 events are sounding this fanfare. Many of the biggest names in classical music – Benjamin Britten, Herbert von Karajan, Bernard Haitink, Georg Solti – will be appearing across the capital, as will several pop and rock artists. Slade stomp the boards at the London Palladium, while The Kinks head for the Theatre Royal Drury Lane. There's also a Festival of European Art, although attempts to borrow the Bayeux Tapestry to exhibit at Westminster Hall are scuppered. As the historian Robert Saunders will later observe, 'it was felt that the subject matter – involving the invasion, conquest and butchery of the native population – struck an unduly sanguinary note'.

The delights don't end there. This being the 1970s, there's a bill of wrestling, a special edition of TV talent show *Opportunity Knocks* (in which, surreally, Johan Cruyff makes a cameo), and a beauty contest. This pageant – Miss TV Europe – will be won by the Netherlands' contestant Sylvia Kristel, a year before she finds fame as the lead character in the ridiculously popular softcore flick *Emmanuelle*.

The festival's first night opens with two gala performances. One is at the Royal Opera House where Britten is conducting and Laurence Olivier performing. The Queen is in attendance, as is Heath, a passionate classical music fan. At just about the time that the PM's arrival in Covent Garden is greeted by the letting off of a stink-bomb by opponents of EEC membership, a few miles to the north-west, the evening's other virtuosos are tuning up for their own recital.

The cream of European football has gathered for a one-off match billed as The Three vs The Six. The Three comprise players from the EEC's just-joined countries (the UK, the Republic of Ireland and Denmark), while The Six are drawn from its half-dozen founder members, so Belgium, France, Italy, Luxembourg, the Netherlands and West Germany. Respectively managed by old adversaries Alf Ramsay and Helmut Schön, there are plenty of star turns to grace the occasion. The Three boast Pat Jennings, Bobby Moore, Colin Bell, Johnny Giles and Peter Lorimer in their ranks, and are captained by Bobby Charlton, who's playing at Wembley for the first time in three years. It will also be the last time for him.

The Six, under the captaincy of the brooding Gunther

Netzer, have a similarly impressive line-up. Dino Zoff, Franz Beckenbauer, Marius Trésor, Johan Neeskens and Gerd Müller are currently keeping the January chill at bay as they go through their respective pre-match stretches.

Despite his absence, Heath trumpets the significance of tonight's match in his notes in the official programme. Announcing the encounter as 'unique in embracing the whole of the enlarged community', he declared the game 'a major landmark in the history of European football'. It appears the nation's football lovers aren't in agreement. The match-day ticket advises attendees 'to take up your position by 7.15pm', but the queues are short to non-existent half an hour before kick-off. This is despite the price of admission being decidedly attractive to watch some of Europe's best strut their stuff; seats start at £1, while standing costs just one of those newly minted EEC-commemorating 50-pence pieces. Wembley will be only a little over a third full tonight.

The general public appear not to be over-enthusiastic about closer European ties. Such indifference is measured by the opinion polls; only 37 per cent of the population favour joining the Common Market. Shadow foreign secretary James Callaghan registers his disapproval of the festival's impact on the public purse: 'It might be thought that because the government cannot give the people bread, they are giving them circuses.' Outside the stadium, disgruntled, placard-waving protesters agree with Callaghan, braving the near-sub-zero temperatures to complain how the £350,000 cost of the festival is a portent of the financial burden of EEC membership.

On the pitch, the game is goalless in the first half, falling short of Heath's hoped-for historic occasion. The two number 10s – Charlton and Netzer – are comfortably the best players on the pitch, the latter coming close to opening the scoring with a nonchalant free-kick that rattles Jennings' left-hand post.

Hopefully Heath, his nostrils now clear of the stench of ammonium sulphide, is having more fun at the opera.

Shortly after the break, Charlton is the chief architect of the first goal, his cross from the left brilliantly directed goalwards by a Henning Jensen flying header. A second goal arrives with twenty minutes left. It's simple and straightforward; Colin Bell's looping cross is headed down by the shortest man on the pitch, Alan Ball, and Scotland's Colin Stein applies the finishing touch from four yards out.

And that's how it ends – 2–0 to the newcomers. It turns out to be a match that doesn't linger long in the public consciousness. And it's certainly not the greatest spectacle to mark what will be Charlton's last appearance at Wembley, scene of the two greatest triumphs of his career. Tonight, he doesn't realise that it's his curtain call. 'Don't write me off,' he protests afterwards. 'You're talking as though I have reached my pension.'

To what extent the other players have believed tonight to have been special, to have welcomed in a new era of fraternity and alliance, is moot. Certainly Alan Ball, not unlike the Brexiteers who would vote for the UK's retreat from the EU forty-three years later, views membership purely in personal terms.

'The only thing that interests me about joining the Common Market is whether or not it will make my family's holidays cheaper.'

The Three 2–0 The Six

Painting the town red

Saturday 5 May 1973

Leeds United vs Sunderland

FA Cup final

The sign in the shop window of Flynn's the jewellers says it all. It's been there for a few days, but comes with extra piquancy this Saturday morning as shoppers shuffle up and down Holmeside, one of Sunderland's busiest shopping thoroughfares.

'As mark of sympathy towards Messrs Bremner, Giles & company, this shop will close at 2pm on Saturday May 5th.'

Featuring the black border of a funeral notice, it's signed, in elegant hand, by the proprietor J. W. Flynn. To say that con-fidence is high – as Sunderland of the Second Division ready themselves to upset the cup holders Leeds United – would be showing restraint. They've already knocked out Manchester City and Arsenal. This is a town that believes. They fully expect that the fiftieth birthday of Wembley Stadium will be marked by the biggest upset in its history.

Human traffic is lighter along Holmeside this morning. A large portion of the town left at dawn, heading south by rail or road, swarms of red and white noisily marching towards either train station or coach stop. One group, numbering around a dozen, were particularly boisterous. Wearing outsized rosettes and red-and-white-striped plastic hats, they parped their horns and swung their rattles and cheered and shouted. There was excitement in their bones, in their lungs. One of them even had a ventriloquist's dummy along for the day, propped over his arm and observing everything. 'Ha'way, ha'way,' the dummy mouthed.

Jimmy Montgomery's mother-in-law was among the swarm engulfing the train station. Montgomery is Sunderland's goal-keeper, the man charged with holding Peter Lorimer and Allan Clarke and Eddie Gray at bay this afternoon. 'He'll keep them out, he will,' she insisted. 'He'll do that.' She also offered up a score prediction. Jimmy will keep a clean sheet in a 1–0 Sunderland win.

By lunchtime, queues are forming at the Top Rank for the right to watch the game en masse, sat on orange plastic chairs and clutching pints of Vaux, the local brew. Those who can't get into the Top Rank, or who don't have access to a television, have to make do with the screens in the windows of television rental companies. The crowd outside Visionhire is five deep; only the first couple of rows can see any part of any screen. The rest just have to imagine.

They have to imagine the sight, at ten minutes to three, of Bob Stokoe, the Sunderland manager, leading out his team. Alongside the straight-laced, straight-dressed Leeds boss Don Revie, Stokoe is wearing a bright scarlet tracksuit, on the reverse of which, in white letters, is his name. All of his players are wearing the same, their names emblazoned on the back of each jacket. A touch of swank and swagger from the second-tier side.

Before the game starts, Stokoe slips a thin, beige raincoat on over his tracksuit, puts his trademark trilby on his head and takes his seat, a blanket pulled up over his legs.

Sunderland get the better of the early exchanges and it's actually no surprise that they take the lead in the thirty-second minute. When Ian Porterfield, the mutton-chopped midfielder from Dunfermline, finds time to control the ball and lash it home on the volley from eight yards out, the Sunderland contingent in the stands erupt. Two hundred and seventy miles directly north, the town erupts too – in people's homes, in the Top Rank, outside Visionhire.

Porterfield isn't the only hero this afternoon. Halfway through the second half, a Trevor Cherry diving header is palmed away by Jimmy Montgomery and Lorimer seemingly can only put the rebound onto the bar. That's not quite the entire story, as the action replay confirms. Montgomery has pulled off a remarkable double save when he had no right to, swiftly diving to his left to divert Lorimer's goal-bound effort. It's every bit as special, as athletic, as spectacular, as Gordon Banks's stop from Pelé three summers earlier in Guadalajara.

He'll keep them out, he will. He'll do that.

When the final whistle blows, Sunderland have become the first Second Division club to lift the FA Cup since West Bromwich Albion in 1931. And their victory offers a blueprint to their contemporaries: over the next seven years, two more second-tier sides will deliver similar upsets to First Division clubs. The romance of the FA Cup, that irresistible urge to root for the underdog, is no stronger than during these times. And Sunderland can claim authorship of this particular brand of fairy tale for which the competition is loved.

Stokoe is up out of his seat and sprinting at a fair lick across the pitch. There's one person he wants to embrace first and that's Jimmy Montgomery. The manager is so taken by the moment – despite the fact that he won the cup as a player in 1955 with Newcastle, that day being charged with marking Don Revie – that he hasn't realised his captain Bobby Kerr has pinched his trilby, revealing a rapidly balding head underneath.

The final yards of Stokoe's charge towards his goalkeeper – long strides, arms aloft, beaming smile – will later be immortalised in bronze and displayed outside the Stadium of Light. Up until his death in 2004, Stokoe will never have to buy a pint of Vaux's Stout in all Sunderland. Having joined the club only a little more than five months ago, he's guided them to an unlikely triumph in a competition they last won before the Second World War. He's made the unbelievable believable.

While Stokoe's statue gets buffeted by the whipping winds coming off the North Sea, his raincoat and trilby are warm and dry in the foyer of the Stadium of Light, behind glass, under lock and key. They've enjoyed a more protected existence than the cup final tracksuit of match-winner Ian Porterfield.

The Scot went on to manage national sides and domestic teams all over the map: Zambia, Zimbabwe, Oman, Trinidad & Tobago, Ghana, South Korea and Armenia. But this doesn't explain why, a good forty years after the '73 final, that red tracksuit – with 'Ian Porterfield' on the back – turned up in a charity shop in Ukraine. It was rescued at the last moment from a pile of unwanted clothes that was on its way to a homeless shelter. Its saviour was a Ukrainian collector of football memorabilia who then alerted a Sunderland-based collector to its existence.

Now one of the prized possessions of the Fans Museum, just across the way from the Stadium of Light, the tracksuit had been hanging on the rails in that Ukrainian shop for quite some time apparently. Unloved, unwanted, unrecognised. Clearly none of the charity shop's regular patrons had heard of Sunderland, let alone Porterfield, Montgomery or Stokoe. Or the Top Rank. Or the Visionhire window.

Leeds United 0–1 Sunderland

'The oxygen disappeared from the air'

Wednesday 17 October 1973

England vs Poland

World Cup qualifier

'It was easy to say it wasn't meant to be, that it was just one of those things. But it wasn't one of those things. The World Cup finals were meant to be. England were expected to win that night. They had always succeeded in qualifying.'

It's nearly fifty years into the future, nearly fifty years after the final whistle sounded, nearly fifty years since England's failure to beat Poland ends their interest in the 1974 World Cup. But Barry Davies still feels the pain of that October evening. It's easy to summon up.

'The place was like a Silesian winter at the end of the game. The oxygen disappeared from the air. People couldn't believe it. It hadn't happened before.'

Two hours earlier, the task had been clear. England had to win to go to next year's finals in West Germany. A draw or defeat would mean Poland would take the one qualifying place from Group 5. A 2–0 loss in Katowice in June had put England in this predicament. Despite this result, though, the collective belief was that victory was inevitable; England expects and all that.

In the ITV studio beforehand, Brian Clough for one was dismissive of the Poles, famously describing the visitors' goalkeeper, Jan Tomaszewski, as 'a circus clown in gloves'. He reprises that taunt during the half-time chat, which fellow guest Derek Dougan and presenter Brian Moore don't leave unchallenged. Dougan and Moore are correct to do so; although sometimes a little unorthodox in his play, in the first half Tomaszewski has pulled off a string of virtuosic saves to deny Colin Bell, Allan Clarke and Mick Channon.

Although Frank Keating's report in *The Guardian* the following morning suggests he sides with Clough (Keating describes Tomaszewski as 'a slackly strung marionette [who] made one think this might be his first game'), up on the BBC gantry, Davies's view differs from that of the man who resigned as Derby County's manager just two days earlier.

'I totally disagreed with Brian Clough. Tomaszewski had a fantastic game. He was diving here, there and everywhere. It was just, in those days, England had the best goalkeepers and their style of play was that you caught the ball if you possibly could and only when you couldn't, you punched. Tomaszewski threw himself at everything and that was his style.'

Having watched them in training, Davies certainly didn't underestimate the Poles. 'I was on record a year earlier when I said the draw was tough on Poland because they were a good side but had England in their group and only one team qualified. I said that if, by some chance, they got themselves into the finals, they were good enough to finish in the top three.' Indeed, Poland would beat Brazil in the third-place play-off. 'That was one of my better forecasts . . .

'I had a pretty good idea of how the Polish team was going to set up at Wembley. There was no doubt that England would go on the attack and Poland would hang on to the point that they had. They, of course, got the bonus of scoring their goal and that made all the difference. Having seen them in training, I knew how quickly they could break and how swiftly they could move the ball.'

The Polish goal feeds off these counter-attacking strengths. A ball out of defence on the left should be cut out by Norman Hunter but is miscontrolled, leaving the balding speedball Grzegorz Lato free to close in on the England goal. The ball is squared to the fast-approaching Jan Domarski, whose first-time shot squirms through Peter Shilton's hands and in.

'England were completely caught out,' says Davies. 'They'd pushed up in anticipation of Hunter winning the ball, which would lead to another attack. It was done so quickly, and suddenly it's a different story. When Hunter went to get the ball on the halfway line, my comment was "Hunter's got to make that".' Hunter didn't make that.

Davies thinks Alf Ramsey dropped two seismic clangers in his time as England manager. One was taking Bobby Charlton off in the quarter-final of Mexico '70 when England were 2–0 up on West Germany, only to capitulate and concede three goals without reply. The second was leaving Bobby Moore out of tonight's starting line-up.

Moore had been at fault for the second goal in Katowice and had been subsequently dropped for a friendly against Austria, which England had won at a canter, 7–0. So Ramsey kept the same starting XI for this final qualifier. 'Hunter was a good player who was just very unlucky that he was of the same generation as Moore,' says Davies. 'But Moore was a calming influence.' It's difficult to be a calming influence on increasingly panicked players when you spend the entire match on the subs' bench.

Nevertheless, from this vantage point, he has the ear of Ramsey and, as the game deepens, he urges him to put Derby's Kevin Hector on. Although England equalise through Clarke's dubiously awarded penalty, given after Martin Peters tumbles to the turf after the lightest of touches, the second required goal isn't forthcoming. Eventually, in the dying embers of the match,

Ramsey finally does send Hector into the fray – although fellow sub Kevin Keegan remains seated. Hector the debutant almost scores with his first touch too, his header cleared off the line by a Polish defender.

England have been profligate all night. They should be out of sight. They manage thirty-nine attempts on goal over the ninety minutes; Poland have just two. England win twenty-three corners; Poland don't have a single one. Rarely has an international football match been so one-sided but has ended in a draw. Davies agrees.

'There were so many good-quality English players who, when having a shot at goal, seemed to be in a desperate hurry. They were the most panicking set of forwards I've ever seen. They had so many chances. There were so many goalmouth scrambles. They could have had a pile of goals. But no one was using their head.'

An England victory would have been long forgotten. Job done, move on. But this draw, this failure to qualify, will leave a scar for decades to come. It's still visible half a century on.

It was left to Barry Davies to introduce the viewing public to the notion of this kind of failure. 'I've never gone searching for a line to say at the end of the match. I wouldn't have thought "What am I going to say?" My style is opening my mouth and hoping that the foot is sufficiently far away.'

No pre-prepared take. No rehearsed line. Just seven blunt words.

'England are out of the World Cup.'

England 1–1 Poland

The quick exit and the long goodbye

Saturday 10 August 1974

Leeds United vs Liverpool

Charity Shield

Very few people can remember the final score in the 1974 Charity Shield, let alone the goals or the scorers.

For the record, it was 1–1 after ninety minutes, with Phil Boersma putting cup winners Liverpool ahead after nineteen minutes and league champions Leeds equalising through a glancing header from Trevor Cherry with twenty minutes left. The Reds eventually took the spoils in an extended penalty shoot-out, when the Leeds keeper David Harvey missed his spot-kick.

What is remembered is the fisticuffs between – and the subsequent dismissals of – Kevin Keegan and Billy Bremner. The annual season curtain-raiser was being played at Wembley for the first time, as the FA attempted to elevate the match's status; until now, the league champions and cup winners hadn't been mandated to take part. The fracas of this Wembley debut – the boiling point of a match that simmered right from the off – was not exactly what the authorities would have wanted. Punches thrown, shirts ripped off and flung to the ground, angry marches back to the dressing rooms. While it wasn't supposed to be an exhibition match, it was meant to be a celebration of the two finest sides in English football. That afternoon, though, charity was a virtue in short supply.

One miscreant – Johnny Giles, deliverer of the right hook to Keegan's jaw that had accelerated the mêlée – remained on the pitch, quite possibly because his reaction to his booking was calm, apologetic and accepting. Keegan, on the other hand, as the tension continued to simmer, became furious. It had been a stormy few days for the Liverpool star. He had also been sent off during the week in a pre-season friendly in Germany against FC Kaiserlautern, again for punching an opponent.

Keegan had plenty of time to cool off. Aside from receiving heavy fines, he and Bremner were both banned until the end of September. One disgusted member of the public even applied to a magistrate requesting that the pair be served summonses 'for behaviour in a public place likely to cause a breach of the peace'.

The summer of '74 had been a strange one for English football. The national team could only watch in frustration as the World Cup happened without them for the first time since before the Second World War. Then the cup winners and league champions both appointed new managers. The seemingly benign and avuncular Bob Paisley inherited Bill Shankly's mantle at Liverpool, while four days later Leeds – after the forensic ways of Don Revie – unveiled the more forthright and gobby Brian Clough.

To say these two new managers would enjoy differing tenures is a gross understatement.

Paisley held his position for nine years, in which time he won six league titles, three European Cups, three League Cups, the UEFA Cup, the UEFA Super Cup and six Charity Shields.

Clough held his position for forty-four days, in which time he won just a single match. When he left Leeds halfway through September, Bremner still had a fortnight of his ban to run.

For Clough, it's the quickest of farewells. *Here's your pay-off. Be gone and good riddance.* For Shankly, it will be the longest of goodbyes. Liverpool had granted him the honour of leading the

team out at Wembley this afternoon, a gesture that acknowl-
edges they're here because of him leading them to cup glory
three months before. After Ian Callaghan converts the winning
penalty of the shoot-out, Shankly wanders onto the pitch,
raincoat in hand. Emlyn Hughes leaps into his arms, while the
others – Smith, Callaghan, Heighway, Lindsay – form a line for
a final embrace. These are his players. Or, rather, *were* his players. They're Bob Paisley's now. But Paisley hangs back, staying
on the sidelines, allowing Shankly these last moments.

It won't end there. When the Liverpool players reconvene at
the Melwood training ground after their summer breaks, they're
somewhat surprised to be welcomed by Shankly in full training
kit. He explains he's just using the facilities to stay fit, but the
players still call him 'Boss' (and continue to call Paisley 'Bob').
Shankly remains a regular visitor to Melwood and even starts
taking over the training sessions. Paisley has a word, reminding the Scot that he's no longer employed here. In the end, it
takes Paisley threatening to resign to get the club's board to ban
Shankly from Melwood. He simply couldn't let go.

The weekend after the Charity Shield sees more thrills and
spills, more bashes and thumps, at Wembley. The cinder track,
more used to speedway tyre and greyhound paw, is the crucible
for the second of that summer's stock car racing meets. Eighty
pence will get you a vantage point on the terraces, and £2
even gets you a seat in the Royal Box, for what the official programme bills as 'a feast of oval action of the kind we all know
is unsurpassed in driving skill and entertainment by any area
of motorsport'.

The Wembley groundsman will want the skill quotient to
be high. Ahead of the first meet in June, he had threatened to
resign over the potential damage an out-of-control stock car
could have done to his pride and joy. For the August meet,
fences have been erected on each side of the track to keep the

cars on the straight and narrow. Once the racing begins, one driver, Gerald Taylor, inadvertently tests whether the fences are strong enough by ploughing into the inner fence, his car finishing inches short of the turf. A close call, but close enough. Stock car racing will never return to Wembley again.

Leeds United 1–1 Liverpool
(Liverpool win 6–5 on penalties)

Once in a lifetime

Saturday 19 April 1975

Hoddesdon Town vs Epsom & Ewell

FA Vase final

It's a quintessential Wembley photograph – one of victory, of celebration. It could almost be a deliberate reconstruction of the triumphant England World Cup team from nine years ago. The winning captain sits on top of his team-mates' shoulders, raising the trophy to the skies. Below him are a sea of smiles from the rest of the proud-as-punch team. One player, inevitably, is wearing the trophy's lid as a hat.

The 1966 equivalent of this picture featured the elite players of a generation, professionals at the height of their careers, at the peak of their powers. This afternoon's photo is of welders and joiners and roofers and signwriters and shopfitters who happen to be half-decent at football. Their captain works in a warehouse. And the trophy he's holding is no Jules Rimet, still gleaming or otherwise. It's a new piece of silverware and he's the first to raise it aloft. It's a cup, even if its name suggests otherwise. This is the FA Vase.

The advent of this new competition signals the withdrawal of the definition and distinction of the amateur in English football. With many supposedly 'amateur' players now being paid to play, whether mere beer money or something more substantial, the FA has ditched the Amateur Cup and brought in this new 'open' cup, one available to those non-league clubs not taking part in the FA Trophy. It could well be something of a hit – perhaps not to a Bay City Rollers level of success (the Scottish group are currently at number 1 with 'Bye Bye Baby', which will turn out to be the biggest-selling single of the year), but more than 200 eligible clubs entered the competition at the first time of asking.

This inaugural season's winning side – Hoddesdon Town of Hertfordshire – play in the Spartan League. Their captain, somewhat less familiar with a razor than Bobby Moore, is also their hero today. Dickie Sedgwick is his name and his two goals have created Wembley history. He almost didn't make it, having been out for weeks with a jaw injury. But even the wildest of horses couldn't have dragged him from a date at the national stadium. Allow someone else to lead the side out? I think not.

Their other hero is their goalkeeper, Fred Gulvin. Another player sporting luxurious, era-specific facial hair, his saves just about hold their Surrey opponents at bay. He once had trials with Chelsea. It shows. Epsom & Ewell skipper Trevor Wales does manage to get a goal back, but Gulvin does enough to ensure it's nothing more than mere consolation.

The final whistle. Cue the photographers. Cue the shoulder-ride for Dickie Sedgwick.

It takes less than an hour for the team to arrive back in Hoddesdon. In Elizabethan times, the town was home to a great many inns, thanks to it being a staging post on the London to Cambridge road. By the nineteenth century, it was one of England's major brewery towns. Tonight the locals are out in force, ready to uphold its beer-flavoured heritage, and taking to the streets when their heroes make their parade. But there's no open-top bus. Instead, the team coach follows behind the chairman's car, the sunroof of which is open to allow this new trophy to be shown off.

It will be the football club's greatest ever day, one it will never repeat. Next season, the holders are dumped out of the competition in the first round by Clacton. But it will be another Essex side, Billericay Town – whom Hoddesdon beat on their path to Wembley glory – who will make their mark on the infant FA Vase. They will win it in 1976, retain it in 1977 and win it again in 1979. The FA Vase has its first legends. The competition is here to stay.

Hoddesdon Town 2–1 Epsom & Ewell

The Kennedy assassination

Saturday 24 May 1975

England vs Scotland

Home international

All eyes, and all cameras, are trained on Kevin Keegan. Last Tuesday, the Liverpool striker walked out of the England camp, having been told by Don Revie that he was being dropped for the following night's match against Wales, despite an impressive performance against Northern Ireland the Saturday before.

Keegan – no stranger to hot-headed behaviour, as the 1974 Charity Shield has already proved – has spent most of the last few days stewing at his cottage in Mold in north Wales, his father's ongoing illness adding further strain. Following two phone calls with Revie, Keegan returned south where, after a candid half-hour face-to-face with the England boss, he's back in the fold. The dust has settled, the air has been cleared.

Keegan knows the cameras are on him as he strolls onto the pitch, playing keepy-uppy with a ball and his head as he walks. In two hours' time, though, the cameras' collective gazes will be elsewhere, focused on the man directly in front of him as the teams march out: Gerry Francis. That's when the cameramen and photographers haven't got Scotland's goalkeeper in their crosshairs.

Stewart Kennedy has had a good season. Not only has he played each and every one of Rangers' forty-two league games as they've cruised to the Scottish title, but he's beginning to establish himself as the national side's first-choice number 1. Kennedy has played four times now for his country; they've won every match.

This is in deep contrast with the state of Kennedy's career even just a couple of years back. Unable to establish himself in the Rangers side, he was supplementing his income working as a miner, which ITV's Brian Moore reminds today's viewers, almost inevitably declaring that at the time Kennedy looked to be 'on the football slagheap'.

It's not the greatest start for him. With just five minutes on the clock, another Rangers man – Francis of QPR – picks up the ball deep in midfield and surges forward. He evades the challenge of Scotland captain Sandy Jardine and, with the ball bobbling up nicely, rifles home from twenty-five yards. Kennedy doesn't even attempt to dive. He's rooted to the spot. Feet of clay.

Two minutes later, England double their lead when a looping Kevin Beattie header evades Kennedy. The goalkeeper actually moves this time, but largely only to haplessly wrap himself around the goalpost in rather comical fashion. When the third England goal goes in – a Colin Bell rattler from outside the area – Kennedy does at least dive, even getting a hand to the rasping shot. But the enduring image, as the England players come together for another celebration, is of him sat on his backside, looking incredulous at what is happening in this first half.

The scoreline exaggerates the difference between the two teams. Scotland have been knocking the ball around well and, within a minute of Bell's goal, are awarded a penalty when Colin Todd handles in the box. Bruce Rioch's successful spot-kick is the least his side deserve. They go into the break 3–1 down.

During the interval, the band of the Coldstream Guards march up and down the pitch, entertaining the fans with their versions of miscellaneous hits of the day, including 'Y Viva España', a hit last summer for Swedish singer Sylvia. The band are still playing the tune as they head towards the tunnel, passed by the Scottish team on their way back out. The beaches of the Costa Brava would undoubtedly be more appealing to these players if they knew the pummelling that awaits them in the next forty-five minutes.

It's that man Francis who gets the fourth, his low drive from a free-kick taking a slight deflection and going in off the post. Kennedy is incredulous again, this time on all fours. The fifth is the final goal of the afternoon, David Johnson poking home after the ball strikes both crossbar and post. The East German referee, Rudi Glöckner, and his compatriot linesman seem blissfully unaware that both Dave Watson and Mick Channon are comfortably offside.

If either Francis or Kennedy look up to Wembley's electronic scoreboard on the final whistle, the bare facts of their contrasting afternoons are laid bare. Francis's reward for his commanding, two-goal performance will be being made England captain. Today turns out to be current skipper Alan Ball's final match for his country; he's the last member of the victorious 1966 team to retire from international football.

Francis will now wear the armband, despite still being just twenty-three. Kennedy doesn't fare so well. Today was his fifth international and, despite it being his first defeat, he will never play in the colours of Scotland again.

While Kennedy slopes away from Wembley, tail tight between his legs, his opposite number remains in the light. Ray Clemence will be back on the nation's TV screens later this evening when BBC One broadcasts a performance from those showboating basketballers the Harlem Globetrotters, filmed across the Wembley concourse at the old Empire Pool. Clemence appears in one particular segment of the show, where he and other members of the goalkeepers' union (among them Bob Wilson, Phil Parkes and Mervyn Day) take on the New Yorkers at their own game.

The Costa Brava – or other holiday destinations – now beckon for the England and Scotland players, but Wembley isn't done yet. In two days' time, on bank holiday Monday, 60,000 souls will file into the stadium to watch a programme of daredevil deeds. Seventy-one-year-old Henri LaMothe will dive from a forty-foot platform into a paddling pool filled with just fourteen inches of water; another high diver, Roy Fransen, will set light to himself and plunge seventy feet into a pool of water onto which petrol has been poured and set ablaze; and the German Traber family will walk a very high highwire, blindfolded and without a safety net.

The headline act, though, is the world-renowned stunt motorcyclist Evel Knievel. He jumps thirteen side-to-side London buses before somersaulting multiple times on landing and getting trapped underneath his motorbike, its engine still running. He breaks both his pelvis and his right hand, and crushes a vertebra in his back. 'You are the last people in the world who will ever see me jump,' he announces to the Wembley crowd before being taken to hospital, 'because I will never, ever jump again. I am through.'

Fewer than five months later in Ohio, Evel Knievel and his motorbike leap over fourteen Greyhound buses.

England 5–1 Scotland

Saint Bobby

Saturday 1 May 1976

Manchester United vs Southampton

FA Cup final

You are twenty-five. You are just about to become immortal. You are just about to score the winning goal in the cup final.

You are Bobby Stokes.

You watch the flight of the ball that's looping forward towards you. You're alone, a single yellow shirt ahead of three red ones.

You might be offside. You don't stop to ask. The ball comes over your left shoulder and drops at your left foot. You shoot instantly, first time. You don't make the greatest of contacts, nothing as crisp and firm as the dipping twenty-yard drive you launched at the Manchester United goal just a few minutes ago. But you've placed it perfectly, across and under their goalkeeper, across and under Alex Stepney. The ball rolls and bobbles into the far corner.

You disappear under an avalanche of team-mates. You've just won yourself a car, a Ford Granada, for scoring the game's first goal. You said you'd win it. You were so confident about it that you booked driving lessons in readiness. In fact, you said you'd score three.

Seven minutes later, you hear the final whistle, you hear the cheers, you see the backroom staff charge onto the pitch. You are more than a new car owner. You're the man whose goal has just won the cup, the man whose goal has just won the cup for your hometown's bitter rivals for the first time in their history.

You're a Portsmouth boy, a Pompey lad, born and bred on the Paulsgrove estate on the north edge of town. You'd have loved to have been doing this – jigging around the Wembley turf, soaking up the adulation of tens of thousands of fans – in the blue of your team. But when you went for a trial with them, back when you were in your mid-teens, they had no money. They were scrapping their youth and reserve teams. You had to head west down the motorway instead. You had to sign for Southampton. Eight years later, you and your left foot have just given them their biggest day in the sun. You'll be on the front pages of the Sunday papers tomorrow, a picture of you drinking champagne from your boot sharing the space with a story about the sexual peccadilloes of a caught-in-the-act magistrate ('Saucy Secret of a Chief JP').

You won't make the front pages again. You play only a dozen or so more times for Southampton. You score only one more goal in their colours. You get sold to play in the United States, to play for Washington Diplomats. It's not too bad. The money's decent, the summers are hot and, in your second season, Johan Cruyff becomes your team-mate. And, for one season, you get to come back to English football for the winter to play in the blue of Portsmouth. The Pompey chimes finally peal for you.

But when you return permanently from the States, only non-league clubs want to sign you. You play a few seasons for a few teams, before jacking it all in and running a pub. Then you do some heating and plumbing jobs. Then you go to work for your cousin in her café down by the ferry terminal in Portsmouth Harbour. You work there for years. Bacon, eggs, tea. Bacon, eggs, tea. Customers in off the boats recognise you from time to time. You're happy to chat about that May day back in 1976. You tell them that if they've got ninety minutes to spare, you'll recall every last detail.

You don't forget, but football forgets you. Eventually you are granted a testimonial by Southampton, a chance to be repaid by the club, by the game. But you had to ask for it. You had to go to Southampton and ask for it.

And within a year, you are dead. You have died from bronchial pneumonia. You have died much too soon.

You are forty-four. But you are also immortal. You scored the winning goal in the cup final.

You are Bobby Stokes.

Manchester United 0–1 Southampton

Thwarted dreams

Saturday 21 May 1977

Liverpool vs Manchester United

FA Cup final

Bob Paisley is smiling. Bob Paisley is laughing. Bob Paisley is on top form.

It's been fewer than three years since he took over as Liverpool boss, three years in which he's already won five trophies. Fifteen more will come during his tenure. You need plenty of Brasso to keep that lot shiny.

Across those nine years in charge, though, Paisley will never get his hands on the FA Cup; he'll never get a chance to buff that famous trophy to a see-your-own-reflection glow. His predecessor Bill Shankly won the cup in his last match as Liverpool boss. Two years after Paisley retires, his successor's successor – Kenny Dalglish – will win it at the first time of asking. But it will forever escape Paisley's grasp. This afternoon will be the closest he gets.

Five days ago, despite losing their final league game of the season to Bristol City, Liverpool retained their First Division title. The first third of an ambitious mission had been accomplished. Next Wednesday, Paisley will take his side to Rome for their first ever European Cup final. For now, though – in approximately ten minutes' time – the second part of a possible, and unprecedented, Treble kicks off.

Between them and immortality stand Manchester United

and their manager Tommy Docherty. As he and Paisley lead their teams into the dazzling Wembley sunshine, they laugh and joke with one another. Docherty, after United's humbling by Southampton twelve months ago, appears confident. He certainly shows confidence in his choice of attire: a blood-scarlet shirt beneath his jacket and tie.

The match hinges on five quick-fire minutes early in the second half. First off, United striker Stuart Pearson latches on to a Jimmy Greenhoff header, outpaces Liverpool full-back Joey Jones and catches out Ray Clemence at his near post to open the scoring. Exactly 120 seconds later, Liverpool are level, thanks to Jimmy Case's edge-of-the-box pivot and piledriver – the most famous goal he'll ever score.

Just 156 more seconds elapse before United nose back in front, courtesy of – whether he knows much about it or not – that man Greenhoff. He was signed six months ago from Stoke City, where he had been captain and general talisman. He hadn't wanted to leave, but the club needed to raise funds to repair the main stand at the Victoria Ground, which had been seriously damaged in a storm. When he was told Old Trafford was the likeliest destination, where he'd link up with younger brother Brian, Greenhoff's protestations dissolved in the air. And here he is now, scoring the winning goal in the cup final.

It isn't one of his finest finishes. A Lou Macari snapshot is heading wide when it ricochets off the Yorkshireman's chest and spins – deceptively, frustratingly for Liverpool – beyond the reach of Phil Neal's attempted goal-line clearance and into the net. 'I remember trying to get out of the way of the winning goal,' Greenhoff will later recall. 'I couldn't, thankfully.'

After just six months in the job, Greenhoff has achieved legendary status in the eyes of the United faithful: the man who denied Liverpool that Treble. And it's not the only time he'll thwart the Merseysiders. In two years' time, in a replayed FA

Cup semi-final at Goodison Park, his deft low header, taken at speed, will puncture Liverpool's hopes of a first domestic Double. A hero twice over, for sure. But, just eighteen months later, Greenhoff will be playing in the Fourth Division for Crewe Alexandra.

That replayed 1979 semi-final will be as close as Bob Paisley will get to another FA Cup final; 1977 is the one and only time he leads Liverpool out at Wembley on a Saturday in May. The disappointment he'll feel at the evaporation of those Treble dreams won't last long, though. The summer of '77 will be a good one for him. He'll take the European Cup back with him to the County Durham mining village, Hetton-le-Hole, where he was born. He'll be awarded an OBE by Buckingham Palace. And he'll pay off the mortgage on his family semi; with the kids having left the nest, he and his wife Jessie move into a detached but still modest dormer bungalow. If it looks like a home ripe for retirees, he has no such plans. Bob Paisley's got all those trophies still to win. Keep that Brasso close to hand.

Liverpool 1–2 Manchester United

Turf wars

Saturday 4 June 1977

England vs Scotland

Home international

It's often – erroneously – said that you're never more than six feet away from a rat in central London. On this particular week, you're definitely never more than six feet away from a Union Jack here in the capital. The ubiquity of the flag, or of representations of it reproduced on any old bit of cash-in tat, proclaims that Britain is in the throes of Silver Jubilee fever. Next week will see a series of 'Jubilee days' – and a special bank holiday – to commemorate the Queen's twenty-five years on the throne. On Tuesday, the bunting will also (ironically) adorn a boat chartered by the Sex Pistols. The band will chug up and down the Thames before playing 'Anarchy in the UK' as they pass the Houses of Parliament.

Flags are very much out in force at Wembley this after-noon as the stadium becomes Little Glasgow for a few hours. Hundreds of travelling fans swing the yellow Royal Banner of Scotland, with that fearsome scarlet lion at the centre of each, back and forth, while the well-lubricated Scottish larynxes lift their songs up and away out of the stadium. Even the Wembley groundsmen have marked the occasion, cutting a tartan pattern into the turf.

The match will be the last home game that England play under the awkward, and underwhelming, stewardship of Don

Revie. Just four days later, the team will be in Rio de Janeiro, playing the first of three South American friendlies. Revie won't be there. Under the guise of a scouting mission to run the rule over forthcoming World Cup qualifier opponents Italy, he will instead slope off to Dubai to thrash out the details of a handsome deal to become the manager of the United Arab Emirates national team. When they discover the subterfuge, the English FA will try to ban Revie from football for ten years.

While England's qualification for next year's World Cup looks unlikely at best, Scotland are on course for Argentina, led by their mischievous boss Ally MacLeod, a man who's been in the job less than a month but whose ambition appears uncontainable.

This afternoon, Scotland take the lead just before half-time through a towering Gordon McQueen header from an Asa Hartford free-kick. It's a meaty, textbook finish, even if it doesn't quite possess the power McQueen has assigned it; he later claims that he met the ball with such ferocity that it rebounded out of the net all the way to the halfway line. It didn't. The ball simply nestled in the bottom corner, its passage back up the pitch made via the left boot of a dejected Ray Clemence.

Scotland double their lead after an hour when Kenny Dalglish – soon to be swapping Celtic for newly crowned European champions Liverpool as the replacement for Hamburg-bound Kevin Keegan – stabs the ball home past the clawing hands of future club-mate Clemence. The singing has not been louder all afternoon, those yellow flags swinging ever more wildly. Although England halve the deficit through a Mick Channon penalty, it's Scotland's day, their first win at Wembley in a decade – and revenge for that 5–1 hammering they received two years ago. Revie makes a swift exit. After all, he's got a flight to catch to the Middle East.

With Wembley due to be fitting high fences this summer,

the Tartan Army take full advantage of the weakened defences. They spill onto the turf in their thousands and a crowd quickly forms around the Scotland captain Bruce Rioch. They hoist him high and he grabs a tam-o'-shanter from the head of a fan to wear. That he grew up in Hampshire and Bedfordshire, and speaks with the clearest of Home Counties accents, is no problem. His father is a son of Aberdeenshire and was a sergeant major in the Scots Guards. Nor is it an issue that another English-accented individual – this one a north Londoner who's wearing a Scotland tracksuit top – is getting the same on-the-shoulders treatment. Rod Stewart will always get a free pass.

The enduring image of the celebrations – the one that will be planted on the back pages of tomorrow's papers, accompanied by tutting editorials – is that of the goalmouth nearest the players' tunnel, where the crossbar has snapped in two under the weight of Scottish flesh. Pocket knives are produced to cut out small squares of the Wembley turf, the owner of each claiming his souvenir to be retrieved from the exact spot that Dalglish scored the winner.

One such square of turf is carried away by a short, red-headed young man of twenty who's currently on honeymoon with his new wife in the capital. He will take the square back home to the Dundee suburb of Broughty Ferry, where it will be diligently planted in his back garden. He will, in thirty-six years' time, become the manager of Scotland. His name is Gordon Strachan.

England 1–2 Scotland

Hammer of the Scots

Wednesday 10 May 1978

Club Brugge vs Liverpool

European Cup final

Twelve months ago, at the Olympic Stadium in Rome, Liverpool won their maiden European Cup with nine Englishmen, a Welshman and an Irishman in their starting line-up. Tonight, the spine of their team – from centre-back to star striker, via midfield enforcer – is Scottish.

Up front is Kenny Dalglish, who's had an excellent debut season at Anfield; before tonight, he'd notched thirty goals in sixty-one games. Behind him in midfield is the fearless Graeme Souness, a mid-season capture from Middlesbrough. And behind the two of them, lining up in central defence alongside Phil Thompson, is Alan Hansen, another summer signing from the Scottish Premier Division, this time Partick Thistle.

Hansen was signed on the direct recommendation of Geoff Twentyman, Liverpool's chief scout. Twentyman is a talent-spotter with a reputation for spying players with promise from the lower leagues and correctly judging their suitability to become part of the best English team of the time. Past prize catches include players like Keegan and Ray Clemence at Scunthorpe United, or right-back Phil Neal at Northampton Town. The East Midlands was about as far south as Twentyman would venture. He tended to be on the search for young players with a 'northern soul', so kept his patch to Scotland and the north of England.

'There was an unwritten rule in our house,' explains Twentyman's son, Geoff Jr, forty-five years later. 'You never asked where he was going nor which player he was watching. You would only get the story after the signing. And that's when he told me about Alan Hansen. Dad would go and watch him at Partick Thistle. One week he'd play centre-back, the next he'd play in the middle of midfield. Whichever position he was in, the opponents could never get the ball off him. He just had this amazing ability, which he had brought into the Liverpool first team, where he could dribble the ball and pass it and get back into position.'

(Occasionally – and presumably in the case of Hansen in particular – there would be a bittersweet after-taste when Geoff Jr heard about his father's travels and travails. The year before this final against Brugge, Geoff Jr was a fixture of Liverpool's reserves, juggling training and midweek matches with his A-level studies. Until, that is, the day Bob Paisley asked for a private audience. 'Your dad tells me that you're going to college to become a PE teacher. Well, I think you'll make a better teacher than player.' Geoff Jr had been let down gently, but the decision would sting within the month when, on Twentyman Sr's direct counsel, Paisley signed Hansen. The young Scot played in the same position as the young Liverpudlian.)

Chief scout Twentyman rarely got to see the first team play, such was his crammed schedule. However, with the domestic season over and no more matches left to travel to, he's here at Wembley this evening, watching over that Scottish spine he'd played a large part in recruiting, watching them play a significant role in Liverpool's retention of the European Cup.

Hansen's been in and out of the team all season, but tonight he starts in place of Tommy Smith, whose leg is in plaster after something of a freak accident: he dropped a pickaxe on his foot, breaking a toe. Ron Jones, BBC Radio 2's lead commentator tonight, notes that 'it must have been a very brave pickaxe to have put Tommy Smith out'.

At twenty-two, Hansen looks a little frail, undeveloped. He's delicate Bambi to Smith's roaring stag. But he's neat and unflustered, and calmly strokes the ball across the line of the back four. He's also blessed with immaculate timing, whether intercepting the ball or putting in a last-ditch tackle, much to the exasperation of Brugge's prolific scorer Jan Simoen, who is largely subdued tonight.

Towards the end of the first half, it's Hansen – not one of the busy attacking players like Dalglish or David Fairclough or Terry McDermott – who comes closest to giving Liverpool the lead, meeting McDermott's free-kick with a firm header that needs to be tipped over by the Brugge goalkeeper, the Dane Birger Jensen.

When the deadlock is broken in the sixty-fourth minute, though, it does come with a Scottish accent. A Brugge half-clearance presents the ball to Souness on the edge of the area and his slide-rule pass carves open the Belgians' defence and plays in Dalglish. The Glaswegian deftly clips the ball over the advancing Jensen from the tightest of angles and it seems to take an age before nestling in the far corner. And he's off, hurdling the advertising boards behind the Brugge goal as if he's Ed Moses, and followed by every ecstatic Liverpool outfield player. At Anfield, the Kop are almost on top of any celebration. Here at Wembley, Dalglish has got to go the extra mile to commune with the Liverpool fans.

Twenty-five nervous minutes are then endured, including a Phil Thompson goal-line clearance after an uncharacteristic Hansen mistake – the only foot he's put wrong this evening. Then the final whistle and the realisation that, here on home turf, Liverpool have become the first British side to win the European Cup twice.

Unlike his compatriots Dalglish and Souness, this is Hansen's last game before the summer break. The other two have the home international tournament starting in three days' time, before the more significant matter of flying out to Argentina for the World Cup. Hansen – no doubt a little jealous, although he'll be a granite fixture of the Scotland team by the time of España '82 – will watch it at home.

For Souness, though, there are more pressing matters to attend to before jetting off to South America. There's tonight's after-party down in Swiss Cottage, for starters. Having won the top prize in just his third match in European football, his date this evening is 21-year-old Swede Mary Stävin, the current Miss World.

Graeme, just where did it all go wrong?

Club Brugge 0–1 Liverpool

'But wait a moment . . .'

Saturday 12 May 1979

Arsenal vs Manchester United

FA Cup final

It was all going so averagely.

Despite being the livelier, more creative side, Manchester

United find themselves 2–0 down by half-time in the 1979 FA Cup final, a scoreline that hasn't been added to during the second forty-five. With just a handful of minutes left, a fair few Mancunians are glancing at their watches, weighing up whether to beat a hasty retreat, to leave now and have a clear run to the Tube station and an early train out of Euston, to not have to endure the pain of another team's celebrations.

But taking such a decision would be woefully premature. For what follows is the most extraordinary five minutes in FA Cup final history . . .

86 mins 4 secs: United have a free-kick, thirty yards out on the right, after David O'Leary climbs on the back of Jimmy Greenhoff. Jimmy Nicholl runs over the ball, leaving Steve Coppell to curl it into the box. It threads its way right through all the players to Joe Jordan at the back, twelve yards out. He swivels and turns the ball back into the danger zone, where Gordon McQueen sticks out a leg and guides it past Pat Jennings.

'Suddenly, United are back in the game with four minutes left,' declares ITV commentator Brian Moore, audibly relieved that the game isn't going to fizzle out anticlimactically. 'And who knows what might be produced in those four minutes?'

86 mins 52 secs: The United fans are now roaring, prompting Moore the soothsayer to continue his theme, even if his words don't come out in the right order. 'Are we in yet for an amazing upheaval?'

87 mins 45 secs: United are relentless, not allowing the ball to leave Arsenal's half. But they lose possession, the ball breaking to the Gunners' left-back Sammy Nelson. He has the time to put his foot on it, to consider his options, but instead hits it first time, attempting to play it down the touchline and take a few seconds out of the clock. Instead, his clearance is poor, ricocheting off Graham Rix and into the path of the darting Coppell. The England winger chips a delightful ball towards

the inside-right channel. Sammy McIlroy controls it, turning inside to leave O'Leary on his backside. Another touch to push the ball beyond Steve Walford leaves the Arsenal substitute in the same helpless position. McIlroy gets just enough on his shot for it to slip under the advancing Jennings and dribble slowly – tormentingly, to Arsenal eyes – into the far corner.

One hundred and six seconds. Two goals.

United have saved the final and now have the upper hand psychologically. Arsenal are on their knees. All afternoon, Moore's co-commentator Brian Clough has been criticising Arsenal's deep defence, noting how having all eleven players behind the ball at set-pieces doesn't aid the free flow of positivity. He's been very much singing the praises of United all game, and now feels they've received their just deserts. 'I'm delighted for them. They've earned it since three o'clock.'

88 mins 52 secs: Arsenal kick off for the second time in a couple of minutes. They've now got to steel themselves for thirty minutes of extra-time, thirty more minutes of United pressure, powered by a figurative following wind. 'Arsenal were preparing their victory speeches,' observes Moore, 'and now they're dumbstruck.'

89 mins 13 secs: Just twenty-one seconds later, another goal is scored. The scales, returned to a fine balance by McIlroy's solo effort, crash down again on the Arsenal side. Liam Brady collects the ball a few yards inside the United half. This is one player not content to see the game out ahead of extra-time. He accelerates, burning past Lou Macari and Mickey Thomas, before offloading the ball to Graham Rix, wide on the left.

Rix's cross is long and looping, inviting Gary Bailey to make it his own. But the young United goalkeeper has misjudged it. The ball eludes his flailing hand, continuing unimpeded on its path towards the far post.

'But wait a moment ...' cautions Brian Moore.

There, at the far post, is Rix's fellow Doncastrian, Alan Sunderland, who slides in to direct the ball into the empty net. The striker is in ecstasy, his head turned to the heavens and his eyes tight shut, as he sprints away into the clutches of his disbelieving team-mates. A hundred and twenty yards away, at the other end of the pitch, goalkeeper Jennings wraps those big hands of his around his ears. He can't believe the cheers of the Arsenal fans. He can't believe what he's just seen. Those two swift goals he's conceded disappear on the wind. He's released from jail in an instant. On the Arsenal bench, manager Terry Neill looks remarkably calm. He straightens his tie. *This was the plan all along.*

90 mins 5 secs: Sunderland receives the ball wide on the right and ushers it along the touchline towards the corner flag. But he's dispossessed and Greenhoff hares upfield with the ball. A long pass to Jordan. A lay-off back to the still-sprinting Greenhoff. Greenhoff to Coppell. A long cross into the box. Jordan's head. Jennings' hands. No final twist, no final turn.

91 mins 27 secs: The final whistle can barely be heard in the cacophony of tens of thousands of whistling Arsenal fans. Neill and his opposite number Dave Sexton shake hands, hug and smile. They understand just how special those last five minutes have been. They know that this is a final that will last long in the memory. So do the 100,000 inside Wembley. So do the millions watching at home.

And it's a final that has left Brian Clough speechless. Well, almost. 'You just want to spend time letting it sink in . . .' is all he can muster.

It's been a climax to silence even the biggest of mouths.

Arsenal 3–2 Manchester United

The 1980s

The five-foot-five giant

Tuesday 13 May 1980

England vs Argentina

International friendly

He measures five feet and five inches, but he will stand a giant tonight. This is Wembley's – and England's – first chance to see Diego Armando Maradona in the flesh, up close and personal, the wonderkid from Buenos Aires, the latest sensation in world football. The sceptics are typically cautious, but the fact that the teenager has already been named the South American Footballer of the Year suggests they might be converted tonight, as does his major contribution to Argentina's young guns winning the World Youth Championship last year. 'Whatever happens,' predicts the BBC commentator Barry Davies, 'the crowd are likely to admire and maybe marvel at the precocious skills of the 19-year-old.' Barry is correct.

Although Maradona played, and scored, against Scotland last year, he remains an enigma, with little known about him other than the minor morsels of trivia revealed in a *Shoot!* magazine Q&A a couple of months ago. Favourite actor? 'Ryan O'Neal.' Favourite food? 'Oven-roasted meat.' Favourite singer? 'The Spaniard Julio Iglesias; and melodical music in general.'

There are a few survivors of Argentina's World Cup-winning side in the team tonight (Daniel Passarella, Leopoldo Luque, the goalkeeper Ubaldo Fillol), while the one-time Birmingham full-back Alberto Tarantini is another familiar face. But there's no Mario Kempes. He's playing for Valencia in tomorrow night's Cup Winners' Cup final against Arsenal. Osvaldo Ardiles is another absentee; he's away with Spurs on a trip to Saudi Arabia ahead of filming his role as prisoner-of-war Carlos Rey in *Escape to Victory* next month.

No matter. Eyes are mainly focused on Maradona, as well as measuring England's progress under Ron Greenwood ahead of the imminent European Championship. The current World Cup holders will offer a stern test, both physically and skill-wise. Maradona alone takes care of the latter, a repository of flicks, tricks and shimmies to beguile and bamboozle. It's six years before BBC Radio's Bryon Butler so memorably describes him as 'a little eel', but that's what he resembles tonight, constantly turning the England central defensive partnership of Phil Thompson and Dave Watson inside out.

England's left-back Kenny Sansom isn't immune to his slippery ways either, and concedes a penalty when he can do nothing but trip the teenager. By then, though, the home side are two goals to the good, both scored by Liverpool's David Johnson. Kevin Keegan will add a third after Passarella converts that penalty. Greenwood will be happy with his squad's progress ahead of the tournament in Italy.

Tonight isn't really about goals, though. The take-home memory is of what is surely Wembley's greatest near-miss. Of course, Maradona is its architect. And it's the prototype, the prequel, of that magnificent solo effort that will end England's interest in the 1986 World Cup, a jinking slalom through the home side's defence that evades dizzied defenders and despairing slide tackles. As Ray Clemence advances from his line,

Maradona slips the ball beyond him – but also narrowly beyond the far post too. It would have been one of the greatest goals to grace this patch of turf.

It's just a practice run. When he scores *that* goal in the Azteca Stadium in Mexico City six years later, Maradona fully accepts the lesson he learnt in 1980. 'I dribbled past all of the England defenders at Wembley, but instead of dribbling past the goalie, I tried to finish it too soon and it just missed the post.' He freely admits it was his seven-year-old brother Hugo – a.k.a. El Turco – who pointed out his mistake. 'El Turco called me on the phone to say "Stupid! You should have faked to one side! The goalie had already dived." . . . In the World Cup in Mexico, I remembered his advice.'

That delicious near-miss isn't all he takes away tonight; he trudges off the pitch wearing Kevin Keegan's shirt. He'll return to Wembley only once more in his career, in 1987, as part of a Rest of the World XI, for which he pockets £100,000. This being less than a year after the Hand of God incident, his every touch is roundly booed by the crowd.

Tonight, though, he's made them purr, as Barry Davies concludes. 'Now you know that the publicity has not lied.'

England 3–1 Argentina

School's out

Saturday 7 June 1980

England Schoolboys vs Scotland Schoolboys

Dentyne Trophy match

If Paul Rideout was your school pal, he'd be the one you'd send into the newsagents to buy cigarettes or into the off-licence for a four-pack. At fifteen, he has the looks, stature and build of someone at least five years older. And at times during this afternoon's match between the young pretenders of England and Scotland, it really seems to be a case of a man against boys. (Indeed, when a quartet of pitch invaders hold up proceedings for a few minutes late in the game, the strapping Rideout joins the police in apprehending the four men.)

That Rideout is head and shoulders above almost everyone else on this large Wembley pitch can be shown in his personal goal tally today. He helps himself to a hat-trick, overpowering and outmuscling the comparative lightweights in the Scottish defence for each goal. As such, he puts himself in venerable company, joining the likes of Johnny Haynes, Jimmy Greaves, Geoff Hurst, Bobby Charlton and Malcolm Macdonald as the scorer of a Wembley hat-trick while representing his country. One thing marks Rideout out as unique among that cavalcade, though: none of those were on the losing side when they did the deed.

The Scottish side edge an extraordinarily close, thrillingly open game. 'I told the English lads I wanted them to win 5–4,' explains Ted Austin, the chairman of the English Schools FA, 'and I told the Scots boys, that if they had to win, to do it 5–4 for the cameras.' The score is even more remarkable bearing in mind these under-15s are playing just forty minutes each way and that the opening goal – Rideout's first, a finish executed with all the aplomb of a seasoned First Division striker – doesn't arrive until half an hour into the match.

Around 69,000 spectators are here at Wembley, mainly pre-pubescent boys judging by the falsetto cheering and chanting. Many have been bussed in from the schools of those playing this afternoon, including an impressive amount making the journey down from Scotland, whether that's from St Mungo's High School in Falkirk (seat of learning of the Scottish centre-forward John Sludden), Musselburgh Grammar (the number 10, Stewart Rae) or Bellshill Academy (the full-back Eddie Macdonald).

Several of the Scottish team will go on to play at the highest level. Paul McStay is one of their standout performers today, scoring twice and showing the quality that will later see him appointed captain of both Celtic and Scotland. The team's number 7, John Robertson, is a future goalscoring legend for Hearts, while Ally Dick, their flaxen-haired left-winger, will go on to play for both Tottenham and Ajax. Highly mobile and sparky all afternoon, Dick, who scores Scotland's fourth, has taken full advantage of this shop window for his talents. He's already been attracting plenty of attention ('clubs phoning me up every night') and by the time he leaves school next summer, he'll be in receipt of no fewer than forty-two offers of apprenticeships. Of the England side, only Rideout – later of Aston Villa, Bari, Southampton, Rangers and Everton – and future West Ham full-back George Parris will make notable careers in the top flight of English football.

Taking place four days before the men's European Championship starts, the match is being televised live on ITV, complete with commentary from Brian Moore and a distinctly impressed Ian St John before they fly off to Italy for the tournament. As such – and aided by the goal-heavy scoreline – it is surely the best-remembered schoolboy international Wembley has ever witnessed. And the game's most remembered moment is undoubtedly Rideout's third this afternoon. It is simply one of the greatest goals in the stadium's history.

Fifteen minutes into the second half, with Scotland 4–2 up, Rideout collects the ball just inside his own half and surges through the Scottish midfield before unleashing an unstoppable thirty-five-yard drive. The ball is still rising as it hits the net. Most 15-year-olds would have gone crazy had they scored such a cracker on the school playing fields, let alone at Wembley on live television. But Rideout remains that cool, taking-it-in-his-stride character. He just walks away almost embarrassed, head bowed and a single arm raised in salute, as if scoring such net-busting goals is a daily occurrence. (It should be noted that, fifteen years later, when he scores the winning goal for Everton in the 1995 FA Cup final at the age of thirty, he won't be anything like as reserved.)

Rideout might have expected to be the toast of Kingsdown School in Swindon come Monday morning, but this is his O-level year and he's already left the education system. Instead, he's a couple of miles away at the County Ground, converting his associate schoolboy status with Swindon Town into a full apprenticeship. After *that* goal on Saturday, the club swiftly get his contract signed before the big guns come calling. It's a wise decision.

England Schoolboys 4–5 Scotland Schoolboys

Teenage kick

Thursday 14 May 1981

Manchester City vs Tottenham Hotspur

FA Cup final replay

As the ball hits the net, the clichés come tumbling out. A supreme piece of individual skill. A masterclass in technique. A goal to grace any final.

It's also one of the greatest goals ever scored at Wembley. Despite this – and while not totally forgotten, while not completely wiped from the collective hippocampus – it's an effort that will soon be cast into shadow by another goal scored this evening, here at the first FA Cup final replay to be played at Wembley.

Ricky Villa's mazy dribble, that twisting, turning journey that ends with the Argentinian sliding the ball under Manchester City goalkeeper Joe Corrigan, is the shade–casting goal, the one that wins the cup for Spurs. But City's opener, a spectacular volley from the teenage midfielder Steve Mackenzie, is a very special goal indeed. Had it been the deciding goal tonight, it would still be lauded all these decades later. But it wasn't. Instead, Villa gets all the praise. The winner takes it all.

Mackenzie deserves a revisit, a revision. There are only eleven minutes on the clock, but the replay has already seen its opening goal when Villa, substituted on Saturday after an underwhelming performance and possibly fortunate to be back in the starting XI this evening, redeems himself and pokes the ball home to score his first of the night and to put Spurs in front.

Three minutes later, City are awarded a free-kick a dozen yards inside the Spurs half. The ball won't touch the ground again until it settles in the back of Milija Aleksic's net. Right-back Ray Ransom pumps the ball forward where, on the edge of the six-yard box, it's met by the head of Spurs centre-half Paul Miller. It's then helped on its way by the left-back Chris Hughton, but the danger is not extinguished. His header just goes straight to Tommy Hutchison, the hero and villain of the first match when he scored at both ends. The Scot twists ninety degrees to his left, goes down on one knee and cushions a header towards his midfield partner Mackenzie, the youngest player on the pitch. Fourteen years Hutchison's junior, the bairn is unmarked on the edge of the D of the penalty box. He's teed up perfectly.

What is Mackenzie thinking as the ball arcs towards him? *Take a touch? Hit it first time? Keep your head down. Don't put it in the stands. Don't do that. Don't do anything to make 50,000 Spurs fans laugh.*

Mackenzie doesn't need to think. Both level-headed and instinctive, his decisions on a football field are made subconsciously. His eye never strays from the ball as it makes its pinpoint descent towards his right foot. Hutchison's set-up has wrong-footed the Spurs players and Mackenzie has sight of enough green around him to know he's got space and time to let the ball fall – and then to let fly. As with Paul Rideout's third goal in that schoolboy international last year, it's probably the sweetest hit of the young man's career. His timing is immaculate and the ball slams into the net before Aleksic even starts diving.

On the TV gantries, the reactions of the respective ITV and BBC commentators are one letter short of being identical. 'Oh, a tremendous goal! Steve Mackenzie!' yells Brian Moore. 'Oh, tremendous goal! Steve Mackenzie!' yells John Motson.

With that graceful swing of his right leg, Mackenzie has become the youngest player to score in an FA Cup final. But individual record-breaking doesn't translate to collective glory. After Kevin Reeves puts City ahead from the penalty spot early in the second half, Garth Crooks equalises for Spurs. Then, six minutes later, Villa embarks on that famous dribble of his. The cup is Tottenham's. City return to Manchester empty-handed.

Villa's goal will, over the next forty years, be celebrated as one of the finest seen in the stadium – the subject of a thousand after-dinner speeches. Mackenzie's equally handsome effort will be less cherished and he will be in less demand on the chicken-in-a-basket circuit. Having joined City from Crystal Palace two years earlier for £250,000 – a vast sum at the time for a 17-year-old, let alone for one who had yet to play for the first team – that volley will be the defining moment of his career.

He's still a teen when City sell him to West Bromwich Albion three months later. He spends six seasons at the Hawthorns, during which time he grows a moustache and makes more than 150 appearances, before heading to Charlton for a further three seasons. Brief spells at Sheffield Wednesday and Shrewsbury Town follow, but he's feeling the effects of an injury-pocked career. He undertakes some coaching back at City, but a life in IT and distance learning provision beckons instead.

There's some distance too between late middle age and that famous teenage kick. Throughout the years, the commentary that accompanied his goal isn't as familiar as the 'And still Ricky Villa ...' line that will become the title of the Argentinian's autobiography. But, in Steve Mackenzie's head, the two-part harmony between Moore and Motson almost certainly never grows faint.

'Oh, tremendous goal! Steve Mackenzie!'

Manchester City 2–3 Tottenham Hotspur

Off to sunny Spain . . .

Wednesday 18 November 1981

England vs Hungary

World Cup qualifier

'As any goalscorer will tell you, it doesn't matter *how* they go in as long as they *do* go in.

'People say, "It was lucky. The ball sort of hit you." Yes, it did hit me, but I'll tell anyone who'll listen that it was Trevor Brooking's fault for hitting such a horrible shot. I just adjusted my feet and redirected it. Happy days. And then, afterwards, lots of silly photos with guitars and sombreros and such.'

The scruffiest goal that Paul Mariner ever scored for his country was also the most important goal he ever scored for his country. Going into their final qualifier for the following year's World Cup in Spain, England's position in Group 4 had been perilous for most of the campaign, thanks to a trio of 2–1 defeats away to Romania, Switzerland and Norway. That final defeat is remembered mostly for that unforgettable piece of broadcasting from Norwegian TV commentator Bjørge Lillelien. Its impressive grasp of public figures from British history makes it well worth one more outing.

'Lord Nelson! Lord Beaverbrook! Sir Winston Churchill! Sir Anthony Eden! Clement Atlee! Henry Cooper! Lady Diana! Maggie Thatcher! Can you hear me, Maggie Thatcher? Your boys took one hell of a beating!'

That hell of a beating left England half-in, half-out of a hole. Escape was possible – probable, even, as they needed only a draw against a Hungary side they had coolly dispatched in Budapest five months earlier. But also possible was a descent into eternal ignominy should they suffer another embarrassing defeat. It would be Mariner's goal that pulled them upwards, upwards into the World Cup finals.

The last time England successfully navigated the qualification process for the finals was two decades earlier in 1961, topping their group and only dropping a single point. No qualification was needed four years later due to them hosting the tournament, nor for 1970 with the side heading to Mexico as reigning champions. Then came the double humiliation of failing to qualify for both West Germany in 1974 and Argentina in 1978.

With those defeats in Bucharest, Basel and Oslo imprinted on the collective consciousness, nerves are far from steady, both in the stadium and in homes across the country. With the game shown live on BBC One, John Motson advises the nation to 'hold tight everybody because here we go'.

From the off, England's pace and harrying is absorbing. Every tackle is strong and committed, every attack charged with intent. The breakthrough is inevitable and, after fifteen minutes, it comes courtesy of that Mariner goal. Ferenc Mészáros's erratic goalkeeping provides the opportunity, wildly flapping at a floated Terry McDermott free-kick. The ball falls at Brooking's feet, but the West Ham man – who scored twice in the corresponding fixture in Budapest – has forgotten to wear his shooting boots. His screwed shot is heading out for a goal-kick when a tumbling Mariner redirects it just inside the post and into an unguarded net. Some will suggest the goal was down to the striker's instinct. Those with a view from behind the goal might offer an alternative take; that Mariner actually falls over the ball and little deliberate technique is applied.

Only fifteen minutes are on the clock, but England – mindful that they took the lead against Norway in their last match, before succumbing to that 2–1 reverse – choose not to defend their slender advantage. Instead, they continue to press forward, creating chance after chance. The more time spent raining shots and headers down on Mészáros's goal, the less time there is for Hungary to score the two goals necessary to stop England's progress. Plus, how inclined the Hungarians are to attack is questionable. They've already qualified for the finals and there's no result this evening that can knock them off top spot in the group. On the final whistle, the stadium erupts. Peter Shilton, the only survivor of the side that drew with Poland in 1973, seems especially ecstatic. He'll finally be going to a World Cup.

'Mariner sets course for Spain,' declares tomorrow's headline in *The Guardian*. Don't forget to pack those guitars and sombreros.

England 1–0 Hungary

The Seagulls have landed

Saturday 21 May 1983

Brighton and Hove Albion vs Manchester United

FA Cup final

Nestled in the Surrey countryside, the seventeenth-century Selsdon Park Hotel has been the favoured pre-match base of many a cup final football team, particularly those with a scent of giant-killing in their nostrils. Sunderland stayed here before the 1973 final, having flown down from the north-east to nearby Gatwick Airport; Southampton also chose to spend the night here, before their showdown with Manchester United. United are in the final this afternoon as well, facing another south coast side. Brighton and Hove Albion have chosen to check in at the Selsdon too.

However, that's where the similarities end. While Sunderland and Southampton headed north up the A23 towards Wembley on their team bus come match-day lunchtime, Brighton are taking to the skies. And that's why twelve footballers in white suits are currently walking across a school playing field towards a waiting helicopter. 'We looked like waiters,' the team's right-back, Chris Ramsey, recalls several decades later, still wincing at the memory.

Despite the suits, they are a raggle-taggle bunch of promising youngsters and, in the likes of Jimmy Case, Tony Grealish and Gordon Smith, weather-beaten, been-around-the-block pros. Case has played at Wembley several times before and of course scored in the 1977 final, also against United. Grealish, the busy, bearded midfielder who will captain the side today in the absence of the suspended Steve Foster, has also previously graced the sainted pitch, playing Gaelic football there for London side St Gabriel's.

The squad are under the stewardship of Jimmy Melia, a balding Liverpudlian who was handed the keys to the manager's office earlier in the season, making the step up from his role as chief scout. Melia is a somewhat flamboyant character. Known for his trademark white shoes, *The Guardian* once described him as looking 'like a *Minder* villain on a trip to Studio 54'. His glamour quotient is largely earned by his girlfriend, the model Val Lloyd. 'She was a good few years his junior,' says Ramsey. 'It was like that Mrs Merton line to Debbie McGee. "What first attracted you to the millionaire Paul Daniels?"'

Travelling to a cup final by helicopter might have looked glamorous, but there were sound reasons behind the decision. The team would avoid traffic queues on the North Circular as they approached the stadium, while the flight offered excellent exposure for their sponsors British Caledonian. The BBC would be broadcasting live on board, gifting the airline extended, unparalleled and free exposure on the cup final edition of *Grandstand*.

It was an attractive proposition for the BBC too, landing a fantastic exclusive ahead of their ITV rivals. Alan Parry, the corporation's roving reporter on the helicopter, explains how fierce the battle for ratings between the two channels was on cup final day. 'There used to be behind-the-scenes wars going on in those days about who could get the first interviewee, who'd get the winning manager, who'd get the scorer of the winning goal. All kinds of skulduggery went on. Bribes being offered and everything. It was so competitive.'

Whether emboldened by their glamorous entrance, Brighton aren't at all overawed and take United into extra-time, thanks to goals from Gordon Smith and Gary Stevens. Then, in the last of those extra thirty minutes, the fairy tale is all set up. Brighton's Michael Robinson breaks away before setting up Smith, unmarked and with acres of time and space inside the United box. Perhaps too much time and too much space. Smith would score ninety-nine times in a hundred in those circumstances, but he fluffs his lines, his shot blocked by Gary Bailey's legs.

The high-flyers of Brighton didn't get handed another such chance. United stuffed them 4–0 in the replay. Back to earth with a bump. An unhappy landing.

Brighton and Hove Albion 2–2 Manchester United

Judge and jury

Saturday 18 May 1985

Everton vs Manchester United

FA Cup final

When Peter Willis wakes up in his hotel room this morning, the biggest day of his football career stretches out in front of him. This afternoon, he will referee the FA Cup final between Howard Kendall's Everton and Ron Atkinson's Manchester United. With just a single season left as a Football League official, he's been handed the big one. This is his golden handshake for all those years of refereeing. It's his carriage clock, his long-service medal.

Willis will hope for as anonymous a day as possible in return for his meagre fee of £43, from which he's had to find the train fare down from County Durham for his wife Helen. An anonymous day, a match in which he's largely invisible, a match in which he doesn't make the headlines. Unfortunately, though, by teatime a significant portion of the nation will know the name 'Peter Willis'.

This afternoon, Everton are chasing an unprecedented treble, having secured the First Division title a few weeks back and won the Cup Winners' Cup the previous Wednesday evening in Rotterdam. Both teams and their managers are wearing black armbands following the tragedy at Bradford City seven days earlier when an horrendous fire in the main stand at Valley Parade resulted in fifty-six deaths. Further tragedy will come later in

191

the month when thirty-nine Juventus fans lose their lives in the Heysel Stadium tragedy in Brussels. It is a tumultuous month for English football. A grave, soot-black month. English clubs will lose the right to play in European competition for five seasons following the events in Belgium. The chance for title-winning Everton to have a tilt at the European Cup – a competition won seven times by three different English clubs over the past eight years – is removed.

The swashbuckling style with which the Toffees beat Rapid Vienna in Rotterdam three days ago is sadly lacking in a lack-lustre, lumpy first half in which both sides' defenders are the most accomplished players. In the seventy-eighth minute, Peter Reid – the busy Everton midfielder who was recently crowned PFA Player of the Year – intercepts a wayward United pass and makes a bolt upfield. The last defender, Kevin Moran, unceremoniously chops him down, sending the Liverpudlian flying and flailing through the air. It's a bad challenge and Willis orders the Irishman over. It's a booking for what is at best a badly mistimed tackle, and at worst a cynical act against a player through on goal.

Except it's more than a booking.

Willis doesn't brandish a red card, theatrically or otherwise (the issuing of cards was removed from the English game four years ago by the FA Council and will return in a couple of years' time). For now, though, his right arm, pointing stiff and straight towards the Manchester United bench, tells the 100,000 people inside Wembley of his decision. Judge and jury. Jury and judge. Moran is guilty. His sentence is instant. He is the first player to be sent off in an FA Cup final.

The United man is incandescent with rage, as are plenty of his team-mates. They surround Willis, ranting and raving. The tall and imposing Willis, a village copper when he's not on the football pitch, doesn't bow or bend. The decision is final. The final becomes this decision.

The press benches and broadcast gantries are united in their condemnation of Willis's interpretation of Moran's challenge. Up in the ITV commentary box, Brian Moore's voice quivers with incredulity. His instinct is backed up by co-commentator Ian St John next to him, who takes a more unequivocal line. 'I think the referee is 100 per cent out of order.' (Even Reid, when he comes back to earth after the challenge, disagrees with the decision. 'There's no way he should have gone. It's an injustice.')

As part of the studio panel, St John's usual television sparring partner, Jimmy Greaves, goes further. For him, Willis has attempted to be the focus of attention, to steal the limelight. 'He wanted to get his name in history before he retired,' he grumbles. Greaves will come to regret letting these eleven words slip out.

While Norman Whiteside's tremendous extra-time goal, curling the ball inside Neville Southall's far post from an unhelpful angle, means that Moran's sending-off doesn't cost United the cup, Willis – the former guardsman, the principled policeman, the straight-backed freemason – doesn't let things lie. Greaves and London Weekend Television are served with letters from his legal representatives, notifying them of the intention to sue for libel.

Thirteen months later, a High Court settlement sees Greaves cover the legal costs of the case and make a donation to the Referees' Association Benevolent Fund. The donation was at Willis's behest. 'It was dirty money and I didn't want it,' he later tells the *Northern Echo*. 'It was the principle that mattered. He'd made me out to be dishonest. He didn't know Peter Willis.'

Everton 0–1 Manchester United

Freight expectations

Saturday 1 June 1985

Brentford vs Wigan Athletic

Freight Rover Trophy final

It's an unlikely piece of pre-match entertainment – and an unlikely prize, to boot. It's 2.30 on a scorchingly hot June afternoon and, squeezed in between no fewer than three performances from the Havering Drum Corps, the chairmen of Brentford and Wigan Athletic have gathered on the Wembley pitch. It's here that they're each presented with a pair of keys, the reward for winning their respective area finals in this season's Freight Rover Trophy. The keys fit the ignitions of a pair of Sherpa minibuses, new additions to each club's vehicle fleet.

This season's Freight Rover Trophy is actually the first Freight Rover Trophy, the paid-for name of the Associate Members' Cup, launched just last season. Its aim is to give clubs in the Third and Fourth Divisions a knock-out competition that will hold their interest until the final, unlike the FA or League Cups, where their early exit is almost guaranteed. Accordingly, it proves a popular addition to English football's domestic calendar, with a range of sponsors – among them Leyland DAF, Auto Windscreens, Johnstone's Paint, Checkatrade and Papa John's – queuing up to attach their name to the competition in the coming decades. This afternoon, even at this early stage in its evolution, Football League secretary Graham Kelly declares it a triumph. 'Who can argue that a competition which has generated around half a million pounds to the League's smaller clubs has not been a success?'

It's also a competition that will, every season, give the players of two lower-league clubs the chance to make what will almost certainly be their only appearance at Wembley. Last season, the inaugural final was played at Boothferry Park in Hull. This year, boosted by the patronage of the Birmingham-based vehicle manufacturer, the national stadium has opened its doors to its grand final, to north versus south.

Freight Rover seems to have fully embraced its sponsorship. Hundreds of its workers and their families have come down from the West Midlands for the game, while the match-day programme is full of gushing praise for the company, with the copywriter somewhat over-egging the football analogies: 'Thanks to an aggressive attacking policy ... beating their rivals hands down on every score ... Start supporting a winning side today' etc. Other adverts in the programme reflect a competition that marries the glamour of Wembley with the prosaic nature of the lower leagues. There's an elegant full-page ad for KLM ('The airline that means business'), while over the page there's a smaller one extolling the virtues of Bucks Bolt & Nut Co Ltd, the Gerrards Cross–based 'stockists of all types of industrial fastenings'.

Wigan have been a Football League club for just seven seasons; their only previous appearance at Wembley came as a non-league outfit in the 1973 FA Trophy final. But Wigan accents have recently been heard around these parts. Four weeks ago, the town's rugby league side won a pulsating, ten-try Challenge Cup final. Can their round-ball counterparts make it an unprecedented double?

The answer is yes. It's been a couple of weeks since their respective area finals, a dead period during which the rest of the players in the Third and Fourth Divisions will have sloped off for some continental sun after another arduous season. Brentford have done so too; they recently returned from a five-day break in Corfu. Wigan steadfastly remained in Lancashire, focused on the task at hand. And it shows.

By half-time, the Latics have one hand on the trophy, having established a 2–0 lead. The first goal is a controversial one. A year before the phrase 'Hand of God' enters the football lexicon, striker Mike Newell clearly controls a through ball illegally before firing home. Everyone sees it, bar the referee and his linesmen. Brentford's players and fans sense a gross miscarriage of justice. Wiganites are prepared to turn a blind eye.

Newell is only twenty years old, as is the scorer of Wigan's second, Tony Kelly. Their manager, the former Northern Ireland international Bryan Hamilton, is clearly a firm believer in blooding youth; their third goal, after Brentford come back into the game with a Robbie Cooke snapshot, is scored by another youngster, the teenager David Lowe. His is a highly impressive strike, one of the best overhead kicks the stadium has ever seen.

This afternoon's guest of honour waiting at the top of the steps isn't a royal, either major or minor. It's Elton John, returning to Wembley little more than a year after his Watford side were beaten by Everton in the FA Cup final. They were the victim of a controversial goal too – Andy Gray's challenge on goalkeeper Steve Sherwood – so he'd be sympathetic to Brentford. Hornets and Bees are united in having the sting taken out of them.

Elton hands over the trophy to Wigan captain Colin Methven and the team pose for the traditional photos back on the pitch. Midfielder Graham Barrow misses out; he's too busy having stitches put in his foot after an over-enthusiastic challenge in the closing minutes by Chris Kamara. But he limps around on the lap of honour nonetheless, blood still leaking into his sock.

That summer, six weeks after those two minibuses head off to their respective new homes, Wembley hosts the most significant concert in its history – and arguably the most significant concert in British musical history. Having welcomed Bruce Springsteen for a three-night residency in early July as part of his seemingly never-ending 'Born in the USA' tour, a week later Wembley opens its gates for an even bigger occasion: some minor, under-sold bash called Live Aid.

It's sixteen years to the day since the stadium hosted its maiden concert, a free event held after 50,000 'tweenagers, teenagers and twenties' had completed a sponsored charity walk to Wembley on behalf of Oxfam. 'It showed that young people,' the Pathé newsreader's script sniffily offers, 'even with their long hair and odd dress, can do important things and do care.'

They care in 1985 too. Live Aid will raise more than £100 million for famine relief, aided by star turns from the likes of Queen, David Bowie, Paul McCartney, U2 and a returning Elton John. The 1969 show was a little less star-studded (Gentle Influence or Grapefruit, anyone?), but one band actually played both events. By the evidence of their Live Aid performance, Status Quo haven't evolved too much over those intervening sixteen years. Not that frontman Francis Rossi cares. 'There's not much music that isn't just three chords.'

Brentford 1–3 Wigan Athletic

Easy street

Wednesday 16 October 1985

England vs Turkey

World Cup qualifier

In September 1983, just fourteen months after taking the role, Bobby Robson offered to resign as England manager. His side had just lost at home to Denmark, putting the Danes in the driving seat for qualification from their group for the 1984 European Championship.

The press, and many former international players, aimed heavy criticism Robson's way. He declared his intention to fall on his sword to the powers that be, specifically to allow the people's favourite, the double European Cup-winning Brian Clough, to take the reins. The FA chairman, Bert Millichip, was having none of it. 'We had a list and your name was top of it,' the genial Brummie assured him. 'You soldier on.'

Despite the Denmark game being Robson's only defeat in four qualifying campaigns, and despite a plus-twenty goal difference from across eight matches, England would fail to make it to France '84, pipped by the Danes by a single point. But, with the backing of the FA bigwigs, the manager had lived to fight another qualification campaign.

Two years later, England's destiny is in their own hands. This morning, they are two points ahead of their nearest challengers in UEFA qualifying Group C for the 1986 World Cup – Romania and Northern Ireland – with two games left to play. Victory against bottom-of-the-table Turkey tonight will secure their ticket as one of the two qualifying teams.

If that state of affairs has relaxed Robson to a comparatively Zen state unimaginable two years previously, something happens this afternoon that mellows the England manager even more. Over in Bucharest, Northern Ireland beat Romania by a single Jimmy Quinn goal. It's a result that means England are highly, highly unlikely not to qualify now. To not be on the plane to Mexico they would somehow have to lose to Turkey (who have just one point to their name in the group) and then lose to Northern Ireland next month at the same time that Romania would have to beat Turkey by a cricket score. It's simply not going to happen. Everyone knows England have made it to the World Cup.

It being October, it's been dark for an hour when England and Turkey head out onto the Wembley pitch for the warm-up tonight. Robson has been suitably buoyed by events in Bucharest and happily acquiesces to an on-pitch pre-match interview by ITV's Jim Rosenthal. He tries half-heartedly to disguise his satisfaction with the situation – there's lots of talk of a determination to finish top of the group to maximise their prospects in the tournament draw – but the smiles keep creeping onto his face. The news is good. 'I'm happy. It's been a good day. And I hope it's going to be a better night.'

And English football could use some good news. The broadcast of tonight's highlights is a rare chance for fans to watch televised football. The domestic game is currently off the nation's screens, as it has been all season as a result of a rights impasse between the Football League and the TV companies. Furthermore, tomorrow is something of a red-letter day. In the next twenty-four hours, the FA will find out whether UEFA intends to ban the national team from the 1988 European Championship following the events at Heysel back in May.

There's plenty around Wembley tonight that screams mid-'80s: the tight shorts, the mullets, the odd moustache and the inevitable booing of the visitors' national anthem. The advertising boards date it too, touting the likes of Farah jeans and Gillette Contour razors. The marketing bods at a certain chocolate manufacturer have been smart too. With an eye on the identity of tonight's opponents, they've taken out advertising space behind one of the goals, reminding onlookers of the dubious pleasure of Fry's Turkish Delight.

The teams change ends after the toss, causing a phalanx of photographers to do likewise. After England's 8–0 dismantling of Turkey in the corresponding fixture in Istanbul eleven months ago, they know the Turkish goal is where most of the action will be and scurry off there accordingly. The snappers' union is two-deep at that end now. A hundred and twenty yards away, Peter Shilton is comparatively lonely.

The flags of both sides are in great number tonight, but it's the England ones that are waved with greater fervour. The home fans' mood is celebratory, especially after Chris Waddle's first international goal – a superb solo effort – gives England an early lead. A Gary Lineker header soon doubles their advantage. Both Waddle and Bryan Robson have further goals ruled out for offside, before Robson – the team's top goalscorer in qualifying, largely thanks to his hat-trick in Istanbul – adds a third. Lineker, earning his ninth cap, makes it 4–0 before half-time. England are coasting, cruising. They're on easy street.

The Everton striker completes his hat-trick ten minutes into the second half. It's his first for his country; he'll go on to score four more hat-tricks over the coming years. At the final whistle, he's surrounded by a phalanx of press photographers, his arms stretched wide in celebration as their flashbulbs pop. The last ninety minutes have confirmed him as the national team's first-choice striker.

Bolton players – including David Jack, the first man to score in an FA Cup final at Wembley – observe the incoming tide of spectators in that famously oversubscribed final of 1923.

The *Graf Zeppelin* airship looms over Wembley during the 1930 FA Cup final between Arsenal and Huddersfield. The crowd's reaction to this interloper was decidedly mixed.

The Earl of Athlone shakes hands with the Wales team ahead of their friendly match against England in 1940. It is one of a series of unofficial internationals played at the stadium during the Second World War.

Blackpool fans swarm to the town's promenade to catch a glimpse of the FA Cup, captured after the thrilling Matthews Final of 1953.

Manchester City have beaten Aston Villa to win the FA Cup in 1956, but goalkeeper Bert Trautmann only has thoughts for his injury. Three days later, a broken neck is diagnosed.

Jimmy Greaves scores England's second goal in their 9–3 mauling of Scotland in 1961. The visitors' goalkeeper Frank Haffey never plays for his country again.

At lunchtime on the day of the 1966 World Cup final, well-wishers see off the England squad from their base at the Hendon Hall Hotel, a short drive from the stadium.

The image of World Cup Willie – the official mascot of the 1966 World Cup – turns up in the unlikeliest of places during the tournament.

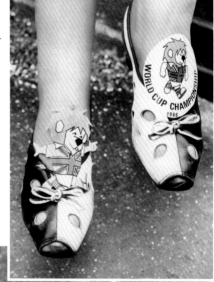

The boys of summer bask in the afterglow of World Cup success. Jules Rimet is most definitely gleaming.

Ahead of the 1968 European Cup final, Manchester United manager Matt Busby can't resist trying out the Wembley turf for himself.

Sunderland goalkeeper Jimmy Montgomery is hugged by his manager Bob Stokoe after their FA Cup triumph in 1973. Montgomery's mother-in-law correctly predicted he would keep a clean sheet against the might of Leeds United.

Norman Hunter cuts a disconsolate figure as the realisation sinks in that, after a 1–1 draw with Poland, the 1974 World Cup will take place without the participation of England.

Scotland's exuberant fans take on a different kind of crossbar challenge after their heroes beat England on home turf in their 1977 Home Internationals encounter.

Kenny Dalglish caps a phenomenal first season in English football by scoring the goal that secures Liverpool's retention of the European Cup in 1978.

It's 1985 and Manchester United's Frank Stapleton attempts to calm down his team-mate Kevin Moran, but the arm of referee Peter Willis indicates that the Irishman has just become the first player to be sent off in an FA Cup final.

Diana, Princess of Wales, looks as ecstatic as Wimbledon's penalty-saving captain Dave Beasant after the Dons' giant-slaying cup final victory over Liverpool in 1988.

Swindon full-back Paul Bodin thumps his penalty home against Leicester in the 1993 First Division play-off final. His spot-kick gives the Robins top-flight status for the first time in their history.

At Euro 96, Paul Gascoigne reminds any England fan who might have lost count that their side are now four-up against the Netherlands.

The first official match under the arch of the new Wembley gets underway in the spring of 2007 as England's under-21 side host their Italian counterparts.

True believers – and their silver-foil replica trophies – can still be found at Wembley, as proven by this young Wigan fan at the 2013 FA Cup final.

At the 2020 European Championships, England's men make their first appearance in a major tournament final since 1966. Marcus Rashford hits the post from twelve yards in the penalty shoot-out against Italy.

Hold the back page! Substitute Chloe Kelly has put England's women back in front in the 2022 European Championship final against Germany. The world can see what it means to her.

England's women have achieved what their male counterparts failed to do the year before and become European champions. For seasoned internationals Ellen White and Jill Scott, their careers close on the ultimate high.

The victorious England players soak up the adoration of the 87,000-plus crowd, the largest attendance for a European Championship match ever, either men's or women's.

The celebratory mood in the England camp is slightly tempered by Robson's annoyance that his team stopped scoring when they reached five, that they didn't add to their tally for most of the second period. He tears a strip off them for not being more ruthless. But by the time he's back out of the dressing room, back in front of Jim Rosenthal's microphone, those smiles have returned. The manager is a happy man, a relieved man.

As they wait to commence the interview, Robson even offers Rosenthal some sartorial tips. 'I like your tie, James. Very nice. The shirt's not too clever but the tie's lovely.'

England 5–0 Turkey

'Sunshine and a trophy'

Sunday 23 March 1986

Chelsea vs Manchester City

Full Members' Cup final

It's fair to say that, in its inaugural season, the Full Members' Cup isn't getting the warmest of welcomes. It's actually become the subject of ridicule. 'The *Few* Members' Cup', snorts Emlyn Hughes in his *Daily Mirror* column.

Hughes – or, perhaps, his ghostwriter – has a point. The competition was drawn up to compensate for the lack of European fixtures for English clubs following their ban, but enthusiasm was decidedly low. As it is, the six clubs who would otherwise be playing in Europe – Everton, Liverpool, Manchester United, Norwich, Southampton and Tottenham – have been given their own mini-competition, the Screen Sport Super Cup, so won't be participating. Then a notable number of other clubs, presumably fearful of unnecessary fixture congestion, politely decline. Only twenty-one teams take up the Full Members gauntlet in this first season. There are just five top-flight sides among them.

John Hollins's Chelsea are one of those five. During the autumn, they top their group, comfortably beating both Portsmouth and Charlton. They draw with West Brom in the semi-final of the southern half of the cup at the Hawthorns before winning on penalties and then defeating Oxford United over a two-legged southern final in December.

Three months later, Chelsea are here at Wembley, ready to take on the winners of the northern section, Billy McNeill's Manchester City. And with nearly 70,000 fans pouring through the turnstiles, the players are belatedly growing an enthusiasm for this new competition. Certainly, thirty-five-odd years later, Chelsea winger Pat Nevin has no recollection of the matches played back in the autumn.

'I don't think we cared about it,' he admits, 'certainly not in the early stages. It wouldn't have been a big deal. We had league games and other cup games to worry about. But as we got nearer the final, you'd go, "Oh yeah, actually . . ." The final was the thing.'

Both teams arrive at Wembley having been in league action just twenty-four hours earlier; Chelsea had narrowly beaten Southampton at The Dell, while City travelled down after a 2–2 draw in the Manchester derby. 'That was the extraordinary thing. It was our second game in two days,' says Nevin. 'But you didn't care. Yeah, you were a bit knack-ered, but you shrugged your shoulders and just got on with it. And we had five Scots in the side for Wembley. Us hardy ones could cope.'

The concertinaed season was the result of decidedly inclement temperatures that winter; the fixture congestion allowed no other option. 'We had no games for almost a month because of the big freeze and the ground was so hard, and then had to play a mental amount of games in a very short space of time. We played nine games in March, which included going over to Iraq to play the Iraqi national team. The pitches here were frozen and Ken Bates knew a good earner when he saw one. The game was held up for forty-five minutes because the guest of honour was late. And he did turn up and, yes, it was a Mr Saddam Hussein. It was a very weird season.'

And this first Full Members' final is a very weird match – especially the last five minutes. Chelsea lead 2–1 at the break, through goals from David Speedie and Colin Lee. Two further goals from Speedie before the hour mark, and another from Lee ten minutes from time gives the Blues an unassailable 5–1 lead. Happy times. Or so they think.

Mark Lillis gets one back for City, before Doug Rougvie puts the ball into his own net for 5–3. Then, with a minute left, the Geordie referee Alan Saunders penalises Chelsea for the lightest of challenges on Andy May. 'I thought it was an incredibly soft penalty,' says Nevin, 'and I was shouting and bawling at the referee. He just smiled. "I'm only having a laugh. I'm blowing the final whistle after this." I thought, *I like that. That's really cool.* Football's supposed to be entertainment, it's supposed to be fun. As long as it didn't affect the actual outcome, that was absolutely fine with me.'

Lillis converts the penalty for 5–4 and, true to his word, Saunders immediately blows for time. Chelsea are the first winners of the Full Members' Cup. No matter that only twenty-one teams have taken part. This means much to both fans and players alike. For Nevin, whose crosses set up two of Speedie's goals, it would be the only time he was a Wembley winner.

'I played at Wembley loads but never otherwise won. I played there for Scotland against England, I played there in an FA Cup final, I played there in a couple more Full Members' Cup finals for Everton . . . Actually, no, I did win there another time. I played for – wait for it – England against the Rest of the World. Well, for a Football League XI. Maradona played in that too. But it was only a friendly. So when it comes to a competitive match where you walk up and pick up a trophy, the Full Members' Cup was it for me. That was the only one.

'Chelsea played really well that day and it felt like it would be the start of something special for us. But we went into meltdown after the final. We fell off the edge of a complete and utter cliff. We had been on course for pushing for the league title. We were right up there. We played QPR and West Ham in our next two games and the combined score was 10–0 against.

'But the final itself was so special and it was a fabulous atmosphere. My mum and dad came down, and a couple of my brothers. They got to see a beautiful Wembley day – sunshine and a trophy. That meant a lot to me.

'Nowadays it would be sniggered at, obviously, but it was a big deal for Chelsea fans back then. They hadn't been to Wembley in so long and they celebrated like they'd won the FA Cup. And with no irony that it was the Full Members' Cup. That's important. Nowadays, as Champions League winners and Premier League champions, it would be quite ironic.

'But back then, it was a cup, a trophy. It was something to be celebrated.'

Chelsea 5–4 Manchester City

Yellow fever

Sunday 20 April 1986

Oxford United vs Queens Park Rangers
League Cup final

Terry Fenwick stretches his limbs as he waits for the referee to call him to the centre circle. He gazes across the pitch to study today's opposition, Oxford United, this season's top-flight new boys following two successive promotions.

In three months' time, the QPR captain will be lining up in England colours at the Azteca Stadium in Mexico City, charged with keeping one Diego Maradona under wraps in a World Cup quarter-final. For now, his task is to contain the likes of quintessential journeyman Trevor Hebberd. On paper, the England defender should have him in his pocket.

At this point, though, Fenwick doesn't realise that, over the next couple of hours, Hebberd will be as much of a handful as little Diego.

By the final whistle, there can't be a single soul in the stadium who thinks that the Oxford number 10 doesn't deserve his man-of-the-match award. It's a unanimous verdict, capping the kind of day he's been waiting for all his career. This could all have happened for Hebberd in this very competition seven years ago. In 1979, he was a valuable member of the Southampton squad that reached Wembley to face Brian Clough's Nottingham Forest in the final. Having played a part in each round, Hebberd could have expected to have occupied, if not a place in the starting XI, then at least the one available substitute berth. But on the eve of the final, his manager Lawrie McMenemy took him aside to break the news that he'd have no role in the match. Tony Sealy would be the twelfth man instead.

Whether or not Hebberd feels he had a point to prove today (McMenemy once described him as 'a Hampshire lad who would be just as happy playing for the village team'), he puts in a shift that's a once-in-a-career performance. He's everywhere, whether opening the scoring towards the end of a lumpy first half with a brilliantly taken solo goal or beating the QPR offside trap with greyhound-like acceleration before setting up Ray Houghton for Oxford's second. Hebberd has a hand in the third goal too, feeding John Aldridge, whose powerful drive is parried by QPR keeper Paul Barron into the path of Jeremy Charles, who taps in to give Oxford a three-goal advantage with just a couple of minutes left on the clock.

Hebberd's transformation into a superhero surprises a number of the Oxford faithful, among them 14-year-old Jeremy Pound, who's positioned low down behind the goal at the eastern end of the stadium. He only knew he had tickets for the final a couple of days ago, when his mum's boss, a genial Irishman by the name of Jim Ryan, suddenly produced a pair for Jeremy and his pal Ed. He even drove the boys down the M40 from Abingdon in his ageing, ailing Peugeot. Pound is delighted he got to see Hebberd's stellar performance in the flesh.

'He was the hero, the really unlikely hero,' he explains more than thirty-five years later. 'He was never crap for Oxford, but he was never spectacular either. You'd expect to see him in the line-up, always in the number 10 shirt, but you never expected to be thrilled by him. At Wembley, we thought either Houghton or Aldridge would be the hero. But Hebberd just played out of his skin. It was definitely the best game he played for Oxford. Something just clicked. Maybe it was the bigger pitch, I don't know.'

Not that Pound saw Hebberd's goal too clearly, scored as it was the best part of 200 yards from his seat. 'It was so distant. We just saw figures in yellow at the far end and we weren't sure who was on the ball half the time. And we didn't have a clue who'd scored until they announced it. "Trevor Hebberd!" I had no idea what happened with that first goal until I watched it back on video, which I've done countless times since.

'And I was so delighted it was Jeremy Charles who scored the third goal. There were not a lot of Jeremys in football. I was pleased enough we had one on our books, let alone the fact that he scored at Wembley.'

Charles's goal gives Oxford a three-goal cushion with just a handful of minutes left, but this causes a little concern to the teenage Pound, who's looking across at his team's bench. QPR are dead and buried, but Oxford manager Maurice Evans doesn't see fit to give his substitute, Andy Thomas, a short run-out on the Wembley pitch. It will be an opportunity that never comes his way again in the rest of his career.

'He must have been gutted,' says Pound with a shake of his head. 'Andy Thomas was a decent player. He wasn't going to let them down, but Evans still didn't put him on. What does the poor guy have to do? And it wasn't as if he was a recent purchase who'd been at the club a short while. He was one of the stalwarts of the two promotion years. He'd already done the heavy lifting.'

Evans instead seems to reserve all his sentimentality for trainer-coach Ken Fish, the club's longest-serving employee who, on the final whistle, he sends up to the Royal Box in his place. The 72-year-old Fish climbs the steps with modesty and shyness, in marked contrast to Malcolm Shotton, the hyperactive Oxford captain. He positively dances his way up while wearing an unsightly yellow baseball cap with a pair of bright blue ox's horns sticking out of it. It looks like it should be a consolation prize on TV darts show *Bullseye*. As he makes his way along the gantry, he shares the heartiest of hugs with the club's owner and benefactor, Robert Maxwell.

As the man who'd tried to merge Oxford and Reading to produce the Thames Valley Royals, Maxwell has forever been viewed with a measure of suspicion by the club's fans. 'He was known to be a complete wrong 'un,' says Pound, 'even back in the 1980s. This is not hindsight. Everyone thought he was a dodgy geezer in charge of our football club, but he was a dodgy geezer who brought us up into the top division. Without him, we'd never have done it. So these are conflicted emotions, where the person to be thanked is not the person you want to be thankful to.'

Today's match has enjoyed more attention than the League Cup final usually does. This is the first such match since the post-Heysel ban, a decision that means more spotlight than normal is being aimed onto domestic competitions. Heysel obviously has a negative effect on Oxford's fortunes; they'll be denied entry to next season's UEFA Cup. Possible visitors to the compact and bijou Manor Ground would have included Inter Milan or Atlético Madrid, Feyenoord or Borussia Mönchengladbach. 'It was our one chance of playing European football,' sighs Pound. 'We knew it wouldn't come round again. And all through no fault of our own.'

That wasn't the only disappointment on the most glorious day in Oxford United's history. That ageing, ailing Peugeot broke down on the way home, leaving Jim Ryan and the teenagers on the hard shoulder of the M40. They didn't get back to Abingdon until half past ten. And the Peugeot never made another journey.

Oxford United 3–0 Queens Park Rangers

The gatecrashers

Saturday 16 May 1987

Coventry City vs Tottenham Hotspur
FA Cup final

The boat makes its short passage across the river and off steps the bride and groom, onto the opposite bank. The knot has been tied just a few minutes ago, the church bells are chiming in celebration, and now the happy couple have become the focus of the unlikeliest welcoming party imaginable.

When they woke up this morning, presumably at different addresses, Macarena Elliott and Mark Duffy couldn't have predicted that their nuptials would form part of the pre-match activity of one of this afternoon's cup finalists. But here comes the welcome from the Coventry City squad, who last night slept at the Compleat Angler hotel here in Marlow, just across the Thames from All Saints Church. All the squad get to kiss Macarena; the belief in the Coventry camp is that meeting a bride today will bring them good fortune when the game kicks off in a couple of hours.

The captain Brian Kilcline is first, offering a generously sized bouquet to the bride. Then comes co-manager John Sillett, with the unusual wedding gift of a signed football. Kilcline's not done, though. With the bride's permission, he slides her garter down her right leg and slips it into his jacket pocket. Another lucky charm? 'I don't know what the wife's going to say about it,' he later confides to the BBC's Tony Gubba.

Never mind gatecrashing a wedding. This afternoon, the Sky Blues, playing in their first-ever cup final, intend to gatecrash the competition's history books. After greeting Macarena and Mark, they're incongruously, inexplicably piped aboard their bus by a bagpiper. The word is that they chose to stay at the Compleat Angler as the hotel manager is a big Coventry fan and has done them a mates' rates deal on accommodation.

Forty miles to the north-east, Spurs are also leaving last night's lodgings, the Ponsbourne Hotel in Hertford. There are no shenanigans here, although – in their immaculate suits, each studded with a white carnation in the lapel – the squad could definitely pass as wedding guests. David Pleat's men are altogether more sober, more serious as they climb aboard their Holsten-branded double-decker. One of the most serious-looking is Clive Allen, a veritable goal machine this season. He's currently on forty-eight goals in all competitions; two more this afternoon will bring up his half-century.

In two hours' time, Allen will give it a good go, opening the scoring with a near-post header from a Chris Waddle cross. There aren't even two minutes on the clock. And before eight minutes have elapsed, Coventry are level after Dave Bennett – part of the Manchester City side who lost to Spurs six years earlier – keeps his balance to round Ray Clemence and slot home. And these opening minutes are a portent for what's to come, with both teams' attacking sensibilities ensuring it's every inch the quintessential cup final. A Keith Houchen cross is touched onto the bar by Clemence, and Cyrille Regis has a goal disallowed before Gary Mabbutt puts Spurs back in front with a scruffy finish from a Glenn Hoddle free-kick. It won't be the winner, although Mabbutt will be the scorer of this afternoon's deciding goal.

Before then, we're treated to a classic cup final goal in what's turning out to be a classic cup final. Houchen plays the ball out to Bennett on the right wing, before hurtling into the box where he meets Bennett's cross with a magnificent diving header – an immaculate example of the art. 'The whole thing looks so spectacular,' Houchen later says. 'It looks like I'm flying. When it is perfect timing, it's like a dance. It all comes together.'

It will become one of the decade's most memorable Wembley goals, one that should decide the destiny of the cup. But it's a mere equaliser. It takes extra-time, and the outstretched leg of a Tottenham defender, to determine whether the trophy will be making the short trip across north London or heading up to the West Midlands. Lloyd McGrath makes a surging run down the Coventry right and his cross is diverted by Mabbutt, the ball arcing perfectly over his own goalkeeper. Like Bert Turner and Tommy Hutchison before him, the centre-back has scored at both ends in a Wembley cup final. His misfortune is what hands the Sky Blues the cup, and the pain he feels this afternoon will be prolonged by a mischievous Coventry fanzine editor who subsequently calls his publication *Gary Mabbutt's Knee*.

The victory is the first in an FA Cup final by a West Midlands side since West Brom's triumph in 1968. Tonight will be a Saturday night unlike any other back in Coventry. In fact, the police warn the club that the city is far too busy for the squad to return home tonight. Tomorrow's open-top bus parade will be a highly memorable occasion, but for now, the team bus diverts to a hotel on the outskirts of Rugby.

The only other guests are a bride and groom. The day, which started on the banks of the Thames this morning, has come full circle. This other happy couple are more than content to spend their evening with the jubilant side. 'They must have had the most unusual honeymoon of any couple ever,' John Sillett later observes, 'celebrating with a cup final side.'

The gatecrashers kept on gatecrashing.

Coventry City 3–2 Tottenham Hotspur

Who's that girl?

Thursday 16 July 1987

Southeast Cardinals vs Millwall Lionesses

London International Football Festival

Twenty-three thousand, four hundred and fifty-five. That's the number of days between the 'White Horse Final' of 1923 and today – the occasion of the first-ever eleven-a-side match at Wembley involving female footballers (following a four-team five-a-side tournament ahead of the 1984 Charity Shield).

Hailing from Cincinnati, the Southeast Cardinals are the current under-14 Ohio state champions and each of the teenagers has had to personally raise $250 to fund the trip. The squad will be in the UK for almost a fortnight and today's game is the opening match of the annual London International Football Festival, an event to which teams from Armenia, Bangladesh, Canada, Denmark, Norway, Taiwan and Vietnam have also travelled.

With the rest of the tournament's matches taking place in

Northwick Park, an unremarkable municipal playing field near Harrow School, the Cardinals are certainly appreciative of walking out at Wembley for the opening game. 'It looks like a matter of pure luck that our girls will just happen to be in the right place at the right time to make soccer history,' their coach, a boat-builder by the name of Mike Tucker, explains to the *New York Times*. 'Just the sheer size of the field and the crowd should be guaranteed to awe the girls. They're used to playing before a couple of hundred people at most.'

While these girls from Cincinnati are the first US soccer team to grace the Wembley pitch, they're not the first US sports team to do so. Nor the first team called the Cardinals. Four years ago, the NFL's St Louis Cardinals lined up against the Minnesota Vikings for an exhibition match, the UK's first taste of live American football. Nearly 33,000 spectators – a mixture of expats (including plenty of those working at US airbases in the UK) and curious Brits – watch the comfortable Vikings victory.

This afternoon, the expected crowd of 15,000 doesn't turn up though, despite free admission. It's closer to 3,000. And the match – consisting of just two fifteen-minute halves – isn't a feast of goals. There are the obvious time constraints, but per-haps the sense of occasion has affected the young players too, among whom is the future England manager Hope Powell, lining up for the Lionesses. Or, more likely, the state of the Wembley pitch, which is still recovering from the footfall of nearly 300,000 Genesis fans over a four-night residency ear-lier in the month, has prohibited a festival of flowing football. History is made, nonetheless.

And there's not such a long wait before the next women's match here. In one year, ten months and seven days, the England team will take to the Wembley turf for the first time when they entertain Sweden – a match, incidentally, that will again feature Hope Powell. The steps might be small and slow, but they're forward steps nonetheless.

Southeast Cardinals 1–0 Millwall Lionesses

Aristocrats and artisans

Saturday 14 May 1988

Liverpool vs Wimbledon

FA Cup final

It was like a scene straight out of a film, where a bustling pub falls silent as a certain person or persons step through the door. But, unlike in the movies, the silence wasn't tension-filled. It was down to incredulity; the regulars were struck dumb. Stepping through the door were their heroes.

Last night, on the eve of the FA Cup final, a handful of the more gregarious members of the Wimbledon squad were causing a little minor mayhem in the refined surroundings of Cannizaro House, the team's hotel for the night, located on the edge of Wimbledon Common. At least a couple of players were reportedly getting stuck into the Bloody Marys. Their manager Bobby Gould, understanding that his Crazy Gang couldn't be pacified, nor persuaded to have a quiet early night, produced a roll of tenners from his pocket and dispatched his charges to the nearest pub. Gould had read the situation masterfully. If his players' high jinks were the product of latent nerves ahead of the biggest game of their lives, he dissolved these by sending them to their favourite, most familiar comfort zone: the saloon bar.

To what extent Gould's man-management has been successful will be judged around quarter to five this afternoon. For now, the hangover-curing pre-match meal, plus the catching of a few rays on Cannizaro House's sun-drenched terrace, has certainly brought a relaxed feel to the team's preparation. And last night's refreshment eradicated the chance of a nerve-shredded, sleep-light night. Although he insists he nursed half a Guinness all night long, captain Dave Beasant slept like a baby.

Whenever they play in London, it's standard practice for Wimbledon's players to make their own way to whatever ground they're playing at. Indeed, they even did so for the semi-final against Luton Town at White Hart Lane (while Gould turned up in Tottenham driving the club's minibus). Today, though, they all travel together. The players' wives and girlfriends have made a surprise visit to the hotel before the bus leaves; Beasant's wife Sandra is there with their second son Sam, born the day before the semi-final.

When the bus arrives at Wembley an hour or so later, Beasant spots his other son, Nicky, in the crowds outside the stadium, sat on the shoulders of his uncle Pete. Beasant's parents are also there; this afternoon will be the first time that his father, Dick, has seen him play professionally. The Wimbledon fans are hugely outnumbered on Wembley Way. There are very few patches of blue and yellow among the tide of red.

Since reaching Wembley five weeks ago, the Dons have gratefully lapped up the limelight. They've recorded a single at Abbey Road Studios and have modelled their cup final suits on *The Clothes Show*. No one can blame them for milking it; Liverpool are expected to steamroller them in the final, so they've clearly elected to make the most of it and have a bit of a giggle. Even though only three members of their cup-winning side from two years ago are named in today's starting line-up, this is arguably Liverpool's most scintillating team ever. A month and a day ago, they played Brian Clough's Nottingham Forest off the park at Anfield. Forest were third in the league and thus no slouches, but Kenny Dalglish's side demolished them 5–0. It wasn't just the scoreline, it was the nature of the performance. 'One of the finest exhibitions of football I've ever seen in my life,' Tom Finney declared afterwards. 'I've seen Brazilians play, but I've never seen the game played at that pace or executed like that.'

Accordingly, Liverpool are expected to run away with things this afternoon as they chase a second Double within twenty-four months, their silky teamplay streets ahead of Wimbledon's bluster and hustle. *Grandstand* presenter Des Lynam bills it as a bout between aristocrats and artisans, a pre-echo of John Motson's famous line about Crazy Gangs and Culture Clubs.

In their dressing room, Wimbledon's players don't believe it to be such a mismatch. And they've got plenty of people willing them to cause an upset. Their manager until the end of last season, Dave Bassett, is here on TV duties and has sent them a telegram that captain Beasant reads out. He does likewise with a similar message from his old PE teacher, before disappearing into a toilet cubicle for fifteen minutes. From there, he can hear the 100,000-strong choir sing 'Abide with Me' through the walls. And before he knows it, the skipper is out on the pitch, chatting to Princess Diana about the suitability or otherwise of wearing high-heeled shoes on the Wembley turf, before introducing her to this ragged band. They might now be managed by Gould, but the essence of the side has been maintained. They are still largely Bassett's allsorts.

Once the game gets under way, the contrast in playing styles isn't as marked as the soothsayers predicted. Although one Liverpool fan notes that Beasant's clearances upfield are 'threatening to take out the BBC's helicopter camera', Wimbledon knock the ball around well, particularly their pocket dynamo of a midfielder, Dennis Wise. Plus, Liverpool are as combative in the tackle as the Londoners – albeit none of their challenges are quite as red-blooded as Vinnie Jones's early reducer on Steve McMahon.

A soft free-kick is awarded to Wimbledon after half an hour, down near the left-hand corner flag at the Liverpool end. It's a decision that comes with consequences. From Wise's lofted kick, Lawrie Sanchez jumps between two Liverpool defenders and guides a flicked header into the net. 1–0. They couldn't, could they?

The major moment in the second half is made by the referee's whistle just past the hour mark, when Wimbledon right-back Clive Goodyear is unfairly adjudged to have tripped John Aldridge in the box. Referee Brian Hill tries to outsprint a brigade of justifiably furious Dons players, while Aldridge looks mildly embarrassed, like a schoolboy who knows a class-mate is being wrongly punished by a teacher for someone else's misdemeanours.

This isn't the first penalty Beasant has faced in this year's competition. On a cowfield of a pitch at Mansfield Town in the fourth round, he saved what would have been a late equaliser from the home side and the prospect of a replay. Beasant's done his homework and refuses to move until Aldridge makes that trademark dummy in his run-up. Diving to his left, he paws the spot-kick away, becoming the first goalkeeper to save an FA Cup final penalty here at Wembley. 'I've saved it,' he mutters to himself. 'I've fucking saved it.'

Beasant will make further history before five o'clock when he becomes the first goalkeeper to lift the trophy as captain. And that's not all he gets his hands on. At the final whistle, he commiserates with his opposite number, Bruce Grobbelaar. The

Zimbabwean had been slating the Dons' chances in the press beforehand. 'Wimbledon, they play tennis, don't they?'

The two keepers will swap shirts in the dressing rooms later, but for now, here on the pitch, Grobbelaar has another gift for Beasant. He gives him a small case, inside of which is a pair of tennis racket-shaped spectacles. They were probably meant as a post-match dig after a comfortable Liverpool victory, but now he hands them over without the glee of a victor. That glee is all Beasant's. Wimbledon have won: game, set and match.

Liverpool 0–1 Wimbledon

The trailblazer

Tuesday 23 May 1989

England vs Sweden

Women's international friendly

If you visited the playing fields of Maryhill Comprehensive in the Potteries town of Kidsgrove in the late 1970s and were told that one of the young footballers there would end up playing for England, you'd put money on it being the tall, goal-hungry centre-forward scoring for fun. And, indeed, Mark Bright did enjoy a glittering career with Crystal Palace, Sheffield Wednesday and Charlton. But he never got to pull on an England shirt.

It was another prolific striker from Maryhill's Class of '78 who did. She wore the Three Lions on no fewer than eighty-two occasions, scoring forty-four times in the process. Her name is Kerry Davis.

That Davis was England women's record goalscorer until 2010 isn't her only significant international achievement. In 1982, at the age of twenty, she became the first Black woman to play for the national side, five years after Laurie Cunningham first played for the men's under-21s and four years after Viv Anderson did so for the full side. Hope Powell and Brenda Sempare would soon follow in her footsteps. Davis did well on her debut, too; she scored twice against Northern Ireland on her home pitch of Gresty Road in Crewe.

As part of tonight's starting XI against Sweden, Davis is making history again. This is the first time that England women have taken to the Wembley pitch for a full, official international. They've played here before – April of last year, in fact, against the Republic of Ireland as part of the Mercantile Credit Festival commemorating the Football League's centenary. But that was far from a full international. The exhibition match lasted just fifteen minutes each way – even shorter than an under-8s game. It was an insulting gesture. Indeed, the Irish side were a late replacement for the Netherlands, who ripped up their invitation, incandescent at such a derisory amount of playing time.

As the England side line up for the obligatory pre-match team photo in the golden early-evening sunshine, Davis gazes around the stadium. It's something of a culture shock. The team is used to playing before modest crowds at modest grounds – the likes of Kenilworth Road in Luton and Elm Park in Reading. Their most recent home game drew just 300 spectators. Wembley is palatial in comparison. The last time they played in the UK was an away game at Stark's Park, home of Raith Rovers of Scottish League Division Two. Toto, I've a feeling we're not in Kirkcaldy anymore.

Davis is in the front row of the team line-up, directly to the right of her fellow striker, Jane Stanley. No longer a Crewe player, Davis is now in her fourth season of playing in Italy, lining up for Napoli after spells at Lazio and ACF Trani. In Italy, she's a full-time professional, but when she returns to Crewe later this year, Davis will have to take up factory work to pay the bills. For now, though, England's front line is, rather surreally, drawn from clubs from the Gulf of Naples and the East Yorkshire coast. Her strike partner Stanley plays for modest Filey Flyers.

Tonight's match is the precursor, the hors d'oeuvre, to a men's friendly between England and Chile. The main course, the fifth and final staging of the Rous Cup, doesn't satiate anyone's appetite, a torrid 0–0 draw played before fewer than 16,000 fans ill-served by a Tube strike. The women's match serves up more satisfying fare, even though there are only an estimated 3,000-odd in the stadium at that point.

The experienced Swedes know England well. Not only did the Scandinavians beat them on penalties in the final of the 1984 European Championship, but they also knocked them out of the same competition at the semi-final stage two years ago. 'The Swedish women have proved a thorn in the flesh of the English side for a good many years now,' reports the correspondent from *The Times*, and they get the better of their hosts this evening too, being savvy enough to soak up the England pressure and hit them on the break. A looping header from their goalscoring legend Pia Sundhage and a fierce volley from Lena Videkull give them a 2–0 victory.

There's no goal for Davis tonight. In fact, in tomorrow's paper, that same *Times* correspondent will moan about England's 'extraordinary profligacy in front of goal'. But the striker will make amends in fifteen months' time. After matches at the home grounds of Brentford, Wycombe Wanderers and Sheffield United, England's women return to north-west London for their second official Wembley international. Lining up against familiar faces from her time with Lazio, Trani and Napoli, Davis scores the only goal in a 4–1 defeat against Italy. It's another record to her name: she becomes the first Englishwoman to score in a full international at the national stadium.

That Kerry Davis's sizeable, ground-breaking achievements will go largely invisible and untold for so long is shown by the fact that it's not until September 2022 – a month after her sixtieth birthday, and forty-nine years after she started playing for adult teams at the age of eleven – that Davis receives a proper acknowledgement from the FA. It comes at the England/Germany Nations League match as part of a Black History Month initiative, with Davis invited as one of the guests of honour. Belated and overdue, it's at least apt that the salute comes here at Wembley. The girl from Maryhill Comp deserves the biggest stage.

England 0–2 Sweden

The 1990s

The twelfth man

Saturday 12 May 1990

Crystal Palace vs Manchester United

FA Cup final

It's 4.24 p.m. and Sydney Pigden's interest in the cup final has just noticeably increased. At home in Lewisham, the former primary school teacher is already enjoying the match, even though Greater Manchester currently has the upper hand over south London, with United leading Crystal Palace 2–1.

It's almost forty-five years since Pigden, a fighter pilot of some renown during the Second World War, flew his Hawker Hurricane over Buckingham Palace as part of a victory flypast. But what he sees on television over the next few minutes gives him as much pride, if not more, as his wartime achievements.

As they go in search of an equaliser, Palace make a change. One of their substitutes rises from the bench, strips off his track-suit and gently stretches his hamstrings. Most of the viewers recognise this to be Ian Wright, the Eagles' 26-year-old striker. Sydney Pigden – Mr Pigden – knows him better as Ian Wright, the seven-year-old pupil of Turnham Primary School on the Honor Oak estate in Brockley.

Wright hasn't played for ten matches. Eight weeks ago, he was chopped down by Derby County's Paul Blades and carried

225

off, his leg broken. He missed the FA Cup semi-final against Liverpool, the classic battle that took Palace to this, their first ever final. And here he is now, ready to make an impression, ready to make an impact.

'All I thought in my mind,' he later revealed, 'was *I don't care where I am, where I get the ball. As soon as I get it, I'm having a shot. I've got to do something in the FA Cup final.*' He is true to his word. Having been playing Sunday league football just five years ago, Wright is seizing the day. His first touch finds him on the left, where he evades Mike Phelan's challenge, then turns inside Gary Pallister, who ends up on his backside. Only goalkeeper Jim Leighton stands between him and FA Cup immortality. The words of Mr Pigden, the man who nurtured and guided his childhood football obsession, come into his head.

'Ian, look for the big part of the goal.'

Wright calmly slides the ball beyond Leighton and then hares off, the pain and frustration of the past eight weeks of recovery suddenly vanishing. He's been on the pitch just 206 seconds. He has brought the scores level.

Down in Lewisham, Mr Pigden is ecstatic. He took the young Wright under his wing at Turnham Primary; the boy had a difficult home life but the teacher gave him the responsibility of being milk monitor, along with helping him with his reading, his writing and, of course, his football. He was a much-needed male influence, stern at times, but also a voice to guide and advise. That goal repays it all in an instant.

But Wright isn't finished there. Two minutes into extra-time, he strikes again, putting Palace in front by stretching for a deep John Salako cross and volleying home. He's off and sprinting again, a second ecstatic release.

Even though Mark Hughes's late equaliser takes the final to a replay, which Palace will lose by a single goal, Wright's world has now been recalibrated. 'People knew me,' he will later explain. 'People were stopping me in the street.' He will soon become a household name, the kind of celebrity who gets documentaries made about him. It will be during one such documentary that Wright will receive an unexpected visitor while filming at Highbury. It's his old teacher, his old mentor. Wright will look as if he's seen a ghost. 'You're alive!' he will splutter. 'Someone told me you was dead.' The tears are quick to flow.

Mr Pigden's advice has steered Wright through a life less ordinary.

'Ian, look for the big part of the goal.'

Crystal Palace 3–3 Manchester United

'I knew what it took to win that trophy'

Saturday 26 May 1990

Cambridge United vs Chesterfield

Fourth Division play-off final

'It wasn't a classic, but who gives a shit if you win?'

Dion Dublin is laughing his way across the Pennines. He's been filming another episode of *Homes Under the Hammer* this morning in Sheffield, and is now driving home to the Wirral. To help melt the miles, he's taking a little time travel, revisiting and reminiscing about the day more than thirty years earlier that Cambridge United won the first play-off final held at

Wembley. Dublin's goal was the only one of the match, making him Wembley's first play-off goalscorer.

The decision to host a single play-off finals at the national stadium – rather than the two-legged home-and-away affairs of the previous three seasons – was an inspired one. Football League official Andy Williamson was the one who had the lightbulb moment, electing to schedule all three divisional finals across the late May bank holiday weekend.

The quality and drama of that first final wasn't the greatest, with Cambridge winning it in their trademark attritional way. Having been appointed manager that January, John Beck had steered the side into the play-off places come season's end. His long-ball tactics drew plenty of criticism, but they got results; he also took the U's all the way to the FA Cup quarter-finals where they only narrowly lost to eventual finalists Crystal Palace. His style of play was highly effective, as Dublin recalls.

'The ball into the channels was called . . . what was it called? It wasn't the Corridor of Uncertainty. Quality Street! That's what Becky called it. "Put the ball into Quality Street." We weren't allowed to play through the middle of the pitch. Everything had to be boomed up to me or John Taylor or Stevie Claridge. It was all about how many corners we could get, or how many throw-ins in the final third. It was stats, stats, stats. "If you get this many crosses in, you'll score this many goals." I bet it was horrible for the fans to watch. I bet it was awful.

'We were a hard-to-beat team. The Abbey Stadium was a horrible place for teams to come to. All the things we did that our opponents didn't like helped us. They'd get no hot water. The dressing-room windows would either be wedged open or wedged shut, depending on the weather outside. We'd put so much sugar in their tea they'd get a sugar rush and then crash. It was silly stuff, but it was any way to get an advantage. We were horrible.'

On the neutral territory of Wembley, the U's couldn't employ these tactics, although one pre-match ritual remained intact. 'We were playing away one time at Carlisle, and we travelled on the day of the game. We left Cambridge early in the morning and when we arrived, we were knackered. So we all had a freezing-cold shower for ten seconds to wake up – everyone had to get in. And then there was a bucket of cold water that was thrown at us as we got out of the shower. After that day, we always had cold showers and a bucket of water on away trips. It got us up for games.'

Not that the team needed such a ritual to energise them in the play-off final. 'We played sixty-odd games that season. It felt like for ever. And this was the moment that defined whether it was ultimately a good season or not. After giving all this effort and being so good all season, we had to get something that day. We had to have *achieved*. That was our mindset. *We have to make sure this one goes our way.*'

Dublin had a couple of chances during the game, a pair of half-volleys from the edge of the box. But then, come the seventy-seventh minute, Cambridge earned another of those precious corners.

'As Chrissy Leadbitter jogged to get the ball to take the corner, I went to the far post. Then Stevie Claridge came over.

'"Dion, go to the near post."

'"No, no, no. I'm here. I'm far post, Stevie. It's an in-swinging corner."

'"Get to the near post."

'"I'm not moving, Stevie. I'm not moving."

'"Dion, get to the near post. The gaffer will go mental. This is where I stand, Dion. You know that."

The junior striker reluctantly does as he's told. He relocates himself.

'Then Chrissy Leadbitter curled this ball into the near post and I headed it in. I got there just before the keeper, an eyebrow in front of his fist. He looked like Superman, flying away past me. I turned to Stevie.

'"Cheers, Stevie. Thanks for that."'

The 21-year-old Dublin – coming up that day against an 18-year-old Chesterfield defender called Sean Dyche – had put one Cambridge foot into the Third Division. With thirteen minutes left, did any part of his brain start to think, *That could be the winning goal. I could be the hero. I could be the headline-maker?*

'My team-mates were letting me know. "Don't get carried away, Dublin." The only time you start to think like that is when the referee says there are three minutes left. *Bloody hell. This could be it.* But we put our heads down and got over the line. Work hard, work hard, work hard.'

Two years later, Dublin signed for Manchester United, winning a Premier League winner's medal in his first season at Old Trafford. But that didn't compare to this play-off triumph. This day at Wembley meant more.

'I think it's because I contributed more to that long season. It just meant so much to us, to get something at the end of it. It made all the blood, sweat and tears worthwhile. I knew what it took to win that trophy.'

Not only is that header still very much treasured ('It's not the best goal I ever scored, but that's my favourite goal by a million miles'), but the souvenirs of that day are cherished even more than Dublin's subsequent achievements: being a member of the Premier League 100-goal club, with a better goals-per-game ratio than Jermain Defoe and Dwight Yorke; being a joint winner of the Premier League Golden Boot; and being an England international.

'I've still got my full kit from that day. It's still dirty, still muddy. We took everything – programmes, team sheets, tracksuits with our names on. It could have been the only time that I played in a game like that, so I didn't want to pass up the opportunity of having a memento.

'It meant the world to us, man. It meant the world.'

Cambridge United 1–0 Chesterfield

'Is Gascoigne going to have a crack?'

Sunday 14 April 1991

Arsenal vs Tottenham Hotspur

FA Cup semi-final

No one remembers the other goals.

No one remembers Gary Lineker's stub-toed grubber after Alan Smith failed to clear his lines. Or Smith's immaculately placed header from Lee Dixon's curling cross. Or the rare solo effort from Lineker, picking the ball up near the halfway line, powering past Tony Adams and angling his shot through David Seaman's butter fingers.

They only remember Paul Gascoigne and the free-kick. Paul Gascoigne and the thunderbolt. Paul Gascoigne and the shot that nearly bust the net.

And rightfully so. It was the kind of goal that would have been the highlight, the headline, of any match anywhere, let alone the first ever FA Cup semi-final to be played at Wembley.

Although staged here in north-west London as a one-off (for reasons of logistics and of allowing as many fans of both sides the chance to watch the clash in the flesh), the anomaly becomes a semi-regular occurrence over the next few years, with the stadium hosting both semi-finals in 1993, 1994 and 2000. The movement away from neutral club grounds is completed when the new Wembley opens its gates in 2007. Many point to the '91 semi-final being a significant catalyst for the devaluing of the FA Cup final's sense of occasion, and thus the devaluing of the competition itself. See here also, of course, the phasing out of replays, the supremacy of domestic league football since the dawn of the Premier League, the parallel supremacy of the Champions League, and top-flight sides selecting weakened teams in the earlier rounds of the cup.

But that's for the future. The headline this afternoon is written after just five minutes of play. Spurs have been awarded a free-kick for a late challenge on Paul Stewart more than thirty yards from the Arsenal goal. The distance is such that there looks to be little direct danger. Most expect Gascoigne to chip the free-kick into the heart of the Gunners' box, in the way he had the previous summer for David Platt to volley home against Belgium at Italia '90.

But the length of Gascoigne's run-up suggests otherwise. Seaman realises this, insisting on a three-man wall to curb the Geordie's ambitious intentions. The third man, Kevin Campbell, gives a look to his fellow defenders that suggests a wall of this nature is unnecessary. Accordingly, he takes a step or two away to his left. This offers Gascoigne a gap into which to aim, but he has other ideas. He charges up to the ball, hits it as hard as he can and watches it swerve round the outside of the jumping Campbell, climbing as it goes. Seaman gets a glove to the ball, but he needs a hand of steel to divert the shot away. It's an Exocet missile.

As the ball hits the net, there's a moment of delay, of disbelief. Has that really just happened? The charge of the Spurs players towards their talisman, and the disappointment of the Arsenal players, confirms it has. Very quickly, everyone understands that this is a special moment, that they have just witnessed an indelible few seconds of Wembley history.

Up on the gantry, Barry Davies understands. And he has the presence of mind to salute the goal with a classic piece of commentary. 'Is Gascoigne going to have a crack? He is, you know. Oh, I say! Brilliant!'

It would be another free-kick that would define Gascoigne's main contribution to the final five weeks later. This time, he was on the receiving end, having conceded the foul with an horrendous challenge on Nottingham Forest's Gary Charles. It would be his last act in a Spurs shirt, the resultant cruciate ligament injury causing him to miss an entire season before being sold to Lazio.

But before Gascoigne was carried off to a waiting ambulance, his England team-mate Stuart Pearce elected to show everyone that anything his Geordie pal could do, he could do as well (if not better). Although closer in than Gascoigne's free-kick in the semi-final, Pearce hit his with even more venom. His was a thunderbolt and a half. But that didn't make the news. Nor did Tottenham's comeback to claim the cup. Instead, the back pages were devoted to the impetuous, irrepressible Spurs midfielder.

That very nasty foul became the main memory of the final, the highlight, the headline. Once again, Paul Gascoigne had upstaged everyone else.

Arsenal 1–3 Tottenham Hotspur

Delayed gratification

Wednesday 20 May 1992

Barcelona vs Sampdoria

European Cup final

It was four in the morning when Joan Gaspart kept his promise.

The vice-president of Futbol Club Barcelona soon found that the River Thames was not the Mediterranean. It was cold, it was polluted, and it was dangerous, with swirling currents not conducive to idle bathing. But a promise was a promise.

'I was asked what I would do if we were champions,' Gaspart told the Spanish newspaper *Marca*, 'and I said I would throw myself into the Thames. I could have said that I would go to breakfast with the Queen of England. It was nothing more than a throwaway comment. But once we had won, the team made a diving gesture with their hands.'

But the stripped-to-his-shorts Gaspart, plus a smattering of colleagues, were quite happy to take the forfeit, to risk hypothermia and hepatitis – drowning, even – in pre-dawn London. Six hours earlier, a few miles to the north, they had witnessed history being made. By defeating Sampdoria at Wembley by a single goal, their club had finally secured their first European Cup, having been beaten finalists twice before: they narrowly lost in 1961 to Benfica, and then again in 1986 against Steaua Bucharest, having failed to convert a single penalty in the shoot-out.

The final marks the fifth occasion that Wembley has hosted the competition's climax, but the first time since

1978 – fourteen long years no doubt extended because of English clubs' ban from European tournaments throughout the latter half of the 1980s.

Two months later, the city of Barcelona would be welcoming the US men's Olympic basketball team – the Dream Team – as they glided to Olympic gold. For now, it's FC Barcelona's own dream team, under the tiller hand of Johan Cruyff and featuring the likes of Ronald Koeman, Pep Guardiola, Michael Laudrup and Hristo Stoichkov, who are aiming for top spot.

The Italian champions Sampdoria, meanwhile, are contesting their first European Cup final, fired towards Wembley by their formidable strike partnership of Roberto Mancini and Gianluca Vialli. The attacking flair of both sides belies how the final score – a 1–0 victory secured in extra-time – might have appeared. This is no attritional, ground-out performance. Both teams have come to London to play football.

The two sides had met three years earlier in the Cup Winners' Cup final, with Barcelona emerging 2–0 winners. Now they have reconvened, both eager to be the winners of the last European Cup before it's rebranded as the Champions League.

The two sides' respective number 10s remain in close proximity most of the game, a pair of future Premier League-winning Manchester City managers: Mancini and Guardiola. Despite wearing the number of the playmaker, the Spaniard patrols the no man's land between his defence and his midfield, in a not dissimilar way to how team-mate Koeman is sweeping up behind his young centre-backs, Nando and Albert Ferrer.

Chances come and go. Both goalkeepers, Barcelona's Andoni Zubizarreta and Sampdoria's Gianluca Pagliuca, pull off sharp saves, while Stoichkov is thwarted by the inside of the post. The stalemate extends into the last five minutes of extra-time. Barcelona are awarded a controversial free-kick and it's no wonder that a seven-strong Italian delegation complains to the

German referee. They know what's coming, they can see the straw-haired Dutchman jogging forward from his sweeper position. Koeman hits it strong and true – a piledriver that pierces a hole through the heart of the white and blue Sampdoria wall.

Guardiola will later describe Koeman's strike as 'the most important goal in the history of our club'. The brakes were now off, the legend could begin to be forged. For Carlos Rexach, Cruyff's assistant coach that night at Wembley, the triumph meant one thing: 'Liberation. There were a lot of people waiting for us to screw it up again. And the feeling was that another life starts. We were released.'

The cold waters of the Thames beckoned, too.

Barcelona 1–0 Sampdoria

The rebel who would be king

Saturday 8 August 1992

Leeds United vs Liverpool

Charity Shield

'Are you watching, Manchester? Are . . . You . . . Watching . . . Man-che-ster?'

The twin terrace choirs of Leeds United and Liverpool ring out, united in song against a common enemy, against a city and in particular against its most conspicuous football team. It's early August and there's a celebratory feeling in the air. Thousands of balloons are unleashed into the north London sky. Spirits are equally high.

A chapter in sporting history is closing today. In seven days' time, English football will never be the same again. Next Saturday, the inaugural season of the Premier League will kick off, radically altering the landscape, shifting the goalposts, redefining the game. This means that this afternoon's match is the final meeting of the FA Cup winners and the champions of Division One. Leeds are the latter, winners of the old championship before this summer's rebadging – 'the last champions', as writer Dave Simpson describes them in the book of the same name.

As the teams march out, the Leeds players absorb the buoyant atmosphere – all smiles and waves to their families in the stands. At the back, the last man out is neither smiling nor waving. Eric Cantona is being Eric Cantona. Having joined the club in January, the Frenchman proved to be something of a talisman as Leeds closed in on their first title in eighteen years, even though he managed only three goals in fifteen league appearances. He will score that number this afternoon alone.

It's a warm August afternoon and supporters fan themselves with promotional flyers for the forthcoming WWE SummerSlam to be held at the stadium at the end of the month. The marketing campaign seems to work: more than 80,000 turn up three weeks later to watch the cartoon antics of 'Macho Man' Randy Savage, The Undertaker and Davey Boy Smith, a.k.a. the British Bulldog.

The last time that Leeds and Liverpool met in the Charity Shield was that tempestuous affair back in 1974. Although such antagonism and outright assaults aren't expected this afternoon, the celebratory atmosphere isn't fooling anyone. As Sky Sports co-commentator Andy Gray observes before a single tackle is made, 'Leeds and Liverpool can't play each other without being competitive'.

Gray is quite correct; it's fierce and combative right from the off, with a breathless first quarter-hour speeding by. The pace of the game is given extra impetus by another historical milestone in the English game. This is the first official match where the new back-pass rule – whereby a goalkeeper can't pick up the ball if it were last touched by a team-mate's foot – has come into effect. Accordingly, the two veteran goalkeepers, John Lukic and Bruce Grobbelaar, are feeling the squeeze by the pressing opposition strikers. The crowd seem to love the extra sense of jeopardy the rule change offers.

Both sides are missing key players this afternoon, with Liverpool particularly hit by illness and injury, and forced to play a three-man defence. This provides plenty of space in which the Leeds winger Rod Wallace can prosper, and one such move ends with the opening goal. A swift counter-attack down the left finds Wallace generously cutting the ball back to Cantona, who thumps it into the corner. Such is its power that Grobbelaar doesn't even bother diving.

Liverpool draw level eight minutes later when a Ronny Rosenthal cross, high and hanging, is headed home by Ian Rush, his tenth Wembley goal for Liverpool. Before half-time, though, Leeds regain the lead through a deflected Tony Dorigo free-kick. Again, Grobbelaar stays on his feet.

The see-sawing tenor of the first half extends into the second period, with Liverpool equalising again with what will turn out to be Dean Saunders' last goal for the club before his move to Aston Villa. Into the final quarter of an hour, Cantona starts to make more of an imprint on the game. First comes a fierce drive off the outside of his boot to re-establish Leeds' lead, before the hat-trick is completed when Grobbelaar flails at, and misses, a Wallace cross, leaving Cantona to nod the ball down and into an untended net. He's the first player to score three times in a Charity Shield since Tommy Taylor for Manchester United back in 1957.

Having signed David Rocastle and Scott Sellars during the summer, Leeds are somewhat overstocked in midfield; joining Rocastle on the bench this afternoon are Steve Hodge and Gordon Strachan. The latter, returning to the fray after being under the surgeon's knife for a back problem, gets to make a six-minute cameo this afternoon, but it's one he'll want to be erased from the collective memory. In those six minutes, the Scotsman contrives to score what may well be Wembley's most embarrassing own goal. Manning the far post at a corner, Strachan is ideally placed to block Mark Wright's shot, but instead the ball hits his right boot, cannons onto his left heel, then back to his right foot, which inadvertently back-heels the ball over the line at the slowest of paces. It's just fortunate that the match is almost into injury-time and that Liverpool don't have time to find yet another equaliser. Leeds hold on to win by the odd goal in seven.

And that's where the happy times end for Leeds. In attempting to defend their title, they will finish this season as low as seventeenth place next May. The hammer blow will be the departure of Cantona in November, a cut-price bargain snapped up by Manchester United. During the title-winning 1991–92 season, he had largely been the impact player rising off the bench. The Charity Shield hat-trick rightfully demanded more of a starring role in a side whose style of play wasn't completely suited to him. It was a tricky conundrum for manager Howard Wilkinson, as the club director Leslie Silver acknowledged when speaking to Dave Simpson: 'Once Cantona had made his name – particularly at the Charity Shield – Howard had an impossible job.'

Wilkinson, clearly noting how Cantona's swift exit mirrored the short spells he'd had at many of his previous clubs in France, knew it too. 'He likes to do what he likes when he likes and then he fucks off.'

Leeds United 4–3 Liverpool

The stars of the stripes

Saturday 3 April 1993

Sheffield United vs Sheffield Wednesday

FA Cup semi-final

As far as you can see, it's coaches, coaches, coaches. Dozens, scores, hundreds. They're parked tight, bumper to bumper, cheek by jowl, in seemingly endless rows in the car parks around Wembley. If you tried to keep a tally, you'd lose count after the first couple of hundred. They've brought tens of thousands of football fans down from Sheffield. There can't be a single coach left in South Yorkshire.

This semi-final, pitching the two Sheffield clubs together, has been moved from Elland Road in Leeds to meet the demand for tickets. Both clubs have sold out their allocations of 35,000 at a canter, so it's small wonder there's congestion on the M1. Seventy thousand are coming here from one single direction. It's a mass evacuation of the Steel City.

Underneath the stadium, the Sheffield Wednesday team bus is the first to arrive. Its driver, Andy Taylor, will become familiar with this route; Wednesday are due back here in a fortnight to take on Arsenal in the League Cup final. Today, though, Taylor is a conflicted soul. He's hoping Wednesday's players will be quiet and morose on the drive back home later. Andy Taylor is a Sheffield United fan.

Actually, it appears he shoulders no client vs club dilemma. A few minutes later, once he's reversed back out and parked up, Taylor returns to the tunnel to await the arrival of United's bus. There, bold as brass, he welcomes each and every Blade off the bus with a hearty handshake. Taylor is probably fortunate that, at this time, Wednesday are taking the traditional, be-suited wander around the Wembley pitch.

He's not the only one with divided loyalties. Ann Colbourne is another Blade working in the service of Wednesday. She's the tea lady at the Owls' training ground and, despite all her seven sons favouring blue, remains hopelessly devoted to the red side of the city. Four miles to the south, for the last couple of weeks Daniel Jarvis has been working in the ticket office at Bramall Lane. It might only be a temporary job, but every day Owls fan Jarvis has to suffer the indignity of wearing a Sheffield United-branded shirt-and-tie combination to work.

Councillor William Jordan, the Lord Mayor of Sheffield, is asked which colour he is. Unsurprisingly, he chooses diplomacy. 'Well, you know what the secretary-general of the United Nations said about being neutral but not impartial? That's really my position. Essentially I shall be supporting United Sheffield this afternoon.' He may have just given us a clue.

The Sheffield rivalry doesn't cut anything like as deep as other football enmities. This can be seen this afternoon with reds and blues travelling down the country, and walking up Wembley Way, together. It's being billed as 'the friendly semi-final'. Lines aren't drawn; there's no great divide. United central defender John Pemberton lives next door to Wednesday full-back Roland Nilsson. The two managers – Dave Bassett and Trevor Francis – even went on holiday to Italy together last week.

And, before the game, there's another vignette that confirms this friendliness. Mel Rees, the Blades goalkeeper recently diagnosed with bowel cancer for a second time, makes a pre-match lap of honour. He is warmly applauded on all sides of the stadium.

Both sets of fans are making plenty of noise ahead of kick-off, but within fifty-nine seconds of the start, it's the Owls who are shouting the loudest. United concede a free-kick thirty-two yards out and Chris Waddle sets up the ball, with almost everyone expecting him to drop it onto the head of one of his strikers, either Mark Bright or Paul Warhurst. Instead, Waddle appears to be sizing up an attempt on goal himself.

This seems either brave or foolhardy on the part of the England man. He isn't among the bookies' favourites to score first this afternoon, and for good reason. Despite Wednesday's progress in both domestic cup competitions, and their impressive standing in the Premier League, Waddle has scored twice this entire season – once against lowly Spora Luxembourg in the UEFA Cup and once at home to Everton in the league. Owls full-back Viv Anderson has scored nearly three times as many.

Up on the commentary gantry, Barry Davies is wise to the Geordie's intentions. It's two years on from his 'Is Gascoigne going to have a crack?' line and here comes the perfect moment to reprise it. 'Chris Waddle . . . Is he going to have a crack? Oh, he does and he scores!' History has repeated itself, at the same end of the same stadium at the same stage of the same competition. 'Anything Paul Gascoigne can do . . .'

This spritely start sets the tenor of the rest of the afternoon. It's a lively, open and attacking affair, with plenty of thrills and spills. Wednesday definitely have the upper hand, with Waddle involved in nearly every attack. But, with a few minutes left before the break, United hit back. From the halfway line, Franz

Carr plays in the bald and bearded Alan Cork, a cup winner five years ago with Wimbledon. Cork slips the ball past the advancing Chris Woods and it just evades the attempted goal-line clearance from a sliding Waddle. Honours even at the interval. Honours even across the city.

Wednesday remain dominant in the second half, with Waddle retaining his position as magician-in-chief, spraying majestic cross-field passes around with the kind of insouciance he developed while playing his football in France. Warhurst, Bright, John Sheridan and the substitute David Hirst all have chances, but are denied either by the woodwork or the alertness of United keeper Alan Kelly. Into extra-time.

'You'd need to be able to read tea leaves to predict this game now,' says Barry Davies' co-commentator, Howard Wilkinson. That's not strictly true – Wednesday are still pouring forth in waves. Eventually, it's Bright who decides the match in the second period of extra-time. Finding himself unmarked, he heads home John Harkes' corner. It's a simple goal. Kelly is heartbroken. His defence has failed him. The Owls are hooting, the Blades have been blunted.

Andy Taylor doesn't get a quiet drive back to Sheffield; Wednesday reaching their first FA Cup final since 1966 ensures the bus is buoyant. They'll return to Wembley the weekend after next for the League Cup final, then again for the FA Cup final four weeks after that. When that ends in a 1–1 draw against Arsenal, Wednesday are back down for the replay five days later. Four visits to Wembley in just thirty-two days.

By that point, Taylor could drive them there with his eyes closed.

Sheffield United 1–2 Sheffield Wednesday

The wheels loosen

Wednesday 28 April 1993

England vs The Netherlands

World Cup qualifier

Graham Taylor didn't sleep well last night. He couldn't stop tossing and turning in his hotel bed, a man ill at ease with what happened a few hours before and with what lies ahead. Throwing away a 2–0 lead against the Netherlands can do that.

This morning, the England manager faces a press pack that can smell blood where there's not even a single trace. Taylor is downbeat but not distraught. The wheels are far from off the qualification campaign and, with five matches still to go, a couple of strong wins will put things back on track. As disappointed as he is with the draw against the Dutch, he's an optimistic guy. Outwardly, at least.

He's also possibly a little too trusting. He admits to the press corps that a certain song was the soundtrack to his fitful night: Buddy Holly's 'Raining in My Heart'. With sleep deprivation possibly clouding his judgement, he gives a rendition to those gathered. He sings of misery, of what's going to become of him. 'Do you want to join in, lads?'

Taylor does himself no favours. If it's an attempt to elicit sympathy, he's playing to the wrong crowd. It's an open goal. The reporters' copy is practically writing itself.

That he's the latest England manager to be the media's punchbag is a little harsh. Last night's match was his thirtieth in charge of the national team, during which time he's lost only three matches. Indeed, his side were beaten just once in his first twenty-three. The problem is that Taylor doesn't win the matches that need to be won. This was most conspicuous at last year's European Championship, where, having qualified as unbeaten group winners, England could only draw with Denmark and France before losing to hosts Sweden. The press have been on his tail ever since. His first match after the Euros was a 1–0 defeat to Spain. The man previously portrayed as a turnip in the tabloids became a Spanish onion.

He could be sitting here reciting a song with a more upbeat lyric. At one stage last night, it looked like that could be the case. Just two minutes in – and three and a half weeks after Chris Waddle's free-kick had given Sheffield Wednesday the lead in their FA Cup semi-final – John Barnes did likewise at the same end, curling his free-kick up and over the Dutch wall and past goalkeeper Ed de Goey. Wembley, a large portion of which had given Barnes an extremely hard time during England's constipated performance against San Marino last month, exploded into ecstasy.

Twenty minutes later, David Platt doubled England's advantage, turning home the rebound after a Les Ferdinand cross-shot hit the post. The midfielder clearly thrives on responsibility. He's been captain for three games now and has scored in each of them.

The two-goal cushion didn't last long, with Dennis Bergkamp planting a nonchalant, sumptuous dinked volley over Chris Woods in the England goal to halve the deficit. Then Paul Gascoigne was withdrawn at half-time with a suspected broken cheekbone. It will turn out to be pretty much a smashed cheekbone, a product of the wayward elbow of Jan Wouters. The Dutch captain wasn't even spoken to by the referee. The cheekbone is so badly damaged that, for future England games, his club Lazio insist Gascoigne wears a protective mask for insurance purposes.

Still, into the last five minutes, England looked like registering an important victory and securing both points. But then Marc Overmars outsprinted the usually fleet-of-foot Des Walker, who grabbed a handful of the Dutchman's shirt and hauled him back. Walker made initial contact outside the area but Overmars stayed on his feet until he was over the white line. The penalty is coolly converted by Peter van Vossen and the Netherlands escape from north London with a point they thought unlikely at one point. They were without Marco van Basten and Ronald Koeman; this really was the chance for England to press home their advantage. They didn't.

This Wembley wobble will be followed by more calamitous results in Chorzów (a late Ian Wright equaliser securing a 1–1 draw against Poland) and Oslo (a 2–0 defeat to group leaders Norway). The final nail in the coffin comes in Rotterdam, where another harsh decision will be to the Netherlands' advantage. Through on goal, Platt is pulled back by Koeman, who is not sent off for the most blatant of professional fouls. The Dutchman later scores from a free-kick. In the final few minutes of the match, Taylor will ask the fourth official to pass on his thanks to the referee for getting him the sack.

In the end, Taylor falls on his sword after the final qualifier against San Marino. If it was raining in his heart after the Netherlands match at Wembley, England's failure to qualify for the World Cup in the US suggests that by now it must be an absolute monsoon.

England 2–2 The Netherlands

Rockin' Robins

Monday 31 May 1993

Leicester City vs Swindon Town

First Division play-off final

'History doesn't repeat itself,' the great Mark Twain once observed, 'but it often rhymes.'

Leicester City have just realised this. Last season, they lost the play-off final to Kenny Dalglish's Blackburn Rovers. The awarding of a penalty was the deciding factor of whether the Foxes would return to the top flight after an absence of five years, this time to the promised land of the brand-spanking-new Premier League. Mike Newell scored that penalty, condemning his old club to another season in the second tier.

Here they are again, twelve months later, back at Wembley on another bank holiday Monday in May, back to stake their claim for a place in that new league. And here they are again, having just conceded another penalty, Leicester's goalkeeper Kevin Poole having been adjudged to have taken out Swindon substitute Steve White. The whistle of referee David Elleray rings out, shrill and decisive. His right arm is pointing, arrow-straight, at the penalty spot. Leicester's players surround him; Poole claims he never touched the striker. But the Harrow schoolmaster is not a man for turning. He's never rescinded a detention handed out to one of his pupils, and he's not about to be undermined by an angry bunch of professional football-ers. And these Leicester players are desperate. With just seven minutes left in the match, and with the sides level, there's a high chance this penalty-kick will decide both teams' fate for next season.

Twelve months ago, Newell's penalty was the only goal of the Blackburn game. This year, the final has been an absolute sizzler. Swindon took the lead just before half-time through a customary classy goal from their player-manager Glenn Hoddle, a curling effort elegantly placed just inside Poole's post. After the break came two more swift goals for the Robins, from Craig Maskell and Shaun Taylor. Fifty-five minutes in, Swindon were three up and dreaming of Anfield, Highbury, Old Trafford . . .

But then came an irresistible twelve-minute passage of play in which Leicester neutralised Swindon's advantage, with rapid-fire goals from the teenager Julian Joachim, Steve Walsh and Steve Thompson. The momentum was surely with the East Midlanders now. But then came a long ball from Hoddle to play in striker White . . .

Swindon's Welsh left-back Paul Bodin steps up for the penalty. Another shrill blast from Elleray's whistle and Bodin drills the ball low and hard past Poole for his twelfth of the season. Advantage Swindon, an advantage they protect until Elleray's final whistle.

Like Leicester, the Robins wouldn't have wanted history to rhyme, let alone repeat. Three years ago, they were in this exact position, winners of the play-off to decide the identity of the last team to be promoted to the top flight that season. Then a series of financial irregularities were exposed, including illegal betting and backhander payments to players. The Football League didn't just reverse their promotion, it demoted them two divisions (although the punishment was halved on appeal). This time, they're clean. This time, they can take their place in the top tier of English football without fear of censure – and for the first time in their history.

But whether the mastermind of their triumph will still be at the County Ground to guide them next season remains a real talking point. Rumours are rife that Glenn Hoddle will soon be taking up a player-manager role at Chelsea, speculation that's fed by Blues chairman Ken Bates being spotted in the stands this afternoon. At the final whistle, ITV reporter Gary Newbon asks the question directly, which Hoddle sidesteps, both verbally and physically, as he makes a swift exit. 'I'm just going to go up to that Royal Box. Might not get another chance . . .'

Hoddle will get another chance the very next season, but it won't be in the red of Swindon. Four days after the play-off final, he substantiates those rumours by succeeding interim manager David Webb as Chelsea boss. And, eleven months later, he's back at Wembley, with his boots on, for a fourth FA Cup final.

While Hoddle continues to climb, Swindon's tenure in the Premier League is short and not particularly sweet. They win just five games all season before being dumped back into the second tier.

As Mark Twain also observed: 'Everything has its limit. Iron ore cannot be educated into gold.'

Leicester City 3–4 Swindon Town

'Oh, he's given another one!'

Saturday 14 May 1994

Chelsea vs Manchester United

FA Cup final

It's all about Eric.

It has been a successful season for Cantona, albeit with a few troughs among the peaks. With squad numbers coming into English football for the first time, he was allocated the sainted number 7 shirt, as previously worn by Old Trafford legends like George Best and Bryan Robson. He's just won the title with Manchester United, his third league championship in as many seasons in English football. He's United's top scorer, with twenty-three goals across all competitions before today. And his peers have anointed him as the PFA Player of the Year.

But in November – and despite being, like England, top seeds in their group – France failed to qualify for this summer's World Cup. Their exit was dramatic: having led at home to Bulgaria through a Cantona goal, the French lost the match in the dying seconds, allowing the Bulgarians to replace them on the plane to the US. Eric would not now get to strut his stuff on football's biggest stage.

Cantona has also been sent off three times this season for United, including red cards in successive league games. For this, he earned himself a five-match ban, a suspension that meant he missed the 1–1 draw in the FA Cup semi-final against Oldham – although he was back in time for the 4–1 victory in the replay.

You can't take your eyes off him. Fascinating, magnetic, irresistible. Certainly that's what the Duchess of Kent seems to think as she's presented to this afternoon's teams. Under a transparent umbrella to ward off the persistent drizzle, the duchess is in no mood to linger and swap too many pleasantries. Until she reaches Cantona that is. The first Frenchman to play in the cup final, his collar up in his trademark rebellious way, he is afforded a longer royal audience than anyone else. Even Alex Ferguson gets nothing more than the briefest of greetings.

The attention on Cantona almost – *almost* – obscures the fact that, this afternoon, United are in pursuit of their first ever league and cup Double, attempting to emulate the feat achieved this century by Spurs, Arsenal and Liverpool. United had a chance of doing so before any of them, but they lost the 1957 final to Aston Villa. Their manager then, Matt Busby, will not witness today's attempt. He passed away in January. Should they be successful by five o'clock this afternoon, their triumph will inevitably be seen as a fitting memorial to the club's greatest ever manager.

That's not the only goodbye to Old Trafford this year. Their long-serving captain Bryan Robson will leave the club this summer, off back to his native north-east and the chance to earn his managerial stripes at Middlesbrough. Despite his exemplary service for the club, there's no room for sentimentality in Alex Ferguson's mind. Robson won't win his fourth FA Cup winner's medal today, nor have the chance to say goodbye to the fans. He's not even been named among the substitutes and will sit a few rows behind the United bench in a suit and tie.

On the opposing bench, there's another sort of goodbye. If he brings himself on as a substitute today, Chelsea player-manager Glenn Hoddle will almost certainly be playing at Wembley for the last time, fifteen years after scoring here on his debut for England, and more than a decade after a double cup triumph with Spurs.

It's Chelsea's first FA Cup final since 1970, so they have every incentive to spoil United's party. With both teams already guaranteed European football next season, it's an open, energetic game from the off. It's also notably physical. Chelsea defender Erland Johnsen is booked in the second minute for an outrageously late challenge on speedy Ryan Giggs. Referee David Elleray could justifiably have issued a straight red.

Chelsea have the better of things in the first half. Their closest effort is when, outside the box and with minimal backlift, their brightest player (and future associate pastor at the Calvary Grace Church of Calgary) Gavin Peacock sends a dipping shot onto Peter Schmeichel's crossbar.

Halfway through the second half come nine minutes that both transform and settle the match. First, Eddie Newton incautiously slides into Denis Irwin, who's sent sky-bound. Cucumber-cool Cantona passes the ball into the net from the resultant penalty, sending Chelsea keeper, the tracksuit-bottomed Dmitri Kharine, the wrong way. Goal number twenty-four.

Six minutes later, Andrei Kanchelskis goes in pursuit of a hopeful long ball, approaching Frank Sinclair in the Chelsea defender's blind spot. The coming together can't be described as anything other than mild but, despite his better-placed linesman not flagging for any offence, Elleray points to the spot.

'Oh, he's given another one!' yells John Motson up on the TV gantry. Even his co-commentator Trevor Brooking – the master of the straight-bat, non-committal aside – sounds positively animated at the decision. 'Look! He's outside the penalty box.'

Cantona steps up again and dispatches a perfect facsimile of his first penalty – low to the right with Kharine heading off in the opposite direction again. As the ball nestles in the corner, Hoddle reaches for the zip of his tracksuit, ready to bring himself on to replace Craig Burley. Once on the pitch, he delivers the kind of sermon he would normally reserve for the privacy of the dressing room. It does little. Within two minutes, Mark Hughes capitalises on a stumble by the clearly shaken Sinclair and United are three up. A fourth United goal arrives in added time, with Paul Ince rounding the keeper but unselfishly squaring to Brian McClair to tap in.

Despite the fact that he had a clear chance to equal Stan Mortensen's long-held cup final hat-trick record, we've seen Cantona in only very occasional fits and starts this afternoon. As *The Independent*'s Ian Ridley will say in his match report, two goals or not, he wasn't his usual ebullient self this afternoon: 'We saw neither the Rimbaud nor the Rambo.' Instead, we had the rarely seen subdued Eric.

Nonetheless, he'll still be the subject of the headlines tomorrow morning, the best of which will be 'General De Goal'. It's always all about Eric.

Chelsea 0–4 Manchester United

The last-chance saloon bar

Sunday 12 May 1996

Dawlish Town Sports & Social Club
vs Grimethorpe Miners Welfare

Carlsberg Pub Cup final

Two months ago, sandwiched between adverts for Fresh Brew's revolutionary foil-packed tea bags ('The freshness can't get out') and Somerfield's latest price cuts ('Save £1.30 on a whole fresh chicken!' gushes Nigel Havers' over-enthusiastic voiceover), another TV commercial had an announcement to make. It was launching a new concept in football, another way of presenting the national game. But a rival to the four-year-old Premier League it certainly was not.

A series of voices – of players, of coaches – told of a particular shared dream. 'Let's get through to the next round. Let's get a win' ... 'It would mean everything' ... 'Instead of watching it, we could be playing it' ... 'Come May 12, we could be at Wembley.'

These voices belong to the plucky amateurs ready to contest a new competition: the Carlsberg Pub Cup. In this first season, 402 teams from pubs and social clubs across the country have contested county, regional and national rounds, with the two finalists rewarded with the chance to play each other at Wembley as the curtain-raiser to the FA Vase final. A similar endeavour has been a fixture of the English cricketing calendar since 1972 – the Village Cup final, which grants the two finalists the once-in-a-lifetime thrill of playing at Lord's.

This lunchtime, with those 402 teams having been whittled down to just two, it's time for the competition's inaugural final. Yesterday afternoon, it was FA Cup final day, when Liverpool's Spice Boys had wandered around the pitch beforehand in their infamous white suits before being felled by Eric Cantona's astute volley. Two more giants of the game are lining up today: Dawlish Town Sports & Social Club and Grimethorpe Miners Welfare.

As the warm-up act for an FA Vase showdown between Brigg Town and Clitheroe, the south Devonians will take on the boys from Barnsley in a sixty-minute match, the idea being that the generous dimensions of the Wembley pitch would be too demanding for the pub sides over the usual ninety. Unsurprisingly, not a single member of either start-ing XI has set foot on the hallowed turf before, but someone among Grimethorpe's management team has: their boss Stuart Barrowclough. Twenty years ago, the former England under-23 international – now a florist and greengrocer back in his native Barnsley – played on the wing for Newcastle in the 1976 League Cup final against Manchester City. Barrowclough knows about the pain of Wembley defeat; Newcastle lost 2–1 that day.

While matches between pub sides might be expected to be error-heavy, high-scoring affairs, the game is goalless after those sixty minutes. By now, the 1,000-strong crowd has been bol-stered by those arriving for the Vase final, and these arrivistes are treated to the drama of a penalty shoot-out. There are two heroes of the hour: the Dawlish keeper Jamie Day is undeniably one of them, batting away two of the Grimethorpe penalties; Dawlish's fourth penalty-taker is the other. If Tony Bowker scores, Dawlish are the first winners of this new competition. It's as simple as that.

His penalty is uncomplicated. The roofer, described by *The Independent*'s Mike Rowbottom as 'a legend in his own social club', does exactly what Gareth Southgate should do next month against Germany. He wallops the penalty high and handsome into the roof of the net, the same net into which Cantona scored yesterday. Bowker is not only the side's co-manager, but today is his thirty-sixth birthday. His gift is Wembley immortality.

The 500 fans who've made the 200-mile trip up to north-west London make the noise of a crowd ten times their number, trying to fill the stadium's near-empty cavern. The difference between the national stadium and the team's regular ground back home in Devon has provided something of a culture shock today. 'It was a bit hard to see,' long-standing Dawlish supporter Alison Barrett good-heartedly grumbles to Rowbottom afterwards. 'Normally we're right by the pitch, two feet away.'

'The best day of my life,' says Bowker, a quarter of a century later, 'except getting married and my children being born. To play at Wembley on your birthday and score the winner at the same end that Cantona scored the day before was unreal. Thanks for reminding me. Not that I will ever forget it.'

Dawlish Town Sports & Social Club 0–0 Grimethorpe Miners Welfare (Dawlish win 4–2 on penalties)

Sheringham's double Dutch

Tuesday 18 June 1996

England vs The Netherlands

European Championship group match

Last Saturday, an impudent, brilliant goal by Paul Gascoigne – the most famous he'll ever score – provided the moment at which England's Euro '96 campaign truly ignited. Until then, a balloon-puncturing 1–1 draw with Switzerland and an underwhelming first half against Scotland had dampened the mood. But Gascoigne's lob over the head of Scottish defender Colin Hendry and volley lashed past keeper Andy Goram secured their first win of the tournament. Blond ambition had well and truly lit the blue touchpaper.

Tonight, seventy-six hours later, a draw against the Netherlands will be sufficient for the hosts to top Group A and progress to a quarter-final back here at Wembley against Spain, who qualified as Group B runners-up in Leeds this afternoon.

But tails are up, spirits are high. A draw won't satisfy the now-voracious squad, nor a nation increasingly gripped by Euro '96 fever, by a hope that those thirty years of hurt could – could – be banished for ever this summer. Over the next two hours, England comply, producing one of their most scintillating victories ever seen at Wembley.

She's inside the stadium, but Carla Jeffries isn't likely to see any of the match. This was the case on Saturday too. Back home in High Barnet at the start of her university holidays, she's found casual work at Wembley in the concession stands – scooping up the chips, flipping the burgers. Six matches. Six shifts. Six ways to be tantalisingly close to the action without seeing a ball kicked.

There's a radio on inside the concession stand, but it's difficult to hear the commentary over the sizzle of all those burgers she's got to prepare throughout the first half. Instead, Carla and her co-workers are forced to imagine what's going on from the crowd noise alone, from the ebb and flow of cheers and jeers.

A little over twenty minutes in and it sounds like England have scored. Word comes through that it's actually a penalty (Carla has to wait until the TV highlights later to see that the Dutch defender Danny Blind conceded it, after a neat piece of trickery by Paul Ince). Alan Shearer, yet to score a penalty for England, will take it. The giant roar tells the refreshments crew that the Blackburn man has broken his duck.

The half-time whistle sounds and England fans pour on to the concourse for sustenance. Happy and hungry. The next fifteen minutes pass by in a blur for Carla and the team as hundreds of mouths need feeding. A couple of minutes into the second half and there are no more customers. Just the next forty-five minutes of scraping and scouring the grill plate, perhaps grabbing a bite or two of any unsold burgers.

Carla has a plan, though. 'I was so gutted that I missed Gascoigne's goal against Scotland and I really wanted to see at least some of one of the games. So I said I was popping to the loo, but actually headed up the steps into the stadium. I was standing at the top of a gangway but a steward saw me and started walking towards me. But he saw my uniform and smiled and left me alone. I'm so glad he did. England were just about to take a corner and when the ball came over, I could see Teddy Sheringham jumping highest and scoring with a header. It was amazing timing on my part. Plus, I'm a Spurs fan, so seeing one of our own score was brilliant. The place erupted. I thought it was noisy down on our concession stand but it seemed twice as loud in the stadium itself.

'I should have headed back down at that point, but the atmosphere was just intoxicating. I didn't want to leave. So I hung on a few more minutes. And, lo and behold, along came another goal. And this one was even better.'

This third goal, Shearer's second of the evening, is a brilliant team effort. Gascoigne turns and twists into the area before pulling the ball back for Sheringham. He shapes to shoot, as any striker would in that position, but instead plays it square, wrong-footing the entire Dutch team, wrong-footing the entire stadium. The unmarked Shearer is the only person not undone by Sheringham's selflessness and he lashes the ball into the top corner for his fourth goal of the tournament. 'Maybe I could have scored,' Sheringham tells Adrian Chiles some years later, 'but if you roll a ball to your top scorer, your main man scoring goals for fun, it seemed the right thing to do.'

As it is, he claims his second five minutes later, pouncing after Edwin van der Sar can only parry Darren Anderton's low, fierce drive. England fans can't believe what they're seeing. Four up against a Dutch team that includes Dennis Bergkamp and Ronald de Boer and Clarence Seedorf. Unbelievable.

Carla can't believe what she's seeing either. 'I was stood there for about ten minutes – longer than I should have done – but I saw three goals! I thought I was pushing my luck then though, so headed back to work. I didn't want to get sacked. I needed the money! As I turned round to leave, that steward gave me a thumbs up.

'When I got back downstairs, all my co-workers were buzzing. "Have you heard? It's 4–0!" I acted all innocent . . .'

That four-goal cushion becomes a three-goal one with twelve minutes left when the Dutch substitute Patrick Kluivert steals in to shoot past David Seaman. Everyone in the stadium sees it as a consolation goal, but that's not the interpretation for those from north of the border. At Villa Park, Scotland are currently leading Switzerland by a single Ally McCoist goal, their first of the tournament. Until a few moments ago, it meant that they would pip the Netherlands to that second qualifying spot. But Kluivert's goal has reversed their positions in the table. Unless they score again, this is Scotland's last match at Euro '96. And score they don't. And home they go.

England are already home, and Spain are the next visitors to Fortress Wembley.

England 4–1 The Netherlands

The new national anthem

Wednesday 26 June 1996

England vs Germany

European Championship semi-final

The front page of this morning's *Sun* is devoted to tonight's Euro '96 semi-final. On it are pictured the comedians Frank Skinner and David Baddiel, dressed in England replica kits and with the England flag painted on their faces. Between them is an actual living and breathing lion.

Also on the front page are the lyrics to 'Three Lions', the song that the pair – along with the not inconsiderable contribution from Lightning Seeds frontman Ian Broudie – have taken to the top of the charts. Printed here are, the paper commands, 'the words the whole nation must sing tonight'. It declares the song to be 'the new national anthem'.

No football song has ever had the impact that 'Three Lions' has achieved over the last few weeks. Already topping the charts before the tournament began, the Wembley DJ played it over the PA before England's opening group game, a lacklustre 1-1 draw against Switzerland. He did the same ahead of the clash with Scotland but then, in the immediate glow of that pressure-releasing victory, he had what Skinner will later call 'a brainwave'. Out of the stadium's speakers came those now familiar piano chords and Broudie's breathy vocals. 'It's coming home, it's coming home . . .' Within seconds, 70,000 England fans were heartily singing along.

At the next two games – that final group match against the Netherlands and the quarter-final against Spain – the DJ barely needed to put the needle on the record. The mass choir of Wembley sang the song throughout both matches. At Paul Gascoigne's insistence, the squad have also had it on heavy rotation on the team bus en route to every match. The new national anthem, indeed.

This evening's rendition, at England's first tournament semi-final on home turf for those thirty years of hurt, is heartier and more fulsome than ever. Skinner, Baddiel and Broudie – in their usual position in the seats just in front of the press box – once again bask in the glow of their song being sung by tens of thousands of people. It's the soundtrack of the summer. 'I can't tell you how it felt,' Skinner will later admit. 'I'm not a good enough writer.'

Echoes of 'Three Lions' can still be heard when England have their first chance of the match, a thirty-yard volley from Paul Ince that forces the German goalkeeper Andy Köpke to punch the ball over the bar. Gascoigne floats the subsequent corner on to the top of Tony Adams' head at the front post and, behind him, an unattended Alan Shearer stoops to nod home from deep inside the six-yard box. The match is only three minutes old.

And the match is only sixteen minutes old when Germany equalise, Stefan Kuntz turning home a low and inviting Thomas Helmer cross. 'It's going to be one of those nights again,' ITV's Brian Moore sagely notes from his commentary post.

One of those nights, indeed. It's tight, cagey and not at all as straightforward as Shearer's early goal might have suggested. The nerves of the nation – shredded when England met West Germany in that semi-final in Turin six years ago – are heading that way again. The game lurches towards half-time, then towards the final whistle and then into extra-time, where the golden goal rule, introduced since Italia '90, may well come into effect. Next goal wins – as long as there is one in the next half-hour.

Darren Anderton is the first to come close to being the golden hero but, in sliding in to meet Steve McManaman's pull-back, he knocks the ball against the post. Four minutes later, Germany – and all of Wembley – think they've won the match when Kuntz heads home from Andreas Möller's corner. The referee's whistle, indicating a foul by the German on Gareth Southgate, ensures we keep going. It's an astonishing first period of extra-time, a high-stakes slugging match with both boxers throwing caution to the wind and leaving themselves open to a sucker punch. As ever, Barry Davies calls it correctly. 'The country's pulse rate must be beyond natural science.'

That pulse rate accelerates even faster when Shearer sends in a low cross from the right that just eludes Gascoigne. Any contact would have found the ball nestling in the empty net, but the midfielder pauses for a millisecond, thinking that Köpke is going to block the cross. On such small margins games – and tournaments – can be won or lost. ITV co-commentator Kevin

Keegan knows this. 'If he'd have had size nine boots on instead of eight and a half, he'd have scored.'

A hundred and twenty minutes draw to a close and, echoing that night in Turin, a penalty shoot-out against the Germans beckons. This time, though, England aren't spot-kick virgins. They exorcised those ghosts four days ago in the shoot-out win against Spain, with Stuart Pearce in particular seeing off the demons of 1990. Hell, some of the England players are actually smiling going into tonight's lottery.

The home side goes first.

Alan Shearer scores. Thomas Hässler scores.

David Platt scores. Thomas Strunz scores.

Stuart Pearce scores. Stefan Reuter scores.

Paul Gascoigne scores. Christian Ziege scores.

Teddy Sheringham scores. Stefan Kuntz scores.

Now it's sudden-death. A nervous-looking Southgate comes forward. He's doing things too quickly; he's rushing. His penalty lacks venom and Köpke makes the first save of the shoot-out. Southgate walks back to the centre circle, muttering. He can't look at anything but his feet.

Andreas Möller steps forward. Andreas Möller scores. Andreas Möller puts both arms on his waist and pushes out his chest, strutting around the pitch like a preening cockerel.

Wembley falls silent. The cameras search out Skinner, Baddiel and Broudie. Their faces wear the dejection of an entire nation. The air has been sucked out of the balloon. The Wembley DJ wisely decides to leave his copy of 'Three Lions' in its sleeve. 'Football did come home,' Skinner will later write, 'but someone parked a big Audi across the driveway.'

An hour or so later, dejection turns to anger for a few fans heading home to Hertfordshire. As their train retreats from London, bound for Welwyn Garden City, one station in particular provokes their ire. A handful leave the train at this juncture, venting their anger on the platform's signage, out to wreak destruction.

That station? New Southgate.

England 1–1 Germany
(Germany win 6–5 on penalties)

Red alert

Monday 25 May 1998

Charlton Athletic vs Sunderland

First Division play-off final

Today will be *the* red-letter day in the footballing life of Clive Mendonca. The striker's boyhood club Sunderland are in the First Division play-off final, ninety minutes away from earning the right to fill their pockets in the increasingly cash-rich Premier League. Mendonca first wore the stripes of Sunderland at the age of five, heading out on Christmas morning in the frost and chill of his housing estate in a box-fresh kit. As a kid, he went to as many home games as his family's straitened circumstances would allow. And when they wouldn't allow, he became adept at cadging free tickets from players via mutual friends.

Now a professional approaching his thirtieth birthday, the play-off final will be the sign-off to a memorable season for Mendonca, a league campaign in which he's found the net twenty-three times. His family have travelled down from the north-east en masse; several have placed bets on their Clive being the scorer of the day's first goal. They have a strong suspicion that, on this humid afternoon, Sunderland's destiny – their hoped-for passage to the promised land of the top tier – will come down to their relative's free-scoring feet.

But that suspicion is actually a fear.

Clive Mendonca won't be gracing the Wembley turf in the red of Sunderland, the red of his boyhood idols. He'll be wearing the red of Charlton Athletic, their opponents, their rivals for that Premier League golden ticket. And, on this bank holiday Monday afternoon, those free-scoring feet will hit the target three times, causing the Black Cats' ship of dreams to list, three damaging blasts to the hull.

Mendonca's personal circumstances aside, the match – eight goals across 120 minutes, plus a fourteen-penalty shoot-out – becomes an instant classic. But it isn't until the second half that it properly explodes. Within thirteen minutes of the restart, Charlton – who led at the break through Mendonca's opener – find themselves 2–1 down. From there on in, it's a matter of catch-up for the Addicks. They equalise, then they go a goal down again. Then they equalise again, only to fall behind once more. It's back and forth 'like a basketball game', says Sunderland's left-back Michael Gray. It's only the goal that clinches Mendonca's hat-trick, a neat swivel and volley, that saves the Londoners' bacon in extra-time. But regardless of what the ultimate result will be after the twelve-yard lottery has taken effect, Mendonca has secured an indelible place in the history books: he's only the fourth player – after Stan Mortensen, Geoff Hurst and Chelsea's David Speedie in that goal-heavy 1986 Full Members' Cup match – to score three times in a Wembley final.

Almost inevitably, it's Mendonca who sets the tone during the shoot-out, his opening spot-kick confidently fired into the top corner. Nicky Summerbee equalises for the Black Cats, after which the next eleven penalties are all successful too. Then Gray – who attended the same Sunderland school as Mendonca – trudges forward, his legs leaden, his lungs empty. The confidence shown by his fellow alumnus of Castle View School is lacking; his penalty barely trickles into the arms of Charlton keeper Saša Ilić. A spent force, Gray doesn't even have the energy to shed a tear.

The sensation experienced by Mendonca is the dictionary definition of bittersweet. As he approaches the autumn of his career, he'll be pulling up a seat at English football's top table for the first time. But he has also condemned his beloved club – along with his family, his friends and the entire population of his home city – to another season out of the reach of the top flight. The Sky Sports commentator jokes about Mendonca 'getting the disguises ready when he goes back to the north-east', but it's a quip that's a little too close to the bone. While later reports that the windows of his mum's house have been smashed by angry Sunderland fans are greatly exaggerated ('My ma is the type of woman, if you put hers out she'd be straight round to put yours out'), death threats are subsequently issued in Mendonca's direction. One Sunderland fan draws a finger across his throat as he stares at the striker during his lap of honour.

Promises of retribution, whether grave or even grievous, never materialise. But a hip injury means that Mendonca plays senior football for only another eighteen months. His premature retirement sees him return home to Sunderland, where he will take up an anonymous job on the assembly line at the city's Nissan factory – back among his people, back among the Black Cats fans whose hearts he broke on that bank holiday in 1998.

Charlton Athletic 4–4 Sunderland
(Charlton win 7–6 on penalties)

'They were home matches. But we weren't at home'

Wednesday 30 September 1998

Arsenal vs Panathinaikos

Champions League group match

'The general feeling was negative. Highbury was our home. It had a brilliant atmosphere on European nights. You'd wander through the streets from Finsbury Park Tube to get to the ground with all that atmosphere along the way. The pitch was small, the fans were close. It was an imposing place to come for potentially technically superior continental teams. Wembley was a money-grab.'

For Arsenal fans such as Rob Williams, the decision to swap Highbury for Wembley for home matches in the Champions League in the late 1990s was a mistake. The official reason given was that a UEFA dictat determined that all pitchside advertising hoardings needed to measure a certain height – that is, to be taller than they currently were at Highbury. Installing these larger hoardings would result in no one occupying the low-down front rows, meaning some of the Arsenal faithful would miss out, or be relocated elsewhere in the ground. Estimates are that as many as 6,000 regular fans would be affected. Of course, a by-product of the move across north London was, as Williams suggests, the potential for much higher gate receipts for these mouth-watering European matches. At 38,000, Highbury's capacity was exactly half that of the now all-seat Wembley.

This shift to the national stadium, which would last two seasons before the demolition crews rumbled through its gates, also serves a research purpose. Should investors wish to pump funds into a future new stadium for the Gunners, proof would be needed that the club could fill an arena of this size. Was the fanbase large enough to sustain the move, however temporary? Arsène Wenger fully understood the long game, the lasting significance. While acknowledging that his players 'may be less comfortable at Wembley', he knows it's a nod towards the future. 'It is a gamble, but it shows that in the long term, you cannot imagine the club staying at Highbury for ever. So what other choice is there than to move from Highbury? Sometimes you're in a situation where you either improve or die.'

Here at the first game at Wembley under the new arrangement, 73,455 souls have set aside any differences they might have about casting Highbury adrift for European nights. But despite the numbers, the visceral atmosphere is lacking, as Rob Williams remembers. 'With that speedway track around the pitch, and the terraces that gently tiered away, you felt a good distance away from the action. That said, it was still Wembley, it was still the twin towers. It retained some romance. It was an event.'

Tonight, Arsenal win their first match of this latest Champions League campaign, adding to their away draw in Lens a fortnight ago. Both goals come from their central defensive partnership. Tony Adams lashes the first one home with all the ruthless panache of Dennis Bergkamp or Nicolas Anelka, while the second comes courtesy of a brilliantly angled Martin Keown header. However, this is the only Champions League victory they will register at Wembley this season. And next season, they'll also manage just one. In neither season will the Gunners progress beyond the group stage. The experiment fails.

'You suspect our rather ageing defenders used the smaller

pitch at Highbury to their fullest advantage,' concludes Williams. 'The bigger pitch did them no favours. And the opposition enjoyed themselves there.

'These matches felt difficult to define. Wembley means cup finals. These weren't those. They weren't even knock-out games. They were home matches in a league. But we weren't at home. Neither were the opposition. It was all a bit weird.'

Arsenal 2–1 Panathinaikos

Standby mode

Sunday 4 July 1999

England under-16s vs Argentina under-16s

Nationwide international

Carl Bell claps his gloved hands together and gazes out across the pitch. The view is somewhat more spectacular than it was last Thursday. Then he was sitting in the stands at the Drill Field in Northwich, home of Northwich Victoria of the Nationwide Conference, watching England under-16s draw 1-1 with France. It wasn't the most salubrious of grounds; indeed, the wrecking ball will reduce it to rubble within three years after failing to meet safety regulations.

This afternoon, 16-year-old Carl is sat in another stadium whose demise is imminent. This is his first experience of Wembley, either as player or spectator. He's both today. As he did last Thursday, he's wearing the colours of England's second-string goalkeeper.

Carl's rise has been rather meteoric. He took up the game only three years ago ('I was picked up by Carlisle as a tall, fat lad before Newcastle bought me off them') and is now into his second year of representing his country. While his exit from the game in a few years' time will be as swift as his ascendancy, several of his team-mates will go on to become established Premier League players. A shaven-headed Jermaine Jenas is in tonight's line-up, as is Jermaine Pennant for whom, at the age of fifteen, Arsenal have already paid £2 million. Bell's Newcastle United buddy Michael Chopra starts as well, becoming the first Anglo-Asian player to represent England at Wembley.

Bell isn't starting this afternoon. Nor did he in Northwich. There are four teenage goalkeepers vying for the top spot in this team, a position currently held by Reading's Shaun Allaway. One of the two below Bell in the pecking order – Andy Lonergan – will go on to play 400-plus games in the lower leagues before, in the twilight of his career, becoming Liverpool's third-choice keeper and winning medals at the 2019 editions of the UEFA Super Cup and the FIFA Club World Cup. 'He's had a better career sat on his arse,' Bell laughs.

Bell doesn't mind sitting on his arse this afternoon, doesn't mind being the substitute. There's a danger of too much, too young. 'Everything was happening at a rate of knots,' he recalls more than twenty years later. 'I probably didn't understand the size of it. I had to take it in my path and it wasn't until I was a little bit older that I could say, "I've done this and I've done that and I've played there". At the time, I was just going along with it.

'I wasn't thinking about Wembley. I was thinking less about the location and more about whether I was going to play for

England. *Am I going to get on?* But there's no remorse or anger from my side that I didn't play. It is what it is.'

A year and four days after England's senior team lost to Argentina in the 1998 World Cup, the juniors exact a little revenge tonight. Midfielder Brian Howard – later to become captain of Barnsley – scores direct from a corner, while Chopra is on the scoresheet again following his winner against France in Northwich. His buddy's goal, and the celebrations, is about the only thing Bell can remember about the match itself. 'Both being from Newcastle, he was the one I was closest to in the team. We were room-mates for quite a long time and my mum and dad had come down with his mum and dad. So the next best thing to playing was having your mate score the winner.'

It was a rare occasion for both of Bell's parents to be present. 'My mum and dad are typical old-school Northumbrian people and they rarely leave the county. If you can't fly somewhere from Newcastle Airport, then they won't go there. My mum refused to go to games because she was always so nervous. But I spotted her in the crowd at Wembley. Even though I was on the bench, she cried the whole game. She was so full of nerves. Her make-up was completely running down her face. "I'm never coming back again. That's it, I'm done."'

His other clear memory of the day is of the soon-to-be-demolished dressing rooms. 'There was the big old bath that holds loads of people and I was sitting in it, thinking about all the people who'd sat in it before – all the stars. These are silly little memories to have more than twenty years down the line, aren't they?'

Bell never got the chance to make further Wembley memories. 'I fell out of love with football very quickly. At the age of seventeen, eighteen, the fun just seemed to go.' Injuries didn't help. He broke his wrist in training, during shooting practice with Alan Shearer and Shay Given. It didn't heal properly and he subsequently broke it three more times. He walked away from the game. 'It was a relief to be finishing more than anything else. I didn't miss it.' He's now a personal trainer in Newcastle.

Six years ago, though, this Wembley day came back into his mind. 'My grandma died and she used to keep old programmes and a scrapbook of newspaper cuttings. Me and my parents were cleaning her bedroom out and came across the programme for the Argentina game. That's when I realised.' He was casting his eye over the two line-ups and noticed a familiar name. Playing up front that day was a 16-year-old Carlos Tevez. 'Me and my dad looked at each other. "Bloody hell!"'

Bell is talking the morning after England Lionesses beat Germany to become European champions. The attention that the side is receiving on each and every media outlet is both a delight and gratifying. It's also a sharp reminder of how far the women's game has come. Before that under-16s match that afternoon in 1999, there was also an under-16s girls international, the first to be played at Wembley. But this historic occasion – England beat Scotland 5–0 – was far from given due respect. The stadium gates opened at 12.45 p.m., with the girls kicking off just quarter of an hour later at 1 p.m. Most of those through the turnstiles at this early juncture would still be putting ketchup on their chips and sugar in their tea out on the concourse, leaving the girls to play in front of empty terraces.

Their historic international isn't even mentioned on the match-day ticket.

England under-16s 2–1 Argentina under-16s

The 2000s

The last long walk

Sunday 13 August 2000

Chelsea vs Manchester United

Charity Shield

It's roughly 140 paces from the entrance of the tunnel under the East Stand at Wembley to the halfway line. It's certainly the most iconic walk in football, one that's been undertaken at some stage by almost every footballing legend the game has produced over the last near eighty years.

This afternoon, though, marks the last time that two clubs will undertake that walk. The opening match of the 2000–01 season is one of the closing matches in the original Wembley's life. FA Cup winners Chelsea take on league champions Manchester United for the right to be the last team to lift silverware here. But first they have to do that 140-pace stroll across the cinders behind the goal and on to the turf itself. Diminutive Chelsea captain Dennis Wise probably has to take a few more than 140.

It's the twenty-seventh, and final, Charity Shield to be played here, at what will become known as Old Wembley, the Wembley that, bought by the FA in 1999 after being in private hands almost all its life, is soon to feel the hammer blows of a wrecking crew. At that first one, the Leeds/Liverpool clash in 1974, the two teams were led out by the immaculately dressed Brian Clough and Bill Shankly. Today, Alex Ferguson – knighted last year following United's treble-snatching exploits – is suitably attired in a blazer and slacks. His opposite number, Gianluca Vialli, has opted for a polo shirt and tracksuit bottoms. His head is shaved.

A couple of the United players share Vialli's haircut. Roy Keane, as fearsome a captain as Billy Bremner was for Leeds back in '74, is one. The other is that style chameleon, David Beckham. His number 1 buzz-cut wasn't his idea, though. Lately, he's been cultivating a *Taxi Driver*-style mohawk, hidden from the manager during United's pre-season training under a beanie. The hat has stayed on at all points today – breakfast at the hotel, the coach journey here – but it's now time to come clean. Off comes the hat. And Fergie hates the haircut.

The Glaswegian instructs his player, in no uncertain terms, that he has to shave the mohawk off. Not later. Not when he's back at home. Right now. A chastened Beckham heads off down Wembley's corridors in search of a pair of clippers. Remarkably, he manages to find some. Cue the bizarre sight, just ahead of the teams going out for their warm-up, of England's star midfielder disappearing into the dressing room toilets to run the clippers over his head.

The day – or, at least, the scoresheet – belongs to Chelsea's two goalscorers: Jimmy Floyd Hasselbaink and Mario Melchiot, both of the Netherlands. New record signing Hasselbaink starts this dose of double Dutch in the twenty-second minute with a shot that deflects off his compatriot Jaap Stam and flies over Fabien Barthez in the United goal. In the seventy-third minute, right-back Melchiot scores his first goal for the club, his unchecked run ending with a low drive that passes through Stam's legs on its way in.

Ten minutes before then, Roy Keane offers an ugly symmetry to the occasion. That 1974 Charity Shield match had been marred by, and largely only remembered for, the double sending-off of Bremner and Kevin Keegan. Keane's own dismissal – in this final Charity Shield before the stadium's demolition – helps to bookend matters. He and Chelsea's Uruguayan midfielder Gus Poyet have been niggling away at each other since the earliest minutes and, after Keane is incensed by an unsightly foul on him by Hasselbaink a couple of minutes before, the Irishman launches himself studs-up at Poyet from behind. The red card is inevitable. It's another crime of passion, and a seventh dismissal in as many seasons at Old Trafford. As he leaves the field of play, Keane at least decides to keep his shirt on.

Just as the long walk from the tunnel will never again be undertaken by a club side, nor will the climb up the thirty-nine steps to the Royal Box. At the final whistle, Dennis Wise leads his men up that staircase, takes possession of the famous octagonal shield and raises it – with assistance from goalkeeper Ed de Goey – towards the Chelsea fans. It's the last time such a roar will travel around the old concrete shell, up under its eaves and into every nook and cranny.

Chelsea 2–0 Manchester United

The double farewell

Saturday 7 October 2000

England vs Germany

World Cup qualifier

'We have to make sure that we do everything we can to ensure that the last game at Wembley is memorable – and memorable for all the right reasons, with a victory hopefully.'

If he didn't already feel the weight of restoring the national team's pride after a wholly underwhelming campaign in this summer's European Championship, which saw them eliminated after the group stage, England manager Kevin Keegan also carries the burden of overseeing the side as they play the last ever football match at the original Wembley Stadium. English fans will expect a departure that does the old place proud, that sends it into the night with an uplifting performance and result. Keegan certainly knows what he wants to avoid.

'I could be known as that man,' he explains at one of the pre-match press conferences. 'The last man to lose at Wembley. I'm in that potential position. But I don't want to be known as that man.' To add additional pressure, three of Britain's gold medallists from last month's Sydney Olympics – Denise Lewis, Steve Redgrave and Audley Harrison – will be introduced to the crowd beforehand. Their golden summer is in marked contrast to that of the England football team.

Tonight's opponents in this opening qualifier for the 2002

World Cup in Japan and South Korea start from an even lower ebb than England. Germany finished last in the same group at the Euros, registering a draw and two defeats, one of which was to England in Charleroi. The only way is up for a team now under the temporary stewardship of Rudi Völler.

The evening is to be a celebratory affair, a final hurrah for a stadium that has hosted so many classic matches over the past seventy-seven years. But, ultimately, no fireworks are needed. The weather, and England's limp performance, turns it into the dampest of damp squibs.

The only goal comes after fourteen minutes when Liverpool midfielder Dietmar 'Didi' Hamann takes a quick free-kick. David Seaman is still trying to construct his wall when the German midfielder strikes hard and low. Out of position and with Paul Scholes as his only protection, the ball skids past Seaman, leaving a look on the goalkeeper's face – somewhere between anger and bemusement – that's only too familiar to England fans whenever the side has just experienced something of a calamity.

And that was largely that. No other goals follow in the remaining seventy-six minutes, no great England strike to sign off with. Instead a German has the last laugh, albeit one who has to face his Liverpool team-mates come Monday morning. But Hamann seems nonplussed about the whole scenario.

'The fact that it was the last game at Wembley probably meant more to them than us,' he will write a few years later. 'We did not go there looking to spoil the party, but we had to get a result and look after ourselves. And that is what we did.'

Hamann will forever be the answer to a pub quiz staple question for years: who was the last man to score a goal at the old Wembley? 'People often bring it up and, yes, it's an honour . . . I guess. But where does it stand in my career? It was [just] a qualifier.' This is, after all, a man with two Bundesliga titles and a UEFA Cup winner's medal on his CV – and with Champions Leagues and FA Cups yet to come.

The significance of Hamann's unanswered goal is felt by others tonight – and by one man in particular. Within minutes of the final whistle, Keegan has tendered his resignation to his boss at the FA, David Davies. And he does so in the insalubrious surroundings of a Wembley toilet cubicle. (It proves to be the right decision. His successor, Sven-Göran Eriksson, will take England to the World Cup, in the process gaining revenge on Germany by thrashing them 5–1 in the corresponding fixture in Munich.)

Keegan's departure also upstages Wembley's final hour. No fireworks, no grand farewell. The lights just go out, those twin towers plunged into eternal darkness.

England 0–1 Germany

Virgin soil

Saturday 24 March 2007

England under-21s vs Italy under-21s

International friendly

The helicopter providing the pre-match aerial shots for TV is still hovering above Wembley when the first goal goes in, the loud chop of its blades joined by ecstatic, and astounded, Italian cheers. To be fair, the helicopter hasn't been lingering unnecessarily. After all, there are only twenty-nine seconds on the clock when Giampaolo Pazzini's strike slightly deflects off Anton Ferdinand's left leg and flies into the England net.

The striker has made history. He has scored the very first goal at the new Wembley. Later this afternoon, he will make history again.

The new stadium has been a slow train coming. It's taken much longer to arrive than was hoped and promised, a tale of delays and problems over the sixty-five months since Didi Hamann's daisy-cutting free-kick said an unsentimental goodbye to the old place. It was initially believed that a 2003 completion was possible; those believers were soon shown to be wildly optimistic, with the demolition not starting until the autumn of 2002, a full two years after football vacated the premises.

It was then hoped that the new gaff would be unveiled in time for the 2006 FA Cup final, as sports minister Richard Caborn announced to the listeners of BBC Radio 5 Live. There was a balance between faith and circumspection in his voice: 'They say the cup final will be there, barring six feet of snow or something like that.' By February, though, the FA had booked the Millennium Stadium to host the final for the sixth successive season. That summer's scheduled concerts – by the Rolling Stones, Take That, Bon Jovi and Robbie Williams – were also relocated.

But now it's here, now it's open for business. And it looks the part. The old twin towers have long disappeared from the skyline. Despite being Grade II-listed, and despite opposition from both English Heritage and Brent Council, the towers – referred to by former sports minister Tony Banks as mere 'concrete blocks' – would have been right in the middle of the repositioned pitch. Relocating the towers wasn't a realistic option; they would have simply crumbled (although the stone base of one of the flagpoles was sufficiently intact to be repurposed as a memorial in a nearby public park). So, instead, down they came, the victims of a German-built excavating machine nicknamed Alan the Shearer. In their place, the 134-metre-high arch becomes the new symbol, the easily identifiable architectural feature, of Wembley Stadium 2.0.

The 55,700 curious souls who take their seats this afternoon are universally impressed with their respective vantage points; there's not a duff view in the whole place. All can thus see the brilliance of Pazzini's quicksilver goal – and see the five that follow this afternoon. David Bentley equalises with a trademark free-kick before Wayne Routledge pounces on a mistake from future Azzurri legend Giorgio Chiellini to put England ahead. Pazzini pulls the scores level with a smart-thinking volley before substitute Matt Derbyshire restores England's lead. Then comes the Italian captain again, showing poise, in spite of the bobbly surface, to secure his hat-trick – obviously the first at the new stadium – and join the likes of Mortensen, Greaves, Hurst, Charlton, Lineker and Shearer in three-goal reverie.

But Pazzini never plays at Wembley again, despite a half-decent international career in the senior side and subsequent spells at Inter and Milan. He never even gets to play ninety minutes there, being substituted towards the end of today's match, but is the recipient of a standing ovation from all inside the stadium. By contrast, James Milner will take to the Wembley turf dozens of times during his career, whether at cup finals, cup semi-finals or Community Shields, or while on international duty. Fifteen years later, he will be here again, scoring Liverpool's first penalty in the FA Cup final shoot-out of 2022.

After this afternoon's game, an anonymous texter contacts the BBC Sport website. There's a reason why he's anonymous: he's surreptitiously texting from the maternity ward. 'My wife went into labour twenty minutes before kick-off, so I've had to miss the game. If it's a boy, I think we should call him Giampaolo.'

Another texter, William from Norfolk, gives his verdict on the new national stadium. 'It's a good thing this game has goals. If it were goalless, I would have fallen asleep. The new seating is far too comfortable.' Those unforgiving, backside-numbing perches from the old stadium, sold off for £59 a piece at the time of demolition, will not be missed. The fifty-four kilometres of new seating isn't all that's notable: the new Wembley also boasts ninety-eight kitchens, 688 food service points, and thirty-four bars capable of serving 40,000 pints of beer during the half-time interval. Like the twin towers, the refreshment queues of old may well have been confined to history.

But while today sees the first official game at the new Wembley, two sides actually took to the turf back at the end of November, when a team from the stadium owners Wembley National Stadium Ltd took on a side representing the stadium builders Multiplex, ostensibly to test the floodlights. Bearing in mind the prolonged disagreements between both companies during the construction process, it wouldn't have been completely surprising if the new stadium had registered its first red card that night.

England under 21s 3–3 Italy under-21s

Gimme shelter

Wednesday 21 November 2007

England vs Croatia

European Championship qualifier

Four days ago, fewer than 100 hours ago, England were on the canvas – bloodied, bruised, bewildered. Almost out for the count.

After goalless draws with Macedonia and Israel, and most recently defeat in Moscow, it appeared that their passage to the 2008 European Championship, to be jointly hosted by Austria and Switzerland, was irredeemably blocked. Their fate in Group E was now not their own. If Russia beat the comparatively weak Israel and Andorra in their final two matches, they would be joining the almost-qualified Croatia next summer.

But then, last Wednesday, a major surprise occurred in the Ramat Gan Stadium near Tel Aviv. Israel pulled out an injury-time winner against Russia, the repercussions of which were huge. The upset meant that a win or a draw in their final group match against Croatia would see England packing their bags come June. A victory by two or more goals would actually make them group winners. The boxer was back on his feet.

That isn't to say that they're immune to another potentially knock-out blow this evening. Lose to Croatia, while Russia notch up that expected win against Andorra, and Steve McClaren's squad will be spending next summer on the beach instead, topping up the tans but also simmering with jealousy.

Tonight's task is made trickier as many of McClaren's senior players are indisposed. There's no Rio Ferdinand, John Terry or Gary Neville. There's no Michael Owen, Wayne Rooney or Ashley Cole. The most experienced of his players – ninety-eight-cap David Beckham – is available, but McClaren has decided to leave him on the bench, the first time Beckham's been there since the World Cup back in 1998.

The manager's thinking has largely been interpreted thus: that, with Peter Crouch in the lone striker role tonight, he needs runners getting beyond the Croatian defence, feeding off the tall guy's knockdowns. That's why he's picked Shaun Wright-Phillips in the right-midfield berth. He's got the legs that Beckham doesn't – and arguably never has.

Most pundits understand the logic. One doesn't – so much so that it was the basis of his newspaper column this morning. He firmly believes Beckham should be in the starting XI. It's an awkward opinion. The column's author is Wright-Phillips's dad. 'It's tomorrow's chip paper' is Ian Wright's defence when Gary Lineker brings it up in the *Match of the Day* studio. 'And hopefully he won't have read it.'

Another pundit – one who's usually Eeyore to Wright's Tigger – is uncharacteristically optimistic. Alan Hansen believes an England win, and a comfortable win at that, is the most likely outcome. Down in the bowels of the stadium, McClaren is showing few signs of nerves or apprehension about the game, let alone about his fragile grip on his job should England exit the competition in a couple of hours' time.

BBC reporter Ray Stubbs asks him about the tenor of the dressing room. 'It's steely resolve. They know they've got the opportunity. They know there are no excuses now. We have to go out and cross that white line. Do the job. Make sure we qualify.'

It's a filthy night at Wembley. Rather than take his usual

perch among his backroom staff, McClaren opts to stand near the entrance to the tunnel under a large, colourful umbrella. It gives him a better view of the first Croatia goal after seven minutes. The elegant Portsmouth midfielder Niko Kranjčar tries a speculative shot from distance. It bounces just in front of the young goalkeeper Scott Carson, who can only spoon the wet ball into the net. 'More Frank Carson than Scott,' BBC co-commentator Mark Lawrenson drily suggests.

The second Croatia goal arrives seven minutes later when Arsenal's Eduardo bisects England's largely inexperienced defence to feed an offside-avoiding Ivica Olić, who calmly rounds Carson. Wembley is a much quieter place now, the England fans' buoyant optimism punctured by their own team. And it's only going to get quieter.

Approaching half-time, the news from Andorra is in. Russia are in front. Had the Russians only drawn tonight, England could have lost and still qualified. But the chances of an Andorran equaliser – they've scored only twice in eleven qualifiers so far – effectively rules that out as a realistic proposition. A minimum of two goals is the requirement for England.

They are booed off at half-time. Up in the *Match of the Day* studio, Hansen is back as Eeyore. He likens them to a pub team. 'Probably the worst forty-five minutes you'll ever see.' Early in the second half, the band in the stands strikes up the theme tune to *The Great Escape*. If ever a song . . .

It seems to work. The slightest of tugs on Jermain Defoe's shirt earns England a penalty, yet another lifeline. Frank Lampard strikes it low and to the left. The equaliser comes ten minutes later when Beckham's first-time cross is chested down by Crouch and swept home. The new Wembley hasn't heard a noise like it before. The boxer is back on his feet. Again.

But, with thirteen minutes left, Croatian striker Mladen Petrić finds himself in space and, unchallenged, unleashes an effort from twenty-five yards. Croatia lead 3–2. The boxer goes down again. The boxer stays down.

The full-time whistle goes. Cue a semi-nervous few minutes while Wembley waits for confirmation of the result in Andorra. But everyone knows. Having found a lifebelt floating towards them and slipped it on, England then decided to jettison it before reaching dry land.

Eeyore is in a disbelieving mood upstairs. 'Out-thought, outplayed, out-fought … It's definitely a low point in English football. It was abysmal. Truly abysmal.'

The last time England lost a competitive game at Wembley, Kevin Keegan resigned as manager shortly afterwards. An emergency meeting of the FA bigwigs is called and McClaren's departure – decided for him rather than self-determined – is announced the following day. His sixteen-month tenure is, until Sam Allardyce comes along, the shortest of any England manager. 'It's the saddest day in my career,' says the man whose playing days ended at the age of thirty-one through injury.

Being relieved of his duties might actually be a source of relief, either instant or slow-releasing. No longer does McClaren have to suffer the slings and arrows of the sports press, at least. No longer does he have to absorb personal humiliation courtesy of the headline writers. No longer will he be referred to as 'a wally with a brolly'.

England 2–3 Croatia

Access denied

Sunday 25 May 2008

Doncaster Rovers vs Leeds United

League One play-off final

In May 2001, Leeds United were striding out under the flood-lights at the magnificent Mestalla Stadium in Valencia, ninety minutes from a place in the Champions League final. Little more than six years later, they found themselves travelling to the Wirral for an opening-day clash against Tranmere Rovers. Their descent had been rapid. They'd become Leeds United of League One. Worse than that, they were starting the season right at the bottom of the table, punished by the Football League for financial irregularities. Their sanction was the docking of fifteen points, a penalty that put them well adrift of everyone else before a ball had even been kicked.

It's now nine months later and Leeds – in a season of flux and turmoil – have managed to give themselves every chance of escaping League One's clutches at the first time of asking. That fifteen-point penalty had been largely offset by wins in the first five matches of the season, a run that continued to leave them unbeaten in the first thirteen games. This upward progress – by the new year, they'd reached the top three in the division – stalled when they slumped mid-season, without a league win for six weeks. During that period, manager Dennis Wise left for an executive directorship at Newcastle United, taking Leeds chairman Ken Bates, godfather to Wise's children, somewhat by surprise. (Wise's assistant manager, Gus Poyet, had already jumped ship to return to Spurs as first-team coach.)

Now under the stewardship of club legend Gary McAllister, after that midwinter wobble Leeds ended up fifth. Following a spirited second-leg win at Carlisle in the play-off semi-final (having lost the first leg at Elland Road), they've made it to Wembley. The clamour for tickets for the final has been intense. At first, season ticket holders could each buy only a single ticket from the club's 36,000 allocation. When the final batch of 10,000 tickets went on sale, allowing season ticket holders and members to buy an additional three tickets each, the most dedicated and hardy fans spent the night before in Fullerton Park, site of the old greyhound and speedway stadium adjacent to Elland Road.

When the sun rose the next morning, bringing with it hundreds of new fans thinking they'd be first in line when the ticket office opened, minor scuffles broke out between the all-nighters and the latecomers, some of the latter trying to queue-jump. Estimates put those gathered as numbering around 7,000, creating the longest queues seen here since tickets went on sale for the FA Cup semi-final against Coventry back in 1987. Hundreds of Leeds fans dawdled back home in the morning light, their pockets unencumbered by tickets. What was crueller is that their play-off final opponents, Doncaster Rovers, won't sell out their allocation and there'll be plenty of empty seats come Sunday.

As disgruntled fans ebbed away from Elland Road on that Wednesday morning, the Leeds squad were already halfway towards London, their destination the distinctly well-heeled health resort Champneys in rural Hertfordshire. From this base, the team could take things leisurely. Thursday would be spent doing some light training at Arsenal's training ground in London Colney, while Friday brought a trip to Wembley to have a look around. For most of their players, it would be their first sight of the new place. The ticket rumpus at Elland Road was a million miles away. 'From that point of view,' McAllister observed at one of the week's press conferences, 'it's been a good decision to get down here behind these iron gates and into peaceful surroundings.'

No one would say it out loud, but there was a strong air of inevitability wafting around. Not overconfidence, not cockiness, just a sense that, having overcome that significant points deduction, the beauty of a Leeds victory in the final couldn't be resisted. A swift return to the Championship appeared to be their manifest destiny. Indeed, as the *Yorkshire Evening Post*'s chief football reporter Phil Hay will later write, 'from the moment Tresor Kandol's header passed through the legs of Danny Coyne at Prenton Park on 11 August, their escape from League One seemed meant to be'.

But sometimes fairy tales go sour right near the end.

This afternoon, Doncaster are out of the traps like the hungriest greyhounds. They're all over Leeds, who look startled in comparison. Only the alertness of their Danish goalkeeper Casper Ankergren maintains the parity between the two teams in the first ten minutes. Leeds warm up as the game lengthens, but their in-form strikers – top scorer Jermaine Beckford and the veteran Dougie Freedman, a loan signing in March from Crystal Palace – can't breach the Doncaster defence.

After a goalless first half, Rovers strike quickly after the break, courtesy of a diving header from James Hayter. It's just reward for their superior all-round play and Leeds have very little response. The final whistle sends Doncaster's players into euphoria, but sinks the crestfallen men of Leeds onto their haunches, onto their knees, onto their backs.

It looked like the League One experience was to be a one-season-only affair. But this is no sojourn. This is no sabbatical. This is home now. Leeds United will be a third-tier club for a further two seasons. Marching on together will have to wait for a while.

Doncaster Rovers 1–0 Leeds United

The 2010s

The 2010s

Mr Tangerine Man

Saturday 22 May 2010

Blackpool vs Cardiff City

Championship play-off final

From his seat in the sunshine, Jimmy Armfield looks across Wembley and calmly takes it all in. In two hours, maybe a little less, his beloved Blackpool could well become a Premier League club for the first time.

He was still playing the last time Blackpool were in the top flight. Their final game as a First Division side was his final game: 1 May 1971, a 1–1 draw against Manchester United. Armfield's team-mates gave him a guard of honour while each and every one of the United side – Law, Charlton, Best and the rest – shook his hand. It was his 627th match in the tangerine of the Seasiders. 'I don't recall being too emotional after the game. I was realistic enough to know nothing goes on for ever.'

This afternoon could be an emotional day, though. Since 1971, Armfield has achieved plenty in football: he's taken Leeds United to the European Cup final; he's been an astute journalist and broadcaster; he's appointed at least two England managers. But, at the heart of the matter, when push comes to shove, he's a Blackpool man right through his very core, like a stick of the town's seaside rock.

In that time, Blackpool have navigated themselves into all corners of the Football League. Up and down, back and forth. This season, they were fancied to be relegated from the Championship, but under the inspiring, attack-minded guidance of Ian Holloway, they're so close to the promised land that they can smell it.

But it's Dave Jones's Cardiff who strike the first blow this afternoon. After he hits the bar in the third minute, Michael Chopra soon makes certain by firing home a low cross-shot to give his side the lead. Blackpool don't leave it long to hit back. Midfielder Charlie Adam, their leading scorer and a £500,000 snip from Rangers last summer, curls a free-kick into the top corner.

Blackpool are dominant now, but Cardiff more decisive, and Joe Ledley puts the Welsh side back ahead with an exceedingly tidy finish. But back come Blackpool. D. J. Campbell – scorer of a hat-trick in the semi-final against Nottingham Forest – attempts an audacious overhead kick from a corner. It's cleared off the line but Gary Taylor-Fletcher is there to head it into the net.

Despite the extraordinary temperatures – the pitch-side thermometer measures 106.7 degrees Fahrenheit at one point this afternoon – it's been a fast, furious and frantic first half. And it's not done yet. With forty-five minutes on the clock, Campbell miscues a shot but the ball runs to the seasoned Brett Ormerod, who toe-pokes it through the legs of Cardiff keeper David Marshall. The Tangerines have their noses in front for the first time.

Ormerod has been here before. Back in 2001, he scored for Blackpool in the Third Division play-off final against Leyton Orient at the Millennium Stadium, the final goal in a 4–2 victory. Since then, he's ventured around the block a fair bit, playing for Southampton (with whom he reached the 2003 FA

Cup final), Leeds, Wigan, Preston, Nottingham Forest and
Oldham. Now he's a tangerine man again and his goal might
just have earned them a promotion – the biggest promotion of
all. He doesn't go too wild with his celebration. He used to
perform a forward somersault when he scored, but not today. He
can do nothing but stroll back for the restart. 'I was absolutely
knackered,' he will later reveal to the Seasiders podcast. 'It was
such a hot day and I just wanted to get to half-time and stick
my head in some ice.'

Ormerod only plays fifteen minutes of the second half, but
when he's taken off, he doesn't sit with the rest of the players,
instead choosing to take advantage of the dressing room's air
conditioning. But that's not the real reason. He can't bear to
watch and so spends the rest of the game pacing up and down.

But Cardiff can't breach Blackpool's defences a third time.
The Lancashire coast will now welcome Premier League football; Ormerod's toe-poke has become the £90 million goal.

Up in the stands, Jimmy Armfield accepts the handshakes of
the friends, family and well-wishers around him. He folds up
his glasses and pops them into the inside pocket of his jacket,
before allowing his finger to dab away a tear.

'They have run, they have chased and they have dragged
themselves up,' he will write in his newspaper column tomorrow. 'We couldn't be prouder of them.'

Blackpool 3–2 Cardiff City

The man with the silver pen

Saturday 28 May 2011

Barcelona vs Manchester United

Champions League final

A Guinness world record is being set tonight. Six hundred and fifty miles north-east of Wembley, around 400 folk have taken their seats at Trädgår'n, a nightclub and live music venue in Gothenburg. They will be watching tonight's Champions League final on what has just been verified as the world's largest LED television screen. From corner to diagonally opposite corner, the screen measures more than 7 metres. Everyone will get a good view this evening.

Elsewhere in Europe, specifically in the small, picture-perfect Swiss village of Moudon, just north of Lausanne, the locals will also be tuning in, hoping to snatch a glimpse of one of their own. For three seasons now, Marcel Ries, the proprietor of the village's sheet metal and laser-cutting business, has been invited by the UEFA bigwigs to attend every European final. 'Invited' suggests a responsibility-free jolly. Not so. Ries is here on business, a man arriving in cities across the continent with the tool of his trade in his hand luggage: a diamond-tipped engraving pen.

For Marcel Ries has an important job to do tonight. He's the man whose hands will be the focus of TV cameras come full-time, broadcast to an audience of 160 million. As the winners congregate in celebration before the trophy ceremony – to hug, to dance, to scream with delight – Ries's steady hands skilfully, but swiftly, inscribe the winners' name on the famous jug-eared trophy. The eyes of the world are on him.

This is the moment he's been waiting for, the reason he's here. While he always gets to watch the first half of European finals, the second forty-five goes unnoticed. By then, he's been handed the trophy and is preparing it in advance of those few tense post-match minutes. Today's task will be straightforward. Barcelona's domination marks them out as likely winners half-way through the second period (not that, of course, he can apply engraving pen to silverware before the final whistle). Plus, Ries has experience of engraving 'FC Barcelona'. Their name is on the trophy from two years ago, when they beat Manchester United in Rome. He was the one who put their name there.

Prior to fulfilling his pressured, contractual duty, Ries does get to see a lively opening to this evening's final, with United taking the game to the Catalans in the early stages. The strike partnership of Wayne Rooney and Javier Hernández is par-ticularly energetic and dangerous. The last time United played at Wembley in a European final, they were victorious against Benfica. Sir Alex Ferguson will be hoping that the spirit of '68 is in his team's blood tonight.

Barcelona soon start dictating the game and it's no surprise when, twenty-seven minutes in, a slide-rule Xavi pass plays in Pedro, who calmly slots home. On the touchline, Pep Guardiola, in a funeral-black suit rather than the kind of chunky knitwear he'll later be noted for, spins around and punches the air with both fists. Ferguson joined him at the side of the pitch just a couple of minutes ago. He stands still – motionless and mute – just staring, trying to work out how his United defence has been sliced open in the simplest manner.

In the aftermath of the goal, the ITV commentary pair of Clive Tyldesley and Andy Townsend speculate how United can get back into the game. Barcelona are rampant, with 66 per cent of possession and having made nearly three times the number of completed passes. Townsend offers his thoughts. 'What you don't try to do is do it in the five minutes after you've conceded, thinking you're just going to turn it around like that, in a nutshell. You're not.'

Precisely thirteen seconds later, Rooney equalises.

While it's a beautifully executed finish, a dipping cross-shot off the inside of his foot, it's also a fortunate goal, with Rooney playing a one-two with an offside Ryan Giggs in the build-up. The equaliser revitalises United, but it doesn't fluster Barcelona. The poise and control that has come to embody the Guardiola era doesn't drop a beat.

The second half becomes the Lionel Messi show as the Argentinian teases and probes and weaves. He puts Barcelona back in front, before supplying David Villa for the Spaniards' third. There are still twenty minutes left, but the white flag is being raised. 'Nobody's given us a hiding like that,' Ferguson later admits. 'In my time as manager, it's the best team I've faced.'

Of course, Marcel Ries doesn't get to see Messi and Villa's masterful finishes. And once he's finished engraving those eleven letters onto the trophy, it's ready for the presentation ceremony. But captain Xavi isn't the one to lift it first tonight. That honour is given to their French left-back Eric Abidal, who just ten weeks ago was undergoing surgery to remove a tumour on his liver. Now he's just completed the full ninety minutes of a Champions League final.

Back in that nightclub in Gothenburg, there's probably not a dry eye in the house.

Barcelona 3–1 Manchester United

The audition

Wednesday 29 February 2012

England vs The Netherlands

International friendly

At 6.45 p.m. on this leap day, the bus carrying the England team for tonight's friendly against the Netherlands pulls up underneath the Wembley concourse. First off is the manager, striding purposely into the bowels of the stadium. He wears a perfectly pressed blue shirt beneath his England blazer and his hair is immaculately parted. This is a man on a mission, this is a man in control.

If the match were being held a month ago, this manager would be Fabio Capello, the England boss since the end of 2007. But the Italian resigned exactly three weeks ago, furious that the FA had gone over his head and stripped the captaincy from John Terry while his court case for allegedly racially abusing an opponent was pending.

The FA called Capello in after he made comments on the matter to the Italian TV station RAI. 'I thought it was right that Terry should keep the captain's armband,' he reasoned on the programme. 'I have spoken to the chairman and I have said that, in my opinion, one cannot be punished until it is official and the court – a non-sport court, a civil court – has made a decision to decide if John Terry has done what he is accused of.' A resignation swiftly followed. Addio, Fabio.

For this first England match since his departure, a caretaker boss has been handed the reins – Stuart Pearce, the under-21s' manager and one of Capello's right-hand men in the senior set-up. It's Pearce who's now striding confidently through Wembley's corridors, who's looking so pristine. The Sex Pistols fan, the player formerly known as 'Psycho', looks every bit the Establishment man.

Pearce has previous when it comes to being caretaker manager, having performed that role at both Nottingham Forest and Manchester City, as well as with the under-21s. Weary of being typecast, though, he's also made no secret of his desire to at least lead the senior team to this summer's Euros in Poland and Ukraine, if not beyond. He has bona fide tournament experience, and not just as a player; three years ago, he led the England youngsters to the final of the European Under-21 Championship. Tonight is – in his head at least, and surely also in the heads of those in the corridors of power at the FA – a chance to prove himself, to stake his claim. No one says it out loud, but the next couple of hours are undoubtedly an audition.

Pearce is handling himself with grace and poise. He sings the national anthem with commitment, if not with quite the gusto he might employ shouting along to 'Anarchy in the UK' at the wheel of his car. He knows poise isn't enough. It needs to be mixed with a measure of passion, which he shows in the goalless first half when bellowing instructions from the touchline. It's not a completely level playing field he's inherited tonight, though. Several key players, including Wayne Rooney and Kyle Walker, are missing, while his three available strikers – Danny Welbeck, Daniel Sturridge and Fraizer Campbell – have a total of four caps between them.

By half-time, the blazer's off as Pearce heads back to the dressing room. He's sauntering rather than striding, suggesting contentment with the 0–0 scoreline, rather than agitation. However, a two-minute period in the second half alters his

demeanour. In the fifty-seventh minute, Arjen Robben brings
the ball from his own half and, astonishingly going unchallenged, rifles the ball past Joe Hart. A minute later, a Dirk Kuyt
cross finds the head of Klaas-Jan Huntelaar. 2–0. Pearce has
withdrawn to the bench, his face morose.

There is light and cheer, though. He hasn't necessarily failed
the audition. With five minutes left, Gary Cahill finds himself
the England player furthest forward (forward enough to actually be offside) and neatly controls a Leighton Baines through
ball before sliding it under the body of Maarten Stekelenburg.
A draw would be perfectly respectable against a team boasting
the stellar likes of Robben, Huntelaar and Robin van Persie,
so when Ashley Young deftly lifts the ball over the advancing
Stekelenburg to equalise in stoppage time, Pearce's frown has
at least been straightened out.

But then comes the killer blow. The Dutch go straight down
the other end and, despite having six Englishmen between him
and the goal, Robben waves that magic wand of a left foot and
places the ball, with unhuman accuracy, into the top corner.
He trots across to the enclave of orange-clad fans behind Hart's
goal and bows before them.

Pearce doesn't bow. He walks off, his feet slightly heavier than
they were a minute or two ago when Young scored. Up in the
press seats, Daniel Taylor of *The Guardian* will soon be ready to
file his copy for tomorrow's paper. 'Wembley hardly felt like a
place where the fans were campaigning for his appointment,'
Taylor writes. 'There was polite applause, an appreciation that
this is a man who would walk through plate glass for this team,
but nothing more.'

Taylor reads the room correctly. This will be the only time
Stuart Pearce will oversee the senior England side. At the start
of May, the FA will appoint the West Brom manager Roy
Hodgson as the team's next permanent manager. Pearce has to

make do with taking charge of Team GB's football squad at the London 2012 Olympics.

For one player, Pearce's caretaker spell had offered some hope, a glint of sunshine. Micah Richards had been recalled to the England set-up for the Netherlands match, having made just a single substitute appearance during the four-year reign of Capello. Pearce had instantly reinstated the right-back into the starting XI, into the role he'd previously performed for Capello's predecessor Steve McClaren. But with the caretaker now jettisoned, so too will Richards be, with Hodgson preferring to take Phil Jones to the Euros instead. Tonight, Richards plays his last game for England. He is twenty-three years of age.

England 2–3 The Netherlands

Five gold rings

Saturday 11 August 2012

Brazil vs Mexico

Olympic Games men's final

If you're Mexican, it's the perfect start. If you're Brazilian, it's potentially calamitous.

Just twenty-eight seconds are on the clock and the men in green are already ahead in the 2012 Olympic final. Manchester United full-back Rafael is caught in possession and the ball is quickly fed to striker Oribe Peralta, whose early shot catches the Brazilian goalkeeper Gabriel off guard. It's one of the fastest goals ever scored here at Wembley, coming just three seconds later than Louis Saha's opener for Everton in the 2009 FA Cup final, which itself was four seconds slower than the Paul Chow header that opened the scoring for Whitley Bay against Wroxham in the FA Vase final the following year.

The whirlwind opening means Mark Clattenburg, the referee, hasn't had a chance to drink it all in. It's a long way from officiating junior matches on the claggy pitches of County Durham as part of his Duke of Edinburgh's Award to the sun-kissed Olympic final.

He's defied the odds. Back then, he was just one of 33,000 referees in England, but now he's the highest regarded of the forty-eight officials selected for the Olympic tournament. Clattenburg's passage through the group stage and knock-out rounds – and, especially, his presence here at the competition's climax – has been aided by the demise of the Great Britain team. After their exit following a penalty shoot-out against South Korea in the quarter-finals, his path to the final has been cleared. There was no longer a national clash or conflict. Daniel Sturridge's missed spot-kick has done wonders for Clattenburg's career.

(The GB team's inability to reach the final four hasn't been mourned too heavily. The country's athletes have more than made up for disappointment on the football field with a hefty medal count over at the Olympic Stadium in Stratford. Tonight, Mo Farah will take a second long-distance gold with another imperious victory, this time in the 5,000 metres.)

Wembley has hosted an Olympic football final before, back in 1948 when Sweden took on and beat Yugoslavia. Another Englishman took charge of that match as well, with Great Britain's defeat to the Yugoslavs in the semi-finals allowing him to be handed the final. His name was William Ling, a referee from Cambridgeshire who, rather remarkably, had yet to officiate a single Football League game. His lack of experience seemed to tell in the final. Not only did he reject two strong Yugoslav shouts for penalties, but he also awarded Sweden one for an offence no more credible than the opposition's claims. As a result, noted the football historian Bernard Joy, 'their behaviour got out of hand for a spell'.

Clattenburg has no such difficulties this afternoon; it's a largely controversy-free affair. Neymar might be playing up front for Brazil but, at the age of twenty, his referee-baiting dark arts – which will go a long way to shaping public perception of him – are yet to be finely honed at this comparatively early stage of his career.

Even if there were to be flashpoints, Clattenburg looks supremely unflappable, despite the Brazilian coach Mano Menezes frequently wafting an imaginary yellow card towards him every time Mexico concede a free-kick. In the end, it's Brazil's left-back Marcelo who's first into the book for a clumsy challenge on goalscorer Peralta. For once, Menezes accepts the Englishman's judgement and sits back down.

With fifteen minutes remaining, a Peralta header doubles the Mexicans' advantage. Brazil are rattled and rupturing, with Clattenburg having to intervene when team-mates Rafael and Juan have a stand-up, in-your-face row. Nonetheless, an injury-time counter-attack goal from Hulk halves the deficit and there's still time for the game to be taken into an additional thirty minutes, but a header from future Chelsea star Oscar misses the target when scoring looked an easier prospect.

Clattenburg brings his whistle to his lips and ends Brazil's agony. Having scored three times in each of their five matches in the tournament, making them unassailable favourites, this afternoon they've largely been firing blanks. They've never won an Olympic gold. That run remains unbroken.

For Mexico, there's no Royal Box to climb up to, no trophy to raise. Instead, there's a podium to step onto and medals to be awarded (third-placed South Korea are here as well to collect their bronzes). These gold medals will be treasured for the rest of each Mexican player's days.

Mark Clattenburg will organise his own permanent reminder of this afternoon. He later visits a tattoo parlour, where he has the five Olympic rings inked onto the inside of his right wrist. It's an indelible commemoration of the most prestigious day so far in his refereeing career.

You can bet, back in 1948, William Ling didn't do the same.

Brazil 1–2 Mexico

Paper lions

Saturday 11 May 2013

Manchester City vs Wigan Athletic

FA Cup final

The difference in preparation couldn't have been starker, but the effect was the same.

Twenty-five years ago, Bobby Gould dispatched the more fidgety members of his Wimbledon cup final squad to the local pub to relieve boredom and/or erase nerves. A quarter of a century on, the notion of a boozy session ahead of a match – let alone the FA Cup final – is unthinkable, inconceivable.

Yesterday, rather than hand over a fistful of cash and allow his players to make a fleeting visit to oblivion, Wigan Athletic manager Roberto Martínez instead delegated the last round of pre-match preparations to a psychologist, a middle-aged man called Michael Finnegan.

Finnegan organised an exercise in which every player wrote down the individual strengths of each of their team-mates and why they would be honoured to walk out with them at Wembley fewer than twenty-four hours later. The players handed back the slips of paper to Finnegan and thought no more about it.

This morning, each player found an envelope that had been slipped under the door of their hotel room overnight. Inside were multiple strips of paper, each containing a personal testimonial penned by either a squad member or one of the backroom staff. They might be praising that player's stamina, his technical abilities, his leadership qualities, his never-say-die attitude. No criticism, just compliments. As a motivational tool, its simplicity was highly effective. Reading these testimonials, the players were pumped. Wigan Athletic, sitting not-so-pretty in the Premier League relegation zone with just one league match to go, were ready to take their A-game to Manchester City, the star-studded side second in the table.

Over the intervening quarter-century since Bobby Gould's unorthodox manoeuvre, the unpredictability of the cup final has been ironed out. The big clubs have applied a tight grip on the destination of the silverware; it's been a frequent visitor to the trophy cabinets of Arsenal, Chelsea and Manchester United in particular. The Nineties and the Noughties failed to produce a single cup final upset.

This changes this afternoon. After last season's last-gasp title win, Manchester City have had to be satisfied with the runners-up slot in the Premier League this year, surrendering their crown to their neighbours in red. Five years into Sheikh Mansour's reign at the Etihad, coming second no longer satisfies anyone in east Manchester. And coming second this afternoon is supposedly unthinkable.

Those in Wigan colours are thinking the unthinkable. While City won both league encounters between the two this season, neither was remotely close to the expected walloping. Indeed, the match at the Etihad less than a month ago was decided by only a single goal. Suspending their relegation worries for ninety or so minutes, this afternoon Wiganites are daring to believe.

And this belief is matched by the Latics' work rate and liveliness. They're sharp in the tackle, swift on the break. There's little to split the two sides. Possession is shared on an equal basis, while both register fifteen shots apiece. But there are two stats that make all the difference and that define the afternoon: red cards received and goals scored. With seven minutes left and the spectre of extra-time looming larger, City's right-back Pablo Zabaleta slides in late on Callum McManaman, the Wigan winger who's caused problems for Roberto Mancini's men all day. It's the Argentinian's second yellow. Like his compatriot Antonio Rattín nearly fifty years earlier, Zabaleta isn't shy in voicing his anger at being ordered to leave the Wembley pitch.

There's blood in the water and Wigan's sharks can sense it in their nostrils. As the clock strikes ninety and an additional three minutes are signalled, they earn a corner, attacking the end packed with their day-tripping fans. The ball's played in and their red-headed substitute Ben Watson produces a near-post flick header that flies past City keeper Joe Hart. It's a mirror image of the Wimbledon goal that downed Liverpool twenty-five years ago. Hart is Bruce Grobbelaar; Watson is Lawrie Sanchez.

Watson is a true fairy-tale hero. He's missed most of the season with a broken leg, only returning to first-team action earlier this month. His is a story that surely resonates with

Wigan's owner, Dave Whelan, who broke his leg in the 1960 final while with Blackburn. It appears to be in the fates.

There are fates in the City camp too. Reports in the *Daily Telegraph* this morning, replicated across Sky Sports News, announced that Mancini is going to be imminently sacked by the City board, regardless of the result this afternoon. While Wigan's players were still on a high from reading those motivational words at breakfast, City's squad were watching TV screens that informed them their leader could soon be driven out of town. Unwelcome uncertainty was the order of the day.

Time was that reaching the FA Cup final could buy a manager a further season or two of job security. Winning it might even earn him the freedom of the city. But within the next month, this afternoon's two managers, the two Robertos, will no longer be at their respective clubs. Mancini will be first to go, leaving Manchester just two days later, those rumours proving correct. The following day, Wigan will lose their penultimate league game of the season – and with it their top-flight status. They're the first FA Cup winners to be relegated from the top tier in the same season. Dave Whelan insists that Martínez's job is safe regardless of Wigan's final league position, but the Catalan's feet are itchy. Following David Moyes's departure to replace the retiring Alex Ferguson at Old Trafford, he's granted permission to talk to Everton about their manager's job, a vacancy that Martínez will fill a week later.

All change. All change.

Manchester City 0–1 Wigan Athletic

Klopps and Robbens

Saturday 25 May 2013

Bayern Munich vs Borussia Dortmund

Champions League final

It's a night of firsts. The first all-German Champions League final. The first time that a stadium has hosted the final twice within the space of two years (the reason being the commemoration of the FA's 150th anniversary). And it's the first time that Jürgen Klopp, the energetic manager of Borussia Dortmund, has brought a team to England's national stadium. Klopp, meet Wembley. Wembley, meet Klopp.

The teams wait in the tunnel while a heavily choreographed re-enactment of a medieval battle supposedly entertains the crowd on the pitch – hundreds of soldiers, archers and drummers, decked out like knights in the respective colours of Bayern Munich and Borussia Dortmund, charging around in perfect order, not a foot out of step. At the rear of the team line-ups, out of shot of everyone bar the long lenses of the TV companies, Klopp and his Bayern counterpart Jupp Heynckes share a warm embrace and an extended conversation.

They part, and Klopp returns to quiet introspection. He puffs his cheeks and lets out a long, controlled sigh. He's wearing a black tie underneath a suit jacket and a dark V-necked jumper, but the top button of his white shirt is already undone. He resembles a member of a funeral party a couple of drinks in at the wake.

This battle for European supremacy between Germany's two best teams is the latest chapter in a distrustful rivalry. And there's extra piquancy because of the elephant in the room. Or, rather, the creative midfielder in the stands.

At the age of twenty, Mario Götze is leaving Dortmund for Bayern in the summer, thanks to the latter triggering a release clause in his contract. It's perhaps fortunate that a thigh injury, gained in the semi-final against Real Madrid, rules him out of playing for his soon-to-be old club against his new employers. Klopp did his best to dissuade him from heading to Bavaria, but not even his charm worked. 'It was like a heart attack,' Klopp told Donald McRae from *The Guardian*, 'like somebody died. I couldn't speak.'

Understandably frustrated by Bayern's dominance of the Bundesliga (especially as his chief goalscorer, Robert Lewandowski, is also rumoured to be heading to Bavaria), in yesterday's press conference Klopp appealed to the neutrals, to those without skin in the game. He likened Dortmund to James Bond, whereas Bayern 'are the other guy' – the other guy being the baddie, the miscreant, the delusional individual hell-bent on world domination. Dortmund's wage bill is half that of Bayern.

This is Wembley's first glimpse of the Kloppian adoption of *gegenpress*, the fast and furious style that he dubiously describes as 'heavy metal football'. And it's Dortmund who enjoy the better of the early exchanges, creating a series of decent chances – but failing to score from any of them. Bayern regroup and strengthen as the game progresses and, on the hour, Arjen Robben is allowed to dance around the Dortmund penalty area and set up an easy opening goal for the Croatian striker Mario Mandžukić.

Klopp keeps any anger about the goal under wraps. He knows when to show emotion and when not to. There's still half an hour left and his players react better to calmness from the bench.

And within seven minutes Dortmund are level, thanks to an İlkay Gündoğan penalty awarded after a studs-up challenge from Bayern's Brazilian centre-back Dante. But, with ninety seconds left, Robben is again allowed to waltz his way through the Dortmund defence before slipping a mishit shot into the net. Klopp's puffed-out cheeks return.

Aside from the odd blast of invective towards his players, the officials and certain decisions, Klopp has been comparatively sanguine tonight. No great histrionics, no great touchline side-show. At the final whistle, he follows his team up to the Royal Box. There's a hand on his shoulder from the German chancellor Angela Merkel, a hug from Michel Platini. But Klopp is in no mood to talk, to receive platitudes, to accept sympathy. Fireworks explode from the Wembley arch into the dark north London night. He doesn't look up. Instead he just slowly saunters across the pitch, his hands deep in his pockets, his mind deep in thought.

For once, James Bond has lost. The other guy has won. 'The result is so shit,' he mutters.

Bayern Munich 2–1 Borussia Dortmund

The exorcist

Tuesday 15 October 2013

England vs Poland

World Cup qualifier

The ghosts are haunting the Wembley concourse tonight, phantom menaces whispering in everyone's ears, reminding all and sundry of horror stories past.

These ghosts have been waiting for four decades. Or, more precisely, four decades minus two days. For this coming Thursday marks the fortieth anniversary of one of the darkest days for the national team: 17 October 1973 – the night England failed to qualify for the World Cup for the first time ever, the night they ushered in seven more years of tournament-free football.

Tonight's parallels with 1973 are too close to ignore. England are one game away from qualification for next summer's World Cup. A win will take them there, but standing in the way again is the Polish national team. A dangerous side. A side able to absorb pressure before hitting their opponents hard on the break. A side with the capacity to break a nation's hearts.

The England players are doing their best to ignore the ghosts and their whispers, the soothsayers and the superstitious. As they walk from team bus to dressing room, some – Daniel Sturridge, Joe Hart, Jack Wilshere – are cocooned from the outside world by their headphones. They don't hear the snappers snapping away. Click, click, click. They avoid eye contact, either looking at their shoes or absently into space. Nerves and tension. Nerves and tension. Other players either don't believe in ghost stories, or they've never heard this particular one. Chris Smalling, Danny Welbeck and Jermain Defoe are more relaxed. Chuckles and smiles. Chuckles and smiles.

The stats suggest that England shouldn't find themselves in this predicament, that by now they should be home and hosed, home and dry. They're unbeaten in all nine qualifying matches before tonight, in the process scoring twenty-nine goals and conceding just four. They should be out of sight. But they're not. Four draws have meant eight points have been dropped. Four draws in nine matches. It should be no more than one or two.

Tonight, England's rivals for top spot in Group H, Ukraine, play San Marino. Currently a single point behind England, they will almost certainly win, and win well. So if England lose or draw tonight, the Ukrainians can start booking the team hotel in Brazil, while the hosts must take the long route to South America via the play-offs (or the second round, as it's officially labelled). Many matches are described as must-win encounters when they're not necessarily. Tonight's is.

Down in San Marino, Ukraine are playing in front of a 1,200-strong crowd. Eighty-five thousand are here at Wembley, but 20,000 of them are Poland fans. That's the official number at least, based on the amount of tickets the FA made available to them. Estimates put the number close to, if not more than, 25,000, with pockets of Poles dotted all around the stadium. 'We're Poland and we're playing at home,' they chant. In his match report, *The Guardian*'s Daniel Taylor will describe 'a night when Wembley often sounded more like Warsaw', a riot of noise created by Poland's 'raucous, beery, fire-cracking supporters'.

England stand in the tunnel. Primed, ready, waiting for the cue. Hart massages Steven Gerrard's shoulders, but the captain carries no outward sign of stress. He looks confident, positive, focused, determined. As ever, he's leading by example. England expects. So does Gerrard.

After those lacklustre draws earlier in the campaign, manager Roy Hodgson deployed much more positive tactics in last Saturday's 4–1 win over Montenegro, an approach that's continued this evening. Andros Townsend, an uncapped player this time last week, is particularly lively, cracking a long-range curling effort onto the bar. Minutes later, Danny Welbeck puts a gilt-edged chance wide. Both attempts show England mean business. But both chances also only come after a swift Poland counter-attack ends with Robert Lewandowski uncharacteristically failing to find the target. Frustration for the Poles, relief for the English. 'Fuck me' is Hodgson's considered response on the bench.

The breakthrough comes four minutes before half-time when Wayne Rooney converts Leighton Baines's cross. Rooney, who's supposed to be protecting a deep cut on his forehead sustained last month during training, had removed his protective headgear just before scoring with that angled header.

It's a slender lead to guard for the entire second half, so England go in search of a second to kill the match. It takes until the eighty-eighth minute when Gerrard is played in by James Milner. One touch. Inside the defender. Another touch. Beyond the defender. Final touch. A toe-poke home. It's a captain's goal, the kind of dogged, no-lost-cause effort that Bryan Robson would score on multiple occasions for his country. Gerrard slides on his knees towards the corner flag, soon to be consumed by a pile-on of team-mates. He's done what the likes of Channon and Bell and Chivers and Clarke couldn't manage forty years ago. England have qualified. The demons of '73 have finally been banished. Steven Gerrard, The Exorcist.

England 2–0 Poland

Early doors

Saturday 17 May 2014

Arsenal vs Hull City

FA Cup final

Arsenal fans have been waiting almost nine years for their club to win a trophy. Comfortably more than three thousand days.

Some would say, with some justification, that they've been spoilt during the Arsène Wenger era – at least during the early years of his reign, when open-top bus parades through the streets of Islington became an exceedingly common sight. The supporters of Hull City would certainly think Arsenal have had more than their fair share. They've had the longest wait to see their team in an FA Cup final. For ever, in fact. The Tigers are here today to make their first appearance at the competition's climax.

Sherard Pearson has certainly been patient. He was seven years old when Hull previously came close to the cup final – a semi-final defeat against, coincidentally, Arsenal in 1930. Sherard was there at Elland Road to watch the 2–2 draw, before the Londoners won the replay at Villa Park. Sherard Pearson is ninety-one years old.

He's one of tens of thousands of Tigers fans occupying the stadium's east end this afternoon. Hull itself is a ghost town, as its two rugby league clubs – Hull and Hull Kingston Rovers – are playing each other at the Etihad Stadium in Manchester as part of the Super League's Magic Weekend. It kicks off at five o'clock, exactly the same time that Wembley fires into action.

This presents a dilemma even for those who've stayed home. Steve Hubbard is particularly vexed. He's something of a Hull KR hero, having scored nine of their ten points, including the only try, in the 1980 Challenge Cup final here at Wembley – also against Hull. But he's a massive Tigers fan as well. 'It's ridiculous,' he sighs of the fixture clash. 'Everyone in Hull is mad keen to go to both.' In the end, he himself has gone to neither. Instead, Hubbard's chosen to watch the football live on TV and to record the rugby, watching it straight after to avoid hearing the score, to sidestep any spoiler alerts.

On the other side of the Atlantic, another hopelessly devoted Tigers fan, Patrick, also has a problem. It's half an hour before kick-off but, as he discloses to *The Guardian*'s online reporter, he's currently standing outside his daughter's ballet class in Bethesda, Maryland, 'praying the teacher lets them out on time to dash back to DC to fire up the laptop and watch the mighty Hull pull off an extraordinary win against the Arsenal'.

'Extraordinary' is definitely the word to describe the first fifteen minutes of the game. After Wigan's shock win over Manchester City in last year's final, Arsenal – who finished fourth in the league table while Hull ended up two places above the relegation zone – will not be going into the final lightly. Nonetheless, they couldn't have been prepared for what's about to happen.

Hull's playmaker Stephen Quinn floats the first corner of the game to the edge of the area in a rehearsed move straight from the training pitch. Tom Huddlestone meets it on the volley, but his shot is miscued and is heading wide – at least until the quick-thinking centre-back James Chester flicks the ball with his left boot, diverting it past Arsenal keeper Łukasz Fabiański. There are just three minutes and five seconds on the clock and Hull are ahead. Last year, Wigan left it late. This year, Hull have gone early.

Fewer than five minutes later, they're two up when another of their three centre-backs, Curtis Davies, pounces to slot home from a tight angle. The third centre-back, Alex Bruce, then almost makes it 3–0 but his looping header is cleared off the line. Arsène Wenger can't believe what he's seeing. No one can believe what they're seeing. We're still only thirteen minutes in.

But that's as close as Hull will come to scoring again. Four minutes later, Arsenal pull a goal back thanks to a scintillating Santi Cazorla free-kick into the far top corner. Hull's resolve is strong, though, and it takes the Gunners until the seventy-first minute to bring the scores level, when Laurent Koscielny bundles home a Cazorla corner. Arsenal smell blood now and want to finish Hull off inside the ninety. They have multiple chances but can't convert them.

Into extra-time and Hull are trying to hang on for a penalty shoot-out, but in the 109th minute, Aaron Ramsey latches on to an Olivier Giroud back-heel to fire Arsenal ahead. And that is that. After all those silverware-free years, Arsenal's trophy cabinet needs to be unlocked again. It's been an excellent final and a terrific comeback. But no comeback would have been required without Hull's sprinting-out-of-the-blocks start. And in that opening quarter of an hour, Steve Bruce's players – his defensive trio, especially – gave their supporters some extraordinary memories that will remain indelible for the rest of their lives.

Whether Patrick the exiled fan in Washington DC got back from ballet class in time to see those incredible fifteen minutes remains unknown.

Arsenal 3–2 Hull City

Sunday service

Sunday 23 November 2014

England vs Germany

Women's international friendly

The smile on the face of Karen Carney's niece is possibly even broader than that of the little girl's auntie. The two are hand in hand, stepping out of the bright lights of the Wembley tunnel and into a dank, damp November afternoon – and into the cacophony created by 45,000 enthusiastic voices.

It's a significant day for Carney. Although still only twenty-seven, today marks the England midfielder's 100th appearance for the national team. In a couple of minutes' time, she'll be called forward and handed a large Perspex cube, inside of which is a gold England cap. Her personal century is being marked, a figurative bat raised towards a figurative pavilion.

But, beyond Carney's short, unfussy presentation, this is not an afternoon for individual attention. The occasion is bigger than that. This is the first time that the new Wembley – if being seven years old constitutes still being 'new' – has welcomed England's women for an international match. A fair few of the starting XI played here during the 2012 London Olympics, when a single Steph Houghton goal gave Team GB victory over Brazil, but this is the first time they'll have done so with three lions on their chests.

It's been almost quarter of a century since England's women last graced Wembley; it was that 4–1 reverse to Italy in the old place back in 1990. In the meantime, they've been shuffling and shuttling between various lower league grounds for their home matches – the likes of Fratton Park in Portsmouth, London Road in Peterborough, Prenton Park in Tranmere and the poetically named Weston Homes Community Stadium, home of Colchester United. Indeed, the Lionesses' last home game before ascending to the national stadium was in Hartlepool.

That their return to Wembley is long overdue is shown in the attendance tonight. Many more would have poured through the turnstiles, but the FA has put a cap on ticket sales with more than an eye on major engineering works in the area, which are likely to affect supporters. The cap was announced after 55,000 tickets were sold, so the actual attendance of 45,619 does indeed show the effects of transport issues – plus the weather's dismal and the match is live on BBC Two. Interest has been high because everyone understands the significance of this afternoon's match. Members of star striker Eniola Aluko's family have flown in specially from Nigeria. 'Making history' says the headline on the front of the match-day programme. It's a fixture that's even been previewed in *Glamour* magazine.

It's just a shame that, for this landmark match, more beatable opponents hadn't been invited. Germany are eight-time European champions; they've won the last six tournaments. This is the nineteenth time England have lined up opposite them. The Lionesses have not won once. The celebratory mood currently bouncing around Wembley surely won't last.

Within just eight seconds of kick-off, the stadium's partially retractable roof nearly comes off when Jordan Nobbs thumps the ball against the German bar. Had it gone in, it would have been the fastest goal in ninety-one years of Wembley. And the crowd's reaction would surely have been heard back in central London. Five minutes later, though, they're largely silenced when, from a German corner, right-back Alex Scott places a glancing header into the corner of her own net. Largely silenced, but there are no moans and groans either. A setback is just a set-up for a comeback. In the stands, the band breaks into the main riff of 'Seven Nation Army'.

Six minutes later, though, a mix-up in midfield puts the German captain Célia Šašić, the Bundesliga's leading scorer, through on goal for Germany's second. With seventy-seven minutes still left, not all the positivity has drained from the England supporters; the more optimistic types are attempting to initiate a Mexican wave. But Šašić's second arrives on the stroke of half-time and effectively kills the game off. Gary Lineker perhaps harshly tweets: 'England's women footballers showing they can match the men by getting bashed by Germany.' The report in *The Independent*, casting its eye towards the forthcoming World Cup, was even less sentimental. 'Any talk of England returning from Canada with silverware next summer must be put in a box labelled "lunacy".'

The Germans continue to be England's bogey team – for just a few more months, at least. Next July, a Fara Williams penalty will be the difference between the two sides in the third-place play-off at that World Cup. But the true revenge for all those years of hurt, all those defeats, will come in 2022, right here at Wembley, right when it matters.

But for the time being, and despite the clamour for tickets for today's game, the national stadium does not now become the permanent home of the Lionesses. It's back to the lower league clubs for the next international match the following February. Destination: Milton Keynes.

England 0–3 Germany

The history woman

Saturday 1 August 2015

Chelsea vs Notts County

Women's FA Cup final

It has been quite a month for women's football in England. On the first day of July, the national team played their first ever World Cup semi-final. Exactly a month later, another threshold is being confidently breached: Wembley is just about to host its first ever Women's FA Cup final.

For centre-back Laura Bassett, the last month is one she will never forget. At the end of that World Cup semi-final, 4,000 miles away in the Canadian city of Edmonton, Bassett had been inconsolable. With the match against Japan poised at 1–1 and having ticked over into stoppage time, she inadvertently lobbed her own goalkeeper and agonisingly watched as the ball hit the underside of the bar and dropped over the line. Japan were through. England were out. She wanted the world to open up and swallow her.

Thirty-one days later and it's an optimistic, dry-eyed Bassett who's just about to lead her Notts County side out here at Wembley. The cliché that everyone's mentioning is that, should she lift the trophy in a couple of hours' time, it would be redemption for the mishap in Canada. Bassett herself doesn't think so.

'I really do believe they're two totally separate entities,' she tells the BBC before kick-off. 'I really don't think that would be cathartic. The only real cathartic moment will be in the future internationally – if we win the Euros, if we win the World Cup. Now *that* would be cathartic.'

Bassett's counterpart lining up next to her in the Wembley tunnel – the Chelsea captain Katie Chapman – has no such concerns. Now heading towards the early evening of her playing career, the midfielder is certainly no stranger to the closing stages of the competition. She's the owner of no fewer than *eight* FA Cup winner's medals, accumulated over a stretched-out club career spent exclusively in the capital, winning them with Millwall, Fulham, Charlton and Arsenal. Her first came when she was just fourteen. Now, at thirty-three, she's attempting to become a cup winner with her fifth club.

Chapman's career is all the more impressive considering she's taken breaks from the game to give birth to three sons. The middle one, six-year-old Riley, is one of Chelsea's mascots today. After the teams line up for handshakes and hymns, Chapman insists that Riley gives her a kiss for luck.

The ninety minutes that follow might be historic, but they're not the most dramatic the stadium has ever seen. The first half-hour is particularly lacklustre – until Eniola Aluko grabs hold of the game. She makes a number of incisive, streaky runs past the Notts County defenders. She sends in some tantalising crosses. She fires in numerous shots from various angles. She makes the difference.

It's fitting that it's Aluko who unlocks the County defence for the opening goal, cutting in from the left and picking a path into the box before setting up Ji So-yun. The South Korean, recently voted PFA Player of the Year by her fellow professionals, pokes the ball home for this historic final's equally historic first goal. And, it turns out, its only goal – despite Chelsea's domination of the second half, largely inspired by the electric Aluko.

It's been a landmark year for the Chelsea number 9. Like Bassett and Chapman, she was a valuable member of the England squad at the World Cup. But there's another reason that 2015 has been an important one. At the start of the year, Aluko qualified as a solicitor, studies that she's dovetailed with a highly successful playing career.

At the final whistle, Katie Chapman sprints off the pitch to leap on top of the Chelsea manager Emma Hayes in jubilation. All three of her sons are here today too; she'll celebrate with them shortly. Meanwhile, Laura Bassett, a Chelsea player last season, faces another dose of heartache. In Edmonton, she was the one being consoled after that freak own goal. This afternoon, she's the consoler-in-chief – hugs and pats on the back to stem others' tears. Then a glum trudge up those steps. At Wembley 2.0, there's extra punishment for the losers. There are 107 these days.

Chapman positively skips up them, arms outstretched to touch hands with dozens of fans. She lifts the cup with left-back Claire Rafferty, bouncing on her toes before kissing the trophy again, kissing it for the *ninth* time. Her team-mates are equally ecstatic. Aluko has comfortably won the player of the match award, her celebrations weighed down by lugging a magnum of champagne around the pitch with her.

It's Chelsea Ladies' first major piece of silverware, but it will be far from their last. In three months' time, they will become champions of the Women's Super League, a title they'll go on to win on five more occasions over the next seven seasons. In that time, Emma Hayes's players will also return to Wembley for three more FA Cup triumphs. Today has been the day that this new era in women's football has been kick-started.

One of those FA Cup wins, in 2018, will be Katie Chapman's tenth. No one else may ever come close to her astonishing record. But reaching double figures is finally enough for the captain and, five days later, she announces her intention to hang up her boots. The History Woman departs.

Chelsea 1–0 Notts County

Hawkesbury Ronaldo and Uncle Albert

Sunday 22 May 2016

Hereford vs Morpeth Town

FA Vase final

It's been a season unlike any other for non-league football, a time when the spotlight has shone brighter than ever before on the semi-pro game. A prime-time BBC One documentary series, *The Class of '92: Out of Their League*, has trailed five ex-Manchester United stars as they take over and run struggling Salford City, putting the trials and tribulations of non-league football into the nation's living rooms. The same club has regularly been the recipient of live BBC coverage of their run through the early stages of the FA Cup. And the rapid ascension of the top flight's current hotshot, Jamie Vardy, from semi-pro to the Premier League is the irresistible football story of the season.

Now, after Manchester United's victory over Crystal Palace in yesterday's FA Cup final, the BT Sport cameras have returned to Wembley for a day of action from further down the football pyramid. The history books start a new chapter today: it's the first time that the finals of both the FA Trophy and the FA Vase are being played on the same afternoon in the same stadium in a new initiative known as Non-League Finals Day.

The arrangement means that supporters will be heading towards Wembley from Herefordshire, Northumberland, West Yorkshire and Humberside, each side being allocated a quarter of the stadium for their fans. Later on, Halifax Town will beat Grimsby Town by a single goal in the Trophy final, but it's the precursor, the Vase final between Hereford and Morpeth Town, that provides optimum interest and intrigue.

Most conspicuous is the vast number of fans that Hereford have brought with them, filling their allocation of 20,000 seats. This would be extraordinary under any circumstances for a club in English football's ninth tier, but it's scarcely believable bearing in mind this is the club's first season in existence. And what a season. Formed from the embers of Hereford United, they have swept all before them, winning the Midland Football League Premier Division title, the Herefordshire County Cup and the Midland Football League Cup. In the league, they finished with a goal difference of plus-108. By 2 p.m., the greatest prize of all for a ninth-tier club could be theirs: will the FA Vase become their fourth trophy in four short weeks?

Not only are the massed ranks of their fans providing great pictures for the BT Sport cameras, but so too is their special guest for the day: a prize bull named Hawkesbury Ronaldo, who's currently being paraded around the outskirts of the pitch as if he were at a cattle auction rather than the national football stadium. It will turn out that Hereford's porous defence could have done with Hawkesbury Ronaldo's sturdy presence in the back four.

It all starts off promisingly for Hereford when those 20,000 are sent into rapture by an opening goal from their midfielder Rob Purdie with barely a minute on the clock. The floodgates appear to have been opened right from the off and there's an inevitability in the air that Hereford's free-scoring ways will be putting Morpeth to the sword. But after such a long, stamina-sapping season, and despite the honour and thrill of playing at Wembley, Hereford soon run out of gas.

Morpeth score a scrappy equaliser ten minutes before the break and then, by the time the clock ticks around to the hour mark, the Northumbrians are 3–1 up. A last-minute fourth goal condemns Hereford to the most disappointing day in their – admittedly short – history.

In overpowering their opponents, Morpeth have upheld the strong Vase record of clubs from the north-east. Since 2009, the region's teams have now won the competition seven times in eight years – single victories for North Shields, Spennymoor and Dunston, plus a hat-trick of triumphs for Whitley Bay. Next year, South Shields will extend the tradition even further.

As Morpeth stretched away in the second half, the focus of attention shifted away from those previously unstoppable Bulls and towards the opposition's number 5. Chris Swailes' chest supplied that scrappy equaliser, an unspectacular finish to an historic goal. At the age of forty-five, Swailes has not only picked up his third Vase winner's medal, but he has also become the oldest player to score in a Wembley final. Old enough to be the father of several of his team-mates, the veteran – nicknamed Uncle Albert – has been around the block many times over, mainly in the lower reaches of the Football League, but also including a short spell in the top flight with Ipswich. He's no stranger to the operating table, either; his limbs have several metal plates inserted into them, while he's also had several interventions for a serious heart condition.

Never mind Hawkesbury Ronaldo. He's halfway back to

Herefordshire. Chris Swailes is now the story of this historic first Non-League Finals Day.

Hereford 1–4 Morpeth Town

Green day

Sunday 14 May 2017

Forest Green Rovers vs Tranmere Rovers

National League play-off final

With their impeccable eco credentials and strict vegan diets, Forest Green Rovers are seen in football circles as distinctly unconventional. Nonetheless, such thoroughly modern ways don't preclude them from being as irrationally superstitious as any other club.

Two seasons ago, Grimsby Town were the beaten finalists in the National League play-off final. Last season, they returned to Wembley and won. Forest Green were their opponents who, back in the final this afternoon, are frantic to emulate the Mariners' achievement of transforming themselves from runners-up to promoted side. So they do like Grimsby did. Ahead of last year's final, Forest Green stayed at the extremely well-appointed Landmark hotel on Marylebone Road in central London. Last night, they stayed at the Hilton in Wembley, barely a goalkeeper's clearance from the stadium's turnstiles. This is where Grimsby stayed twelve months ago. They're hoping for the magic to rub off.

(Something else that Forest Green do differently this year is choosing not to sack their manager on the eve of the play-offs. They took this extraordinary measure twelve months ago to a collective raised eyebrow from the entire football world.)

Not all the Forest Green backroom staff were put up at the Hilton last night. Back in rural Gloucestershire, the club's press officer Richard Joyce wakes early ahead of previewing the game on the local BBC radio station, before driving the 110 miles to north London. Usually he operates solo, but today he's recruited a couple of helpers to assist him with the media duties. It's going to be a busy day, especially if they win. And if they do win, Joyce has an innovative idea he's aiming to execute on the final whistle.

Come three o'clock, Joyce and his team are all set up on Wembley's press benches. He's also employed the services of a couple of freelance photographers; one behind each goal to ensure any golden Forest Green moments aren't missed. Further along, in the Royal Box, the club's owner Dale Vince takes a deep breath. Wearing a leopard-print shirt that's undone to halfway down his chest, the environmentalist isn't the usual buttoned-down figure found in the posh seats. But he doesn't feel out of place. He was here last year, of course. They've had the dress rehearsal; now it's time for the full performance. Will Forest Green's status as a non-league club for the last 128 years end this afternoon?

They might be a highly principled, free-thinking football club, but they're not sentimental either. Only two players in last year's starting XI are on the pitch come kick-off. One of the new players – the winger Kaiyne Woolery – will play a starring role. It's been quite a season for the Londoner. Back in August, he was playing for Bolton in League One before transferring to Wigan of the Championship. He then headed to Gloucestershire on loan to play in his third different division this season. And now he's at Wembley.

It's Woolery who breaks the tension just a dozen minutes in when, unchallenged by a single Tranmere player, he closes in on goal and fires a low, firm shot past goalkeeper Scott Davies. The delight is short-lived. The Merseysiders hit back ten minutes later thanks to a Conor Jennings thunderbolt from the edge of the area.

Forest Green reassert themselves when their top scorer Christian Doidge collects the ball wide on the left. His lengthy strides (he used to play basketball for Wales) swiftly take him to the eighteen-yard line from where he rifles home. And three minutes later, they make it three when Woolery catches Tranmere captain Liam Ridehalgh in possession and, through on goal, passes the ball into the net.

Forest Green's two-goal margin goes unthreatened in the second half and football's eco-warriors are a non-league club no more. Here in the departure lounge that is the play-off final, they've been cleared for take-off. Tranmere are grounded for another season.

Richard Joyce prepares himself for the post-match deluge. 'The coverage we got was unbelievable,' he recalls five years later. 'Apart from maybe Salford City because of their Class of '92 connections – and with the greatest respect to other clubs – I can't imagine another football club winning the National League play-off final being on the BBC six o'clock news. That was down to the club's unique identity. We were on 5 Live, we were on Radio 1's *Newsbeat*. When we turned up at our stadium the following evening for our party, ITV News were broadcasting live as the coach pulled up. It was quite stressful because my phone was constantly buzzing as everyone was going through me. But I would never swap that for the quiet life of finishing mid-table and achieving nothing. I'd take the stress all day long.'

Before all these media demands, though, Joyce unveils his secret plan. With phone in hand, he follows the players up the

Wembley steps, sneaking behind them to broadcast the experience to the nation on Facebook Live. 'People could watch what the players' eyes were seeing when they were collecting the trophy. It was as if a player was wearing a GoPro.' Wembley has come some long way from the cumbersome, static cameras of Pathé News.

But no matter the innovation, no matter the success, Forest Green's ascension to the Football League would be bittersweet for Joyce. That summer, after three years as full-time press officer and match-day announcer, plus three part-time years there while a student, the club will announce he's on his way. 'Following our promotion to the Football League and increased interest from press around the world, we needed to reorganise our communications team and created a more senior position. His current press officer role was made redundant and Rich did not want to apply for the new job.'

Innovative but unsentimental.

Forest Green Rovers 3–1 Tranmere Rovers

Sitting tenants

Sunday 20 August 2017

Tottenham Hotspur vs Chelsea

Premier League match

As ever, Daniel Levy's face is inscrutable, unreadable. Immaculately dressed in crisp white shirt and spotless club blazer, the Tottenham chairman and his fellow directors take in the scene. They need to get used to the view; this is their perch for this season. Some take out phones and snap away, keen to commemorate the occasion. Levy doesn't. He's not one for quick snaps. He's more about the long game.

Instead, he looks upwards at the Wembley arch, admiring its geometry, appreciating the engineering underpinning it. In recent years, Levy has gained a strong understanding of the complexity of large-scale engineering projects, gained as he's steered the protracted rebuild of White Hart Lane over in N17. When it's completed, the new Spurs stadium will be even more impressive than the 10-year-old, not-so-new Wembley. For now, though, the national stadium will do.

Today's match isn't the first league fixture to be played at Wembley. Halfway through the 1930–31 season, Clapton Orient of Division Three (South) played two of their home matches at Wembley, against Brentford and Southend United, while alterations were being made to their Lea Bridge Road ground – namely the removal and relocation of wooden fencing that opponents complained was too near the pitch.

Fewer than 2,000 made their way across London for the Southend game.

In contrast, there are 73,587 Londoners of both persuasions here today. The fixture computer has been kind, giving the occasion a match to savour. Tottenham were runners-up in the Premier League last season and their opening home game of the new campaign pitches them against the reigning champions.

There are concerns among the Spurs faithful that the dimensions of the Wembley pitch – significantly larger than White Hart Lane, the smallest in the Premier League last season – won't allow their team to play its customary pressing game, one that worked so well over the last twelve months. They went the entire campaign without losing a single league game at home; in fact, they won all but two. As the curtain fell on White Hart Lane, it became a fortress. But now, three months on from the charging bulldozers and swinging wrecking balls moving in, the fortress has been flattened. It is no more. A new citadel needs to be established.

That doesn't happen this afternoon. Chelsea take the lead after twenty-four minutes when Marcos Alonso's curling, eye-of-a-needle free-kick proves to be an opening goal befitting the occasion. Harry Kane comes closest for Spurs when he smacks a shot again the post, but then, inside the last ten minutes, unlikely intervention comes courtesy of Chelsea striker Michy Batshuayi, who neatly heads home into his own net. There's still time to turn this draw into all three points, but Spurs don't take it. Chelsea do, though, the wing-back Alonso bagging his second with a low shot from the left. That unbeaten home league run has come to an end at the first time of asking in the new place. Indeed, it will take Spurs until mid-October to register their first league win underneath the arch.

Levy and his directors leave their perch. The phones stay in the pockets; they don't want to commemorate this particular scene in photographs. Still immaculate, still unreadable, Levy will be hoping for better days than this in the months to come.

Tottenham Hotspur 1–2 Chelsea

Home turf

Saturday 18 May 2019

Manchester City vs Watford

FA Cup final

With every week that passed, the kids could see the monster growing. It loomed larger and larger, visible in the gaps between the buildings on the Harrow Road until its arch appeared over the tops of the shops, above the laundrette and the greengrocer's and the fried chicken outlets. The centre of gravity, the meridian line, of English football was right here in their backyard.

Raheem Shaquille Sterling was one of these kids, passing within a couple of hundred yards of the new stadium twice a day on his way to and from his secondary school – Copland Community School, just off Wembley High Road. He was five years old when the last match was played at the original Wembley, that damp squib between England and Germany. He had recently arrived from Jamaica with his mum, Nadine Clarke, and was living on the nearby St Raphael's estate, a sprawl of low-rise streets squeezed in between the national stadium and the North Circular. As a primary school kid, he would see the wrecking balls reducing the skyline to rubble, flattening the twin towers to dust. Then he would see the cranes move in, ready to build the new monster from the ground up.

By this point, Sterling — a fine athlete, like his former national-standard sprinter mum — was the hottest football property in all of the catchment area of Brent. Despite his diminutive size, he was playing in, and dominating, matches well beyond his age group. A career as a pro surely beckoned. It seemed that Raheem Sterling might just be destined to make the new stadium his second home. It seemed it was being built just for him.

This afternoon, Sterling is back on his old stomping ground, just a few hundred yards from his childhood front door. He's been back since, of course — playing here eighteen times for England, as well as appearances for Manchester City, including twice this season in the EFL Cup final against Chelsea in February and the FA Cup semi-final against Brighton last month.

But this is the FA Cup final — the fixture of the footballing calendar that made this stadium known across the world, from Kathmandu to Caracas. And this afternoon it's Raheem Sterling's first FA Cup final too. The local boy is keen to make an impression. And he will, with the team's all-round performance delivering the biggest margin of difference in a cup final. Watford will be hit for six.

It could all have been so different.

Ten minutes in, with the game still goalless, a swift Watford counter-attack sees Gerard Deulofeu playing in Roberto Pereyra. The Argentinian is straight though on goal but City goalkeeper Ederson is quickly at the edge of his box to stifle the shot. Then Watford have a strong shout for a penalty after Vincent Kompany appears to handle, but their claims are waved away. It's not going to be their afternoon. It'll be City's.

David Silva gets the first goal after twenty-six minutes before

Gabriel Jesus doubles the lead. Sterling tries to steal the goal for himself, but the Brazilian's shot has just crossed the line before he smashes it into the net. The master magician Kevin De Bruyne doesn't enter the field of play until ten minutes into the second half, but it takes him only six minutes to conjure up City's third. (Indeed, he plays just thirty-five minutes but still wins the man-of-the-match award.) By now they're cutting Watford to ribbons and Jesus soon adds the fourth.

With nine minutes left, Sterling belatedly makes his impression on the scoresheet, first converting a Bernardo Silva cross and then doing likewise to a De Bruyne centre. He used to score goals for fun on the football pitches of Copland School just over the way and he's doing so again this afternoon. The dream – shown in the tattoo on his right arm that depicts the young Sterling, number 10 on his back and ball under his arm, gazing up at the Wembley arch – has come true.

When that sixth City goal goes in, Pep Guardiola buries his head in his hands, not out of frustration, but in embarrassment that today has been so easy. It's the final's largest margin of victory for 110 years and secures an unprecedented domestic treble for the Spaniard and his club – Premier League, EFL Cup and FA Cup.

It's the perfect time for Vincent Kompany to bow out. A true City legend, tomorrow the captain will announce his return to his boyhood club Anderlecht, this time in a player-manager role. That'll be his homecoming. Today, Raheem Sterling has had his.

Manchester City 6–0 Watford

The 2020s

The sound of silence

Saturday 1 August 2020

Arsenal vs Chelsea

FA Cup final

Kris Temple isn't where he would usually be found on cup final day. Normally he'd be stationed just behind the team benches, within easy earshot of the substitutes and backroom staff. And with one of the best views in the house.

This year, he's positioned further up Wembley's North Stand, just below the press boxes. His view is no worse – and today it's unencumbered by anyone obscuring his view. This afternoon's cup final, rescheduled from May, is like no other that's ever been played before. There isn't a single fan of either side – no Arsenal red, no Chelsea blue – in the stadium. This is football in the time of Covid-19.

This makes Temple's task more than a little strange this afternoon. Some might say it makes him redundant. He is the official announcer here at Wembley: the person to gee up the crowd beforehand, to introduce the pre-match entertainment, to run through the line-ups, to detail the substitutions, to announce the scorers, to hail the winners. Last year, he had a captive audience of nearly 86,000, half of whom were deliriously cheering his goal announcements as Manchester

City hit those six past Watford. Today, he's talking to no fans at all.

'During the pandemic, and depending on a club's point of view, a stadium announcer has either been seen as an essential part of the staff or not. After all, why would they be using you? Who are you talking to? Fortunately, I was seen as essential. The FA decided they needed an announcer at Wembley. There's a lot of protocol stuff – the possible presentation of trophies, the national anthem in the case of England matches – and someone is needed to lead that over the PA.

'Announcers are also there for the players. That's an overlooked part. In this situation, you're trying to create as much of an atmosphere as you can without the supporters. If a player scored and there was no announcement, it would feel less like a real occasion.' With no crowd reaction, it falls on Temple and his cohorts to fill in the silence as much as possible, to try to make it not sound like a practice match or behind-closed-doors friendly. 'I'm not saying that players listen to everything I say, but there is at least the sound of me in the stadium, if only in the background. Plus, the broadcasters want some genuine noise. They want any part of the atmosphere that they can get.'

Nonetheless, having an announcer as full-on as normal in an empty ground is a little misplaced. 'Obviously you have to scale back what you're doing. You can't be the shouty person that many are in a full stadium as that would just sound ridiculous. Yes, you might still announce a goalscorer with a little bit of energy to make that player feel good or to come across on the broadcast, but ultimately you've got to wind back the enthusiasm at least a few per cent.'

This can be hard sometimes, especially if a goalscorer's name itself is conducive to a shout-out. Take Pierre-Emerick Aubameyang, for instance. His surname lends itself to an exclamation. 'Au-bam-e-yang!'

'Some names definitely work better than others,' agrees Temple. 'Some are a nightmare, with nothing to get hold of. Take Harry Kane, for instance. His surname is just one syllable. There's not much you can do except elongate it. "Aubameyang", though, has a few bits you can get hold of.'

Temple will have a couple of opportunities to exclaim Aubameyang's name over the next couple of hours. After Christian Pulisic gives Chelsea an early lead, in the process becoming the first American to score in a cup final, the Gunners captain equalises with a twenty-eighth-minute penalty. On goes the mic. 'The goalscorer for Arsenal is number 14, Pierre-Emerick Au-bam-e-yang!' Temple's voice echoes around the empty stands, a sound he's still getting used to. 'When you're greeted by silence, that would normally mean your mic isn't on or you've made such a hash of someone's name that everyone's quietly giggling rather than reacting.'

Temple reprises his Aubameyang goal announcement exactly halfway through the second half when the striker clips a dinked finish over Willy Caballero's head, which turns out to be the winning goal. Mikel Arteta has now won the FA Cup with Arsenal as both captain and manager.

As much as his name is an announcer's dream, Aubameyang gives Temple a headache after the game. Covid restrictions dictate that there's no traditional presentation at the top of the steps. Instead, the celebrations take place at ground level on the pitch, with the winning captain retrieving the famous cup from a plinth before carrying it back to his ecstatic team-mates. He might be highly adept at scoring multiple times in a cup final, but Aubameyang is showing difficulty with simpler tasks.

'Leave the base! Leave the base!' calls out an official, but Aubameyang seems deaf to his pleas, and instead carries both trophy and base across to where his team-mates are waiting. It's too much of a handful and, just as he's about to lift the trophy, he clumsily drops it to the turf. As it is, the trophy presentation is a potentially tricky climax to the announcer's day; even more so if the winning captain has butter fingers.

'One of the hardest things to nail is that trophy-lift moment,' explains Temple. 'You have to choose your moment to start the sentence. I know how many words I have to say before I get to the name of the winning team. And are they going to do the 'Woooooooooo-aaaaaah!' wiggly-hands thing? Plus, you've probably got someone waiting to press the button on the fireworks and streamers, so getting it right isn't just an ego massage for me. It's that other people are waiting on my cue too. The fireworks and streamers need to go off as the cup is raised into the air.'

Despite the trophy drop, Temple does get it right this afternoon. He's already started his sentence, but fortunately has yet to reach the word 'Arsenal'. A ten-second pause puts things back on track and Aubameyang raises the trophy just as 'Arsenal!' comes over the PA and the fireworks erupt.

The explosions echo around an empty Wembley.

Arsenal 2–1 Chelsea

The final countdown

Wednesday 7 July 2021

England vs Denmark

European Championship semi-final

'It's the biggest game of our careers,' says Gareth Southgate. 'We won't be content unless we pick that trophy up on Sunday.'

Ahead of a European Championship semi-final at Wembley, Southgate is in an ebullient mood. But this isn't Southgate the bearded, suited-and-booted fiftysomething, the England boss. These are words from a quarter of a century ago, uttered by Southgate the clean-shaven, tracksuit-wearing twenty-something, the England defender. But the sentiment remains. You can imagine him saying a very close approximation of these words in the dressing room this evening, motivating his players, a good few of whom weren't even alive during the summer of '96.

Southgate won't need reminding of that semi-final against Germany all those years ago. But the scar could finally heal tonight if his young charges can overcome Kasper Hjulmand's Denmark.

There are so many parallels with the pre-match fervour of twenty-five years ago. The excitement, the anticipation, the inescapable sense of destiny. There are even visual echoes of 1996: one of England's mercurial midfielders, Phil Foden, has opted for the same short, peroxide haircut as Paul Gascoigne sported back then. The word is that, should England win the tournament come Sunday, the whole squad will also go perox-ide. Foden's barber – Sheldon Edwards of Clapham Junction, also the hairdresser of choice of Raheem Sterling and Jadon Sancho – needs to keep his diary clear.

As before the Euro '96 semi-final, the country is gripped by an irresistible fervour. Yesterday, the band of the Queen's Guards performed a big-band version of 'Three Lions' on the front lawn of Clarence House, Prince Charles's pad when he's in London; this morning, Atomic Kitten reformed on Heart's breakfast show to sing a new version of their old hit 'Whole Again'. Its lyrics have been revised. Apparently Southgate is the one who still turns them on.

Some of the nation's broadcast journalists have been in posi-tion outside Wembley since 6 a.m., some fourteen hours before kick-off. At the fan zone in Trafalgar Square, the more dedicated England supporters will be putting in a similar-length shift.

Writing in *The Guardian*, the journalist Barney Ronay shares a note of concern. Too often England performances at the national stadium have been limp, dispassionate affairs. He's hoping for Wembley to become a sizzling cauldron against the Danes, for it not to be witness to 'the anti-energy of those midweek friendlies when the national stadium carries all the fierce, scalding passion of a night at the Ideal Home Exhibition'.

Ronay needn't have worried. By early evening, the place is buzzing. The crowd won't stand for any limp performance. This time, the song of choice in the stands is 'Sweet Caroline' rather than 'Three Lions', a song of celebration rather than expectation. Standing on a platform high above one of the goals and bathed in golden late-evening sunshine, ITV's anchorman Mark Pougatch rightfully interprets this giddiness as a response to the comparative release from Covid restrictions, to 'the sense of human beings expressing some joy and normality'.

There certainly isn't the intensity of a clash against an old enemy. The tournament has seen Denmark become most people's second team of choice, after their midfield magician, Christian Eriksen, suffered an on-field cardiac arrest during their group match against Finland three and a half weeks ago. No one can deny them their place in the last four. Their squad has been through the ringer. Although ongoing travel restrictions mean no Danish fans can come here from home, 6,000 expat Danes have created a sea of red at their end of the stadium.

Before kick-off, England captain Harry Kane presents his opposite number, Simon Kjær, with an England shirt. Signed by the entire squad, 'Eriksen 10' is printed on the back. It's an especially poignant gesture for Kjær. It was he who, when his team-mate collapsed in the Finland game, was first on the scene, sprinting the length of the field to clear Eriksen's airway and commence CPR. It's no exaggeration to say that Kjær saved his life.

There's no repetition of Alan Shearer's early goal in the 1996 semi-final tonight and that's possibly to England's advantage. No overconfidence, no feeling of inevitability. Indeed, Denmark are the last team to have beaten England here. Instead, a sense of jeopardy will keep minds focused. And, in the twenty-ninth minute, that sense of jeopardy is made flesh in the form of an immaculate free-kick from the baby-faced Danish winger Mikkel Damsgaard. As a measure of England's march in the last fortnight, it's the first goal they've conceded all tournament.

Fired up, England go into attack mode and Sterling sees his shot manfully blocked by Kasper Schmeichel from point-blank range. But the Leicester keeper can't do anything six minutes from half-time when, in attempt to stop Sterling getting on the end of Bukayo Saka's cross, the unfortunate Kjær slides the ball into his own net. The national hero does not deserve this.

Schmeichel comes to the rescue again to thwart England's best chance in the second half, making a flying one-handed save to deny his former club team-mate Harry Maguire a headed goal. Sterling remains in the thick of things and when, fourteen minutes into extra-time, he's tripped by Joakim Mæhle, England are handed their ticket to the final. Kane's penalty is saved by Schmeichel, but the captain smashes the rebound home. And when Denmark are reduced to ten men through injury for the second half of extra-time, Danish hopes are extinguished.

Twenty-five years on, the young Southgate's blushes are finally spared. His older self has created redemption. He has reached the final.

England 2–1 Denmark

The madding crowd

Sunday 11 July 2021

England vs Italy

European Championship final

Sunday morning and John Murray wakes up in his room in a central London hotel. He's woken up in many rooms in many hotels during his twenty-seven years with the BBC, but today may turn out to be the most significant day of his career. With the England men's team gracing the final of a major tournament for the first time since 1966, Murray is entrusted to call all the shots – and the fouls and the tackles too – for BBC Radio 5 Live. For those unable to be in front of a television screen at eight o'clock this evening, he will be their guide. A Wolstenholme moment may just await the man from Northumberland.

As lunchtime approaches, Murray has the chance to sink into his own thoughts, to reflect in the calm before the storm. 'I wouldn't want to build up my role in it because I know where I am in the pecking order, but I was thinking, *This could be the greatest experience of my career.*

'I'd been asked a lot that week, "What are you going to say if England win?" I had no idea. Wolstenholme's commentary wasn't pre-prepared. He just said what he saw and encapsulated it perfectly. So that's always my fall-back position. If I can't think of anything profound, I'm just going to say what I see.

'That morning, I wanted to go and have a walk to see what the feeling was like as I'd read a lot about what it was like at Wembley ahead of '66. I walked out of the hotel, thinking there'd be England fans on the streets and how this would have been just how it was back then. Around two or three o'clock in the afternoon, I got on the Tube and went to the stadium. When I stepped off the train, there were a lot of England fans at the station getting back *on* the Tube. I remember thinking that was strange, but not thinking anything more about it. But when I look back, that was the first indicator that all was not well. Even when I reached the top of the steps at the Tube station and looked down on Olympic Way, which was absolutely packed, I thought, *Oh, fantastic. Look at this. It's the middle of the afternoon and they're here already.*'

But all was indeed not well.

'As soon as I got down to ground level, it became very clear what was going on, that there were a lot of very, very drunk people there. People were climbing lamp-posts and full cans of drink were being thrown into the air. A lot of people with families were clearly quite worried and concerned.'

Although travelling alone and notably tall, Murray's progress towards the stadium is slow. A veteran of commentating at Wembley, he knows this patch well, but his local knowledge is failing him; his short cuts are all fenced off. He's concerned for his safety too. 'I thought, *I'm going to get hit on the head by a can and I'm going to be out of the match. I'm not even going to get into the stadium.*'

Ninety-eight years after 13-year-old Ernie Thunder and his Auntie Hilda squashed and squeezed their way into an oversubscribed Wembley, the man from the BBC is doing likewise. Once he eventually gets into the stadium and up to his commentary eyrie, Murray is broadcasting almost straight away. 'It was the Wimbledon men's final that day and we went on air during one of the breaks to do a turn. Almost the first thing I said was that if anyone was coming to Wembley, try to find a different route and not come up Olympic Way.'

Once Novak Djokovic has dispatched the Italian Matteo Berrettini to win his seventh Wimbledon singles title, all ears are tuned to Wembley. By then, Murray and his colleagues are well aware of what's occurring both inside and outside the stadium, of hundreds of ticketless fans trying to surge their way in. They feel duty-bound to describe it to the nation.

In five months' time, Baroness Casey's report on the day's events will be published – a damning indictment of bad behaviour and poor organisation that explains how there were seventeen mass breaches of the stadium's security with 2,000 fans, fuelled by drink and cocaine, targeting disabled entrances to gain entry. One fan even posed as a steward and hijacked a child in a wheelchair, separating them from their father, to gain access into the ground. The report describes the events as a 'perfect storm of lawlessness', consisting of 'a series of "near-misses" which could have led to significant injuries or even death'.

The Casey report is for later. The match is now about to kick off. Murray might not know what he's going to say in the event of an England victory, but his introduction meets the scale of the occasion. 'Here we are. The moment has arrived at Wembley. This is the biggest football match for England for fifty-five years.'

He doesn't have to wait long to describe an England goal. There aren't even two minutes on the clock when Luke Shaw makes a pitch-long run along the left flank to arrive unannounced in the Italy area and thump home his first ever England goal. 'Shaw scores! On the volley! England lead!'

Even though England hold that early lead until halfway through the second half, when Leonardo Bonucci equalises for Italy, Murray hasn't been holding optimistic thoughts. 'It felt like there was an inevitability that it wouldn't go England's way. Chris Sutton was with us that night and I remember saying to him at half-time: "England aren't going to win this. It just doesn't feel right, the whole thing."' It was something more than the usual England fatalism that emerges on the big occasion, when the match almost inevitably lurches towards being decided on penalties.

The shoot-out is a notably topsy-turvy affair, one to test a commentator's maths skills along with their powers of description. Both sides score their first kicks, before the advantage swings England's way after Andrea Belotti fails from twelve yards. Then Marcus Rashford, brought on as a sub in the final minute of extra-time specifically to take a penalty, misses England's third. It's even-steven.

Jadon Sancho, another 120th-minute sub, takes England's fourth penalty. He too fails to convert. Advantage Italy. Up steps Chelsea's Jorginho, arguably the most consistent penalty-taker in the Premier League over the last few seasons. If he scores, Italy win. But Jordan Pickford's big right hand tips his kick onto the post. A lifeline. Up in the press box, John Murray is having trouble forming sentences. 'Oh! Ohhh! Have you ever . . . ?'

But Bukayo Saka still needs to score England's fifth penalty to take it into sudden-death. There's fear in his teenage eyes and he joins the pantheon of those who've missed crucial spot-kicks in knock-out tournaments for England. His manager knows just how he feels. This was him twenty-five years ago.

The difference between the two occasions, though, will be the reaction. In 1996, it was only the infrastructure of New Southgate station that bore the brunt of frustration and anger. In 2021, cowardly keyboard warriors take to social media to unleash disgusting racist vitriol towards Saka, Sancho and Rashford. The bad taste of the evening just became even more poisonous.

Murray hasn't got any words prepared to describe a defeat. He just says what he sees. 'Gareth Southgate's England lose in a penalty shoot-out in the final. What a twist, what a terrible twist for England.'

The following days offer Murray a chance to gather his thoughts. Even though he may never get to commentate on an England team in a major final again, he's almost relieved that his Wolstenholme moment didn't come that evening.

'My reflection afterwards was that I didn't think it would have been right for England to have won that night. A lot of people had behaved exceptionally badly and I felt it would have been wrong for them to have been rewarded after what happened. That might be looking at it in a small-minded way, bearing in mind it would have given great joy to millions if England had won, but that's how I felt having been there on the night.

'Plus, if England had won, that bad behaviour would have

been airbrushed out. It would have just been about the euphoria of winning. It was important that it wasn't forgotten.'

England 1–1 Italy
(Italy win 3–2 on penalties)

'I just couldn't see us getting beat'

Sunday 31 July 2022

England vs Germany

Women's European Championship final

Three hundred and eighty-five days after the men's team graced the European Championship final, England's women have arrived at Wembley, keen and eager to show their male counterparts how to win the continent's biggest trophy. And their fans are showing exactly how to behave before such a significant match. The place is buzzing.

England's tournament has, in large part, been defined by their substitutes. Well, by one substitute at least. Manchester United striker Alessia Russo has played in all five games leading to the final, coming off the bench in each of them and scoring four times, earning the inevitable 'supersub' tag in doing so. Her fourth was as audacious as international goals come, an extraordinary back-heel from a tight angle during the semi-final against Sweden at Bramall Lane in Sheffield. Russo's impudence left BBC TV commentator Robyn Cowen near speechless, unable to find the words to describe what she'd just seen. 'Oh . . . oh . . . oh . . . wow.'

The goal was the third in England's 4–0 win, the one that effectively sealed the team's place at Wembley. If ever a substitute appeared to have a date with destiny, for whom it seemed to be written in the stars that they'd score the winner in the final, it was surely Russo. In the past fortnight, she'd been transformed – in the eyes of the wider English public, at least – from unknown squad member to household name.

That the England fans making up the vast majority of the 87,192 packed into Wembley this afternoon – the highest ever attendance for a European Championship final, either men's or women's – believe this is Russo's destiny is clear from the reception she receives when she replaces Ellen White after fifty-six minutes. With the score goalless and England having more of the play (aided by Germany's star striker and captain Alexandra Popp withdrawing before kick-off after aggravating an injury in the warm-up), it's all set up for her. But Russo won't make the breakthrough, nor will Golden Boot contender Beth Mead. Instead, it'll be another sub who does. Ella Toone has been on the pitch for only six minutes when a sumptuous pass from Keira Walsh puts her through on goal and, with Russo-esque audacity, she loops the ball high above the oncoming German keeper and in. Wembley erupts. North London erupts. The country erupts.

On the England bench sits Jill Scott, England's second most capped player. She has spent sixteen of her thirty-five years as an international footballer. Today will almost certainly be her last match for her country, possibly the last match of her entire career. That's if she gets on the pitch, of course. Team boss Sarina Wiegman has named the same starting XI for the entire tournament, the first coach to ever do so in the Euros. Scott has been on the bench for every game. In total, she's played less than half a half over the past five matches. There's no guarantee she'll get to make a cameo this evening, to make her swansong. Not that Scott's thinking of herself right now.

'Hand on heart,' she later explains, 'I don't think any part of me thought like that. I didn't care what I did that day as long as England won that final. That's all I was thinking of. I didn't care how. I didn't care if it didn't involve me. I just wanted us to win for all those years of not winning.'

But Scott will be involved. With England now having a lead to protect, the defensive midfielder is given the nod. *Go and warm up. England needs you.*

However, while she's stretching her muscles down the touchline, Germany equalise with a sharply taken goal from Lina Magull. The irresistible momentum that England have built up over the last five matches – scoring twenty goals and conceding just one – has just hit a pothole. Scott finishes her warm-up but retakes her seat. Magull's goal has changed things. The Manchester City midfielder isn't needed. For now, at least. Nonetheless, sat there with the scores level again, her confidence remains high, thanks to England's performances en route to the final.

'It seemed too perfect in a way, but it didn't feel inevitable as just one moment can knock you out of a tournament. You can't be complacent. But when we beat Norway 8–0 in the group stage, I thought that something was happening. I just couldn't see us getting beat.'

Scott eventually gets the nod with a minute left of the ninety and the game – barring a dramatic late goal from either side – heading into extra-time. Her experience at international level, gained from 160 caps, is being harvested one last time.

'I didn't really get given too many instructions,' she recalls. 'Or maybe I wasn't concentrating because I was fully in the moment. But I knew what my role was. When I crossed over the white line, I was so calm. I was so focused on my job. I knew I was there to smash a few people. And that was it, really.'

Into added time at the end of the first period of extra-time, Scott gets into an altercation with the German midfielder Sydney Lohmann, and, thanks to the positioning of the cameras, the nation receives a sense of the passion surging through her veins. No lip-reading training is required. 'Fuck off, you fucking prick!' she yells at Lohmann. So much for being calm.

'I can have a passionate moment in a game,' she defends, 'but I'm very good at switching myself back into the zone. In that moment, the girl had my leg trapped in her legs and she was swearing at me, but the camera didn't get that. Don't get me wrong. I'm not proud of the language that I chose. But having been an England fan since, well, since birth, I think it was just all that emotion coming out. That moment showed what I've probably been like my whole career. It's just that, back in the day, there weren't thirty million people watching.'

With Scott helping to baton down the hatches in midfield, it's left to another substitute to create the headlines. As delicious as Toone's chip had been, England's second goal, from Chloe Kelly, was as scrappy as they come – a toe-poke from three yards out after a scramble in the Germany box. No one in Wembley cares. And nor does Kelly, ripping off her shirt to celebrate. It's an instant classic of a celebration, one to be fondly recalled over subsequent decades, just as, say, Nobby Stiles's dainty jig or Gazza's dentist-chair delight.

There are still ten minutes to go, though. These will be ten of the tensest minutes any England fan will endure. Hands across the eyes, fingernails chewed down to stumps. But England hold on until the final whistle. The men's team might still be accumulating all those years of hurt, but the women have extinguished theirs. Their joy is unbound. In her post-match touchline interview with the BBC, Chloe Kelly grabs the mic to sing 'Sweet Caroline'. Later, Wiegman's press conference is invaded by the whole squad; goalkeeper Mary Earps dances on the desk. This time their choice of song is 'Three Lions'. England's women have brought football home.

Three weeks later, Jill Scott announces her retirement from football. Admirably, she's chosen to bow out at her career's pinnacle, its zenith. In the biggest game of her long footballing life, the fairy tale has the happiest of endings. Those sixteen years in the service of her country have rewarded her with her greatest medal.

But Scott knows what people will remember her most conspicuous contribution to her last match to be. Like Ella Toone's dinked goal or Chloe Kelly's shirtless celebration, it's seared into the national memory, an indelible moment in the greatest day of women's football in England.

'I got sent a picture today from Jodie Taylor, who used to play for England and who's now out in San Diego. Her mum's gone to visit her and the first thing she gave her was a mug with 'F*** off, you f***ing prick' on the side.

'My grandma's got a similar mug at home in Sunderland. But I don't think she's worked out what the asterisks mean yet . . .'

England 2–1 Germany

STATISTICS

ENGLAND MEN'S TEAM AT WEMBLEY

Matches at old Wembley: 223
Matches at new Wembley: 85

Summary

Played	308
Won	193
Drawn	76
Lost	39
Goals for	669
Goals against	233

By competition

Friendlies	138
Home International Championship	53
World Cup qualifiers	48
European Championship qualifiers	46
European Championship	11
World Cup	6
Nations League	6

Opponents: 61 teams

Scotland	33	Greece	3
Northern Ireland	18	Luxembourg	3
Wales	18	Slovenia	3
Germany/West Germany/East Germany	16	Montenegro	3
Brazil	12	Ukraine	3
Switzerland	10	USA	3
Hungary	9	Albania	3
Spain	9	Andorra	2
Czech Republic/Czechoslovakia	8	Cameroon	2
Denmark	8	Colombia	2
Netherlands	8	Estonia	2
Poland	8	Finland	2
Portugal	8	Lithuania	2
France	7	Malta	2
Ireland	7	Moldova	2
Italy	7	Nigeria	2
Argentina	6	Rest of the World	2
Bulgaria	6	Slovakia	2
Serbia/Yugoslavia	6	Belarus	2
Croatia	5	Cyprus	1
Russia/USSR	5	Egypt	1
Sweden	5	Georgia	1
Austria	4	Ghana	1
Belgium	4	Iceland	1
Mexico	4	Israel	1
Norway	4	Ivory Coast	1
Romania	4	Japan	1
San Marino	4	Kazakhstan	1
Turkey	4	Peru	1
Uruguay	4	Saudi Arabia	1
Chile	3		

England's highest scores

England 9, Luxembourg 0	European Championship qualifier	15 Dec 1982
England 9, Scotland 3	Home International Championship	15 Apr 1961
England 8, Mexico 0	friendly	10 May 1961
England 8, Turkey 0	European Championship qualifier	14 Oct 1987
England 8, Northern Ireland 3	Home International Championship	20 Nov 1963

England's highest conceded

England 3, Hungary 6	friendly	25 Nov 1953
England 1, Scotland 5	Home International Championship	31 Mar 1928
England 4, Rest of the World 4	friendly	21 Oct 1953

Highest individual tallies

5 goals:

Malcolm Macdonald	England 5, Cyprus 0	European Championship qualifier	16 Apr 1975

4 goals:

Dennis Wilshaw	England 7, Scotland 2	Home International Championship	2 Apr 1955
Jimmy Greaves	England 8, Northern Ireland 3	Home International Championship	20 Nov 1963
David Platt	England 6, San Marino 0	World Cup qualifier	17 Feb 1993

3 goals:

Roy Bentley	England 3, Wales 2	Home International Championship	10 Nov 1954
Tommy Taylor	England 5, Ireland 1	World Cup qualifier	8 May 1957
Johnny Haynes	England 5, USSR 0	friendly	22 Oct 1958
Jimmy Greaves	England 9, Scotland 3	Home International Championship	15 Apr 1961
Bobby Charlton	England 8, Mexico 0	friendly	10 May 1961
Terry Paine	England 8, Northern Ireland 3	Home International Championship	20 Nov 1963
Geoff Hurst	England 4, West Germany 2	World Cup final	30 July 1966
Geoff Hurst	England 5, France 0	friendly	12 Mar 1969
Luther Blissett	England 9, Luxembourg 0	European Championship qualifier	15 Dec 1982
Gary Lineker	England 5, Turkey 0	World Cup qualifier	16 Oct 1985
Gary Lineker	England 8, Turkey 0	European Championship qualifier	14 Oct 1987
Paul Scholes	England 3, Poland 0	European Championship qualifier	27 Mar 1999
Alan Shearer	England 6, Luxembourg 0	European Championship qualifier	4 Sept 1999
Jermain Defoe	England 4, Bulgaria 0	friendly	3 Sept 2010

3 goals:

Raheem Sterling	England 5, Czech Republic 0	European Championship qualifier	22 Mar 2019
Harry Kane	England 4, Bulgaria 0	European Championship qualifier	7 Sept 2019
Harry Kane	England 7, Montenegro 0	European Championship qualifier	14 Nov 2019
Harry Kane	England 5, Albania 0	World Cup qualifier	12 Nov 2021

Most appearances at Wembley for English league clubs or England men's team

Harry Kane	76
Eric Dier	60
Peter Shilton	56
Tony Adams	54
Dele Alli	54
Kyle Walker	50
Son Heung-min	50
Kieran Trippier	49
Bobby Charlton	48
Christian Eriksen	48
Bryan Robson	48
Wayne Rooney	48
Stuart Pearce	47
David Seaman	47
Raheem Sterling	47
Bobby Moore	46

Most goals at Wembley for English league clubs or England men's national team

Harry Kane	52
Bobby Charlton	25
Gary Lineker	25
Wayne Rooney	22
Son Heung-min	22
Jimmy Greaves	18
Alan Shearer	18
Geoff Hurst	17
Frank Lampard	16
David Platt	16
Raheem Sterling	15

ENGLAND WOMEN'S TEAM AT WEMBLEY

23 May 1989	friendly	England 0, Sweden 2
18 Aug 1990	friendly	England 1, Italy 4
23 Nov 2014	friendly	England 0, Germany 3
9 Nov 2019	friendly	England 1, Germany 2
23 Oct 2021	World Cup qualifier	England 4, Northern Ireland 0
31 July 2022	European Championship final	England 2, Germany 1
7 Oct 2022	friendly	England 2, United States 1

CLUB HOME GAMES AT WEMBLEY

Tottenham	2016–19	51
Arsenal	1998–2000	6
Leyton Orient	1930–31	2
Ealing Association	1928–29	8

MAJOR FIXTURES

FA Cup finals

88 (72 old stadium, 16 new stadium): 1923–39, 1946–2000, 2007–

5 were also replayed at Wembley: 1981, 1982, 1983, 1990, 1993

First match at old stadium: 1923, Bolton Wanderers 2, West Ham United 0

First match at new stadium: 2007, Chelsea 1, Manchester United 0

Teams with most wins: Arsenal 11, Manchester United 10

Highest score: 2019, Manchester City 6, Watford 0,

FA Cup semi-finals

37 (7 old, 30 new): 1991, 1993–94, 2000, 2008–

First match at old stadium: 1991, Tottenham Hotspur 3, Arsenal 1

First match at new stadium: 2008, Portsmouth 1, West Bromwich Albion 0

Teams with most wins: Chelsea 10, Arsenal 5,

Highest score: Stoke City 5, Bolton Wanderers 0, 2011; Chelsea 5, Tottenham Hotspur 1, 2012; Hull City 5, Sheffield United 3, 2014

League Cup finals

49 (34 old, 15 new): 1967–2000, 2008–

First match at old stadium: 1967, Queens Park Rangers 3, West Bromwich Albion 2

First match at new stadium: 2008, Tottenham Hotspur 2, Chelsea 1

Teams with most wins: Manchester City 8 (including 2 via a penalty shoot-out), Liverpool 5 (2 via a penalty shoot-out)

Highest score: 2013, Swansea City 5, Bradford City 0

Women's FA Cup final

8 (all new): 2015–

First match: 2015, Chelsea 1, Notts County 0

Teams with most wins: Chelsea 4, Manchester City 3

Highest score: 2017, Manchester City 4, Birmingham City 1

Football League Trophy finals

31 (16 old, 15 new): 1985–2000, 2008–

First match at old stadium: 1985, Wigan Athletic 3, Brentford 1

First match at new stadium: 2008, Milton Keynes Dons 2, Grimsby Town 0

Teams with most wins: Birmingham City 2, Bristol City 2, Carlisle United 2, Rotherham United 2, Stoke City 2, Wigan Athletic 2

Highest score: Bolton Wanderers 4, Torquay United 1, 1989; Southampton 4, Carlisle United 1, 2010; Rotherham United 4, Sutton United 2, 2022

Full Members' Cup finals

7 (all old): 1986–1992

First match: 1986, Chelsea 5, Manchester City 4

Last match: 1992, Nottingham Forest 3, Southampton 2

Teams with most wins: Chelsea 2, Nottingham Forest 2

Highest score: Chelsea 5, Manchester City 4, 1986

League play-off finals

81 (33 old, 48 new): 1990–2000, 2007–

First match at old stadium: 1990, Cambridge United 1, Chesterfield 0, fourth-tier final

First match at new stadium: 2007, Bristol Rovers 3, Shrewsbury Town 1, fourth-tier final

Team with most wins: Blackpool 6 (one second-tier, two third-tier, three fourth-tier), Huddersfield Town 4 (one second-tier, two third-tier, one fourth-tier)

Highest score: Bournemouth 5, Lincoln City 2, fourth-tier final, 2003

European Cup/Champions League final

7 (5 old, 2 new)

1963	AC Milan 2, Benfica 1
1968	Manchester United 4, Benfica 1
1971	Ajax 2, Panathinaikos 0
1978	Liverpool 1, Bruges 0
1992	Barcelona 1, Sampdoria 0
2011	Barcelona 3, Manchester United 1
2013	Bayern Munich 2, Borussia Dortmund 1

Cup Winners' Cup final

2 (both old)

1965	West Ham United 2, 1860 Munich 0
1993	Parma 3, Antwerp 1

OTHER FINALS

World Cup final

1966	England 4, West Germany 2

European Championship finals

1996	Germany 2, Czech Republic 1
2021	Italy 1, England 1, Italy won 3–2 on pens

Women's European Championship final

2022	England 2, Germany 1

Olympic men's final

1948	Sweden 3, Yugoslavia 1
2012	Mexico 2, Brazil 1

Olympic women's final

2012	United States 2, Japan 1

LARGEST ATTENDANCES

Old stadium	Bolton Wanderers v West Ham United	FA Cup final	28 Apr 1923	126,047*
New stadium	Portsmouth v Cardiff City	FA Cup final	17 May 2008	89,874

*Official figure – in reality it was much higher

BIBLIOGRAPHY

As well as the exclusive interviews I conducted, the following books all broadened and coloured in my understanding of particular matches and/or people.

Eniola Aluko, *They Don't Teach This: Lessons from the Game of Life*, Yellow Jersey Press, 2019.

Dave Beasant, *Tales of the Unexpected: The Dave Beasant Story*, Mainstream Publishing, 1989.

Charles Buchan, *A Lifetime in Football*, Phoenix House, 1955.

Jimmy Burns, *Barça: A People's Passion*, Bloomsbury, 1999.

Matt Busby and David R. Jack, *Matt Busby, My Story*, Souvenir Press, 1957.

Sir Bobby Charlton, *1966: My World Cup Story*, Yellow Jersey Press, 2016.

Hunter Davies, *The Glory Game*, Weidenfeld & Nicolson, 1972.

Matt Dickinson, *Bobby Moore: The Man in Full*, Yellow Jersey Press, 2014.

Paul Donnelley, *Arsenal's Greatest Games: The Gunners' Fifty Finest Matches*, Pitch Publishing, 2018.

Paul Gascoigne, *Gazza: My Story*, Headline, 2004.

Jimmy Greaves, *Greavsie: The Autobiography*, Time Warner, 2003.

Paul Harrison, *The Black Flash: The Albert Johanneson Story*, Vertical, 2011.

Paul Hayward, *England Football: The Biography, 1872–2022*, Simon & Schuster, 2022.

Jon Henderson, *When Footballers Were Skint: A Journey in Search of the Soul of Football*, Biteback Publishing, 2018.

Ian Herbert, *Quiet Genius: Bob Paisley, British Football's Greatest Manager*, Bloomsbury, 2017.

Nick Hornby, *Fever Pitch*, Gollancz, 1992.

Gary Imlach, *My Father and Other Working-Class Football Heroes*, Yellow Jersey Press, 2005.

Simon Inglis, *Played in London: Charting the Heritage of a City at Play*, RIBA Publishing, 2014.

Bernard Joy, *Forward, Arsenal! The Arsenal Story, 1886–1955*, Phoenix House, 1952.

Kevin Keegan, *My Life in Football: The Autobiography*, Macmillan, 2018.

Sue Lopez, *Women on the Ball: Guide to Women's Football*, Scarlet Press, 1997.

Lawrie McMenemy, *The Diary of a Season*, Arthur Barker, 1979.

Diego Maradona, *El Diego: The Autobiography of the World's Greatest Footballer*, Yellow Jersey Press, 2004.

Harry Pearson, *The Farther Corner: A Sentimental Return to North-East Football*, Simon & Schuster, 2020.

Mark Sanderson, *Bobby Stokes: The Man From Portsmouth Who Scored Southampton's Most Famous Goal*, Pitch Publishing, 2016.

Robert Saunders, *Yes to Europe! The 1975 Referendum and Seventies Britain*, Cambridge University Press, 2018.

Alex Scott, *How (Not) To Be Strong*, Century, 2022.

Dave Simpson, *The Last Champions: Leeds United and the Year That Changed Football Forever*, Transworld, 2012.

Frank Skinner, *Frank Skinner*, Century, 2001.

Rogan Taylor and Andrew Ward, *Three Sides of the Mersey: An Oral History of Everton, Liverpool and Tranmere Rovers*, Robson Books, 1993.

Steve Tongue, *Turf Wars: A History of London Football*, Pitch Publishing, 2016.

David Tossell, *All Crazee Now: England Football and Footballers in the 1970s*, Pitch Publishing, 2021.

David Tossell, *The Great English Final: 1953 – Cup, Coronation and Stanley Matthews*, Pitch Publishing, 2013.

I also scoured the archives of a great many newspapers, magazines and periodicals, including *The Guardian*, *The Times*, *The Independent*, *The Observer*, the *Sunday Times*, *The Sun*, the *Daily Mirror*, the *Daily Mail*, the *News of the World*, *The Scotsman*, the *Yorkshire Evening Post*, the *Northern Echo*, the *Liverpool Echo*, the *Sunderland Echo*, the *Blackpool Gazette*, the *Sunday Pictorial*, the *Sunday Chronicle*, the *New York Times*, *Marca*, *FourFourTwo*, *The Blizzard*, *When Saturday Comes* and the pages of *Hansard*.

The BBC website was a reliable fount of information, while YouTube filled the gaps in my knowledge with its old BBC and ITV broadcasts, and Pathé and Movietone newsreels. The excellent englandfootballonline.com remains an extraordinary repository of information pertaining to the national sides, both men and women, including details not found anywhere else.

ACKNOWLEDGEMENTS

Big thanks . . .

. . . to all those who shared their first-hand testimonies of particular days or nights at Wembley, especially Carl Bell, Barry Davies, Dion Dublin, Carla Jeffries, Richard Joyce, Fred Knotts, John Murray, Pat Nevin, Jeremy Pound, Jill Scott, Kris Temple, Geoff Twentyman, Jim White and Rob Williams. Also thanks to Emilie Hagan, Jo Tongue and Remmie Williams for their help in organising interviews.

. . . to my editor Frances Jessop, for her good taste in commissioning the book, her wisdom as the book took shape, and her trademark enthusiastic marshalling of the production process. Also at Simon & Schuster, thanks to David Edwards for his meticulous copy-editing, and to Sophia Akhtar, Alex Eccles, Victoria Godden, Ben Murphy, Craig Fraser and Laurie McShea. Thanks to Matthew J. I. Wood for the jacket illustration and to Bill Edgar for the statistics section.

. . . to my agent, Long Tall Kevin Pocklington at The North Literary Agency.

. . . and to the folks back home – Jane, Finn, Ned and Ralphie the faithful hound. Thanks, as ever, for your love and patience.

INDEX